TO RWANDA AND BAC

G000090481

Also by Mary C. Grey:

The Outrageous Pursuit of Hope

Pursuing the Dream: A Jewish–Christian Conversation (with Dan Cohn-Sherbok)

TO RWANDA AND BACK

Liberation Spirituality and Reconciliation

Mary C. Grey

DARTON · LONGMAN + TODD

First published in 2007 by
Darton, Longman and Todd Ltd
1 Spencer Court
140–142 Wandsworth High Street
London SW18 4JJ

© 2007 Mary C. Grey

The right of Mary C. Grey to be identified as the author of this work
has been asserted in accordance with the Copyright, Designs
and Patents Act 1998.

ISBN-10 0-232-52664-8
ISBN-13 978-0-232-52664-6

A catalogue record for this book is available from the British Library.

Printed and bound in Great Britain by
The Cromwell Press, Trowbridge, Wiltshire

CONTENTS

Foreword   vii

Introduction: 'Ah, but your land is beautiful'   ix

1 THE DYNAMICS OF THE RWANDAN GENOCIDE:
   ITS IMPLICATIONS FOR A THEOLOGY OF
   RE-MEMBERING   1

2 THE GENOCIDE, THE CHURCHES AND THE
   BETRAYAL OF SACRED SPACE: SEEKING A
   FEMINIST SPIRITUALITY OF RECONCILIATION
   BEYOND THE DISTORTION OF SACRIFICE   21

3 THE WORLD WAS SILENT — AND ABANDONED:
   RWANDA: SEEKING A SPIRITUALITY OF CARE
   AND COMPASSION   56

4 FRAGILE BRIDGES OVER TROUBLED WATERS:
   BUILDING COMMUNITIES OF
   RECONCILIATION   81

5 LISTEN TO THE CRYING OF THE EARTH:
   POVERTY, STRUCTURAL JUSTICE AND
   RECONCILIATION WITH NON-HUMAN
   CREATION   109

6 MOVING ON: HOW TO BRING BACK THE
BEAUTY OF LIFE? HOW TO BRING BACK
HOPE?   141

7 STRUGGLING WITH RECONCILING HEARTS
AND HOLDING FAST TO OUR DREAMS   168

  Notes   199

  Bibliography   216

  Index   225

FOREWORD

Even though this book originated in a journey to Rwanda, and the complexity of the issues around reconciliation are at its heart, it is not simply another book about Rwanda. I pretend no expertise in an area where so many have suffered and others have witnessed as peace activists and conflict-resolution professionals all their lives. But the experience was so intense, as I hope these pages will show, that it reawakened profound questions about spirituality. It also forced me to confront the difficulties for feminist theology around areas like forgiveness and sacrifice that I had largely avoided. I had to ask if what I have come to believe now contradicts what I wrote earlier. Lastly, an opportunity was given for me to confront some personal faith issues, mostly painful areas pushed below the surface.

So this book does not fit neatly into one category. There is an autobiographical strand, a journey theme and plenty of theological wrestling. The core centres on the meaning of reconciliation both for conflict-resolution, in the struggle for justice and healing for the whole planet, as well as for personal practice. There are jagged edges, where I let the events of the world act as a filter, be these the latest conflict, or where I happen to be journeying. I ask the reader to be patient with a certain sense of untidiness with this method, because I feel that this is exactly the way many of us write, facing the turbulence of events on the larger screen at the same time as in personal life. I also ask forgiveness that in some places I could not properly answer my own questions. To keep struggling with them was all I could do. While writing, my own life has become increasingly complex, with a growing extended family and intense involvement in academic and activist areas: you have all contributed to this book and I am grateful to you all. I want to thank the team at Darton, Longman and Todd for their continued interest and encouragement for my writing, and especially Brendan Walsh who made valuable comments: without him the book would be much more uneven. Also thanks to Hannah Ward, my copy-editor, who has journeyed with me in creative ventures in much more than correcting errors.

But I especially want to thank the group who journeyed to Kigali in December 2004, as well as our generous and courageous hosts in the Presbyterian Church in Kigali and the WCC Faith and Order Commission who invited us in the first place.

I can never express enough thanks to Nicholas who puts up with all of our holidays being dominated by my writing – and has done so for nearly thirty years. And I dedicate this book to the Revds Elizabeth and Stanley Baxter of the Centre for Theology and Health, Holy Rood House in Thirske, as a contribution to their valuable work for peace, non-violence and justice.

Mary Grey
Michaelmas 2006

INTRODUCTION

'Ah, but your land is beautiful'

A JOURNEY TO RWANDA

This book's immediate spark issued from a short journey to post-genocide Rwanda, a journey that will haunt me for ever. It raised troubling questions about human failure of solidarity with the victims of violent injustice. It also raised questions about how Christian spirituality could genuinely be based on justice, questions for me personally, and what this meant for the Christian Church, a church still accused of complicity in the Rwandan genocide of 1994. These questions take on a new seriousness in the wake of the death of Pope John Paul II, recognised internationally as a great spiritual leader. The direction in which Pope Benedict XVI will take the Church is the great anxiety. What kind of space will he make for the concerns of justice and liberation theology, given his past record as Cardinal Ratzinger when he severely curtailed its development in Latin America? What priority will social justice now be given, in a climate where issues of obedience, discipline and tradition seem paramount? I wondered, too, how those areas of reconciliation addressed fruitfully by Pope John Paul II would be furthered, as well as how those issues that he ignored or blocked – like the ordination of women – would be treated.

This anxiety evoked in me deeper questions about the theology and spirituality I have been developing for the last twenty years. First, the new space we are in – in the Roman Catholic Church, as well as in areas of ecumenism and interfaith relations – drives me to ask questions about the interconnections between reconciliation and justice, areas that are fraught with difficulty for feminist theology, where women have often been forced into peacemaking and reconciling roles that have swept justice issues under the carpet. So this book will weave many strands together. Beginning with a journey into understanding Rwanda's search for justice and reconciliation thirteen years after the genocide, it makes connections with other struggles and explores the blockages that prevent reconciliation and wholeness at the deepest level, *our unreconciled hearts and spirits*, while seeking pathways into healing and hope.

PIERCING THE CLOUDS

The journey to Africa began auspiciously – apart from a three-hour sojourn on the runway of Nairobi airport. This was because of thick clouds over Rwanda: our plane was not allowed to take off until a safe landing was ensured. The subsequent journey flying over Lake Victoria and then over Rwandan mountains was breathtaking. I felt thrilled to be offered this opportunity, never having ever been to Africa before. I had realised that my twenty years of very valued involvement with India's semi-desert state of Rajasthan as part of the small NGO, Wells for India,[1] had meant I had gained no first-hand knowledge of Africa, something this present opportunity would begin to address.

As I looked around at my fellow passengers on the aircraft, I wondered what their relationships to Rwanda could be. Could they be returning exiles? Were some of them survivors of the genocide that had occurred more than ten years earlier in 1994? A couple beside me told me they now lived in Germany and it was the first time they had plucked up the courage to come back to their home country since those devastating events. Later, I discovered that quite a few passengers were actually part of the same team of theologians and activists as myself, invited to Kigali by the Faith and Order Commission of the World Council of Churches to write a document on 'Affirming Human Dignity and the Integrity of Creation' as part of the preparation for the Council's next Assembly in Porto Allegre, Brazil, in 2006. This was part of the World Council of Churches' Decade against Violence, and the location of our colloquium in Rwanda was deliberately chosen as a site that had experienced violence on a massive scale. But it would be the tragic situation of post-genocide Rwanda as much as our allotted task that would draw us together in the next few days.

As we drew near our destination, we encountered the thick clouds the pilot had feared. These were clouds the like of which I had never seen before: everyone held their breath as the pilot attempted to descend through these creamy, mountainous clouds, seemingly fathomless abysses, only to re-ascend! We began to fear a return to Nairobi as he told us that he would make a last attempt and then think of another plan. What a huge relief for all that this attempt was successful and we found ourselves, thankfully, on the runway at Kigali airport in brilliant sunshine.

On arrival at the airport the first thing I saw was a UN plane. I was struck with the realisation of what the airport had meant in the days of the genocide and its crucial importance as a gateway to the outside world. But in the capital, Kigali, it was the sheer beauty of the land that first impressed me. I thought of Alan Paton's book on South Africa – written already almost four decades ago – entitled *Ah, But Your Land is Beautiful*.[2] After fog and frost-bound England in December, the warm sunshine, blossom and greenery of Kigali were a delight to behold. The panorama ringing the capital was striking, as Kigali is built on hills, a reminder of the frequent description of Rwanda, *the land of a thousand hills*, with most of the country above 1,000 ft. 'If only Rajasthan had some of this rain', I would often think in the next few days. Indeed, Rwanda seemed to be blessed with a generous climate, as well as great beauty and fertility. Its reddish brown earth is striking. I remembered reading how General Romeo Dallaire, the commander of the UN peacekeeping mission, UNAMIR, in Kigali in the days of the genocide, being homesick for this very soil of Rwanda during one of his brief breaks home in Canada. I remained amazed by the signs of this fertility, by the banana plantations, avocado trees, maize, cassava and coffee plantations and thought of the traditional saying: 'God spends the day elsewhere but always comes back to spend the night in Rwanda.'

A bittersweet expression – clearly I would need to revise some of these first rather superficial impressions, and understand that poverty comes in different guises. To get to grips with understanding the country I – like all the group – had done as much homework as we could. I knew that Rwanda was a very small country, about 26,000 sq. ft., about the size of Wales or Belgium. Like Belgium it is ringed by other countries, in this case Tanzania, Burundi, Uganda, the Democratic Republic of Congo and Kenya. This very fact already sends out signals as to its vulnerability. With no mineral wealth, Rwanda is heavily dependent on agriculture (90 per cent of its people are rural-based), with coffee and tea being its only exports. Despite the beauty of the country, its only internationally known attraction has been the Kagera National Park with its famous gorillas. It is only when I began to learn the significance of the poverty indicators that the superficially rosy picture began to crumble. Of Rwanda's 8 million people, 60 per cent of the population are now under 20 years old, 49 per cent under 14 years; 42 per cent of women are widowed, and 400,000 children are orphaned – and many of these head their own household.[3] Life expectancy for men is 48.1 years – some say even less – and for women, 50.1. A shocking story lies behind these figures.

None of these statistics was automatically visible. But, driving through the streets of Kigali, the landmarks of the events ten years earlier were already very clear. We were the guests of the Presbyterian church in Kigali, whose Centre d'Accueuil was very close to the very luxurious Hotel Mille Collines, whose manager, Paul Rusesebagina, had played such a heroic role in saving the lives of many terrified Tutsi people when the genocide was at its height.[4] Not many hundreds of yards away in the valley below I glimpsed the Catholic Church of the Holy Family, *La Sainte Famille*, where a particularly horrifying story had been played out and its sequel has not ended. But it was now Saturday night in Kigali and young people were doing what young people do on Saturday nights everywhere in the world where they can – congregating in bars and clubs and starting the weekend. In contrast with India's huge cities that I know better, the streets of downtown Kigali did not seem crowded. Soon darkness fell and even though the city had electricity, I could see the hundreds of small dwellings studded across the many hills ringing Kigali, where kerosene lamps were lit and people were beginning to cook their evening meal.

Our group began to get to know one another. We were a mixture of scholars, church-based leaders and human rights activists from all over the world, joined by representatives and leaders of the Presbyterian Church in Rwanda (our hosts), the Congo, Kenya and Burundi. We knew that many of our African colleagues had been personally touched by the genocide, without knowing any details. Some of our German colleagues were very familiar with the background and legacy of the Holocaust and aware that comparisons had been made with the Rwandan genocide. For most of us, the superficial story of events was still the one we were most aware of. We knew that there were two main groups of Rwandans, Hutus and Tutsis (Hutus being the majority 85 per cent), with another small group, the Twa, who formed 1 per cent and who have been derogatively named pygmies. (In fact the Twa have experienced racial injustice from both Hutu and Tutsi alike.) We knew that on 7 April 1994, President Habyarimana's plane had been shot down and that it remains a mystery to this day as to who was actually responsible. The newly elected President of Burundi was also in the plane, killed along with President Habyarimana and other colleagues. This event sparked off a massive wave of killing. In fact it was a hundred days of brutal murdering in which almost 1 million Tutsis and moderate Hutus had been killed in spectacularly horrible, inhuman ways. This came to an end – as the official story goes – only in July when the army of the RPF (the Rwandan Patriotic Front), under its leader Paul Kagame, currently President of Rwanda, swept through the country, 'liberating' it from the Hutus and stopping the genocide. The RPF – now RPA, Rwandan Patriotic Army, immediately set up an interim government. Then a further 1 million people (Hutus) – including many leaders – fled in fear, or were driven, out of the country across the borders into Tanzania, Uganda, Kenya and the Congo. There another story began, as the refugees settled in huge camps and vast amounts of international aid flooded in. But to their dismay, the NGOs (among them were Oxfam, Care International and Médicins sans Frontières) now found themselves feeding the leaders of the genocide, *les génocidaires*, as they were referred to. These huge camps were controlled by the leaders, who now organised armed resistance. And so the story of violence carried on, as we shall see.

But for this first evening in Kigali, the consciousness of our group as to the complexities of what had happened and its continuing effects was limited. We were grateful for the wonderful hospitality offered to us, aware to some extent of what the background experiences of our hosts must comprehend. At the same time we were united by a sense of the gravity of what little we already knew and at the implications and questions raised for the Christian Church and faith far beyond Rwanda's borders.

As I hinted above, the Rwandan experience caused other urgent questions to emerge for me. The spirituality that has inspired my life was from the start rooted in the social justice traditions of the Roman Catholic Church. Challenged deeply by the Christian feminist and then ecological movements I had been developing a spirituality motivated by mutuality-in-relation:[5] so I saw God's grace embodied in the way relationships were transformed from domination and oppression to those fostering justice, integrity, truth and mutual love. Later, this search for just connection between people extended to connectedness with the earth, prophetic justice and a search for a holistic notion of wisdom. I had tried to understand redemption within the metaphor of right relation, and Divine revelation as communicated through all interwoven relational processes. But I had never completely lost the hope that this prophetic justice would be expressed and embodied in the lived faith of Christian community, in an ecumenical dimension that would radiate to other faiths. That was the focus of another two books, *Beyond the Dark Night: A Way Forward for the Church?* and *Prophecy and Mysticism: The Heart of the Postmodern Church*.[6] More recently my work in India brought a consciousness of the plight of the 200 million Dalits (former Untouchable people) who suffer caste discrimination and humiliation on a daily basis. Dalit women experience the worst of this.[7] This, together with the so-called war against terrorism following September 11th 2001, raised the question of the possibility of sustaining even a fragile hope, hope of peace, hope of the transformed world that all liberation movements long for, and the solution to some of the seemingly most ineradicable conflicts. I had written optimistically of the *Out-rageous Pursuit of Hope* in 2000[8] and now, tragically, this hope appeared to be receding beyond the horizon. Such a context again raised urgently for me the whole area of reconciliation. As I wrote earlier, this is a fraught area for feminist theology, not only because women have been forced to 'reconcile' in contexts where they are the victims of injustice, but because there are issues of power, domination, coercion, and histories of colonialism and racism where lines of truth and innocence are blurred in competing justice claims. Not only this, but one key area in feminist spirituality continues to be the search for a healed, responsible self, especially where sense of self has been damaged by abuse, or has never had a chance to be discovered: all too often it had been concealed or prevented from emerging through an overwhelming criss-crossing of multiple oppressions. In this situation it is highly problematic to speak of reconciliation, where lack of justice is so glaring that the priorities are for truth-seeking and truth-telling, and the creation of safe spaces for this to take place.

I am very conscious of all of this: yet the subject of reconciliation will continue to raise its head as a burning issue in multiple contexts. Not only is it a continually troubling area for women, and countless people trapped in powerless situations, but it has become an international phenomenon, with, for example, the Truth and Reconciliation Commission in South Africa,[9] the Recovery of Historical Memory Project (REMHI) in Guatemala and the call for similar processes elsewhere, for example in East Timor. Reconciliation is a daily project in personal life: hardly a family (including my own) is untouched by misunderstandings and hurts, at one end of the spectrum, and intergenerational feuds at the other.

The roots of these intergenerational hurts are sunk deep in history, as even the one example of the IRA demonstrates. I learnt this painfully in a recent project with a Jewish colleague and friend, Rabbi Dan Cohn Sherbok, where we embarked

on a dialogue on reconciliation, *Pursuing the Dream*, through a
series of letters written in the space of 13 months.[10] Although
we agreed on many ethical issues such as peace and justice for
the earth, there were intractable doctrinal issues that we failed
to solve. These had been the underpinning of much historical
suffering on the part of mostly Jewish communities and
continue to haunt relationships between the faiths. To keep
wrestling with them seemed as much as we could do – in that
particular context.

Rwanda's wounds are also sunk in history, I would learn,
although these do not go so far back in time as the tensions
between Christianity and Judaism. But reconciliation in the
context of genocide like this presents unavoidable challenges
as to integrity for the entire Christian community as I hope
this story will reveal. For the moment the only issue I want to
highlight is this: in my childhood the world was beginning to
come to terms with the Holocaust, to recognise its truth and
the degree of culpability of not only the Nazis, but the Church
and the international community. With Rwanda's experience
we have a replay of genocide, as we do in Bosnia, with both
similarities and differences. We have to ask the questions as to
what was learnt from the Holocaust, if anything. And now
that the world has moved on, what meaning has the continuing suffering of the Rwandan people for the Church and
world? Are their voices to be heard any more? Make Poverty
History focuses on Africa, but even so, its attention is partial
and risks being short-lived. (For example, during the heady
days of the Live Aid Concerts around the world in July 2005,
not a word was heard about the escalating famine in Niger.) It
is said that the possibility of genocide haunts the situation in
Darfur, in the Sudan, and, as I write, intervention is being
urged, to prevent an escalation into genocide, and a replay of
Rwanda and Bosnia: the outcome is still uncertain.

If reconciliation is at the heart of the meaning of church,
how does the Church come to terms with its own complicity

in genocide? And given the problematic area of reconciliation for a feminist spirituality of justice, what answers can be gleaned by looking again at what happened in Rwanda in 1994, before and after?

So, first, in Chapter 1, I will ask the question as to what actually happened in those dreadful days, focusing not so much on re-presenting the horror in dreadful detail, but in asking what the meaning of 'remembering' is for Christian spirituality and a theology of peacemaking today. Chapter 2, through the story of the massacre at the Catholic Chapel of Ntarama, begins to explore the role of the Churches and to struggle with some of the difficulties of feminist theology with reconciliation and sacrifice. In Chapter 3, through the desperate efforts of General Dallaire to get the world to listen, and the terrible stories of the refugee camps on the borders of Rwanda, the issue of responsibility is tackled and the deeper question as to the blockages to compassion and conversion opened up. The key role of compassion in spirituality is explored through a focus on people and communities of compassionate action, as a resource for conflict-resolution.

Reconciliation on many levels – beginning with efforts in Rwanda and Burundi – is tackled in Chapter 4, which is actually the heart of the book: here Christian traditions of truth-telling, peace and non-violence are explored and connections made with other conflict situations. Chapter 5 opens up issues of poverty and justice: the often-missed link is made here between justice and reconciliation with the earth. The Holy Spirit as the Green Face of God is the inspirational image for this and the following chapter. Chapter 6 focuses on discovering new spiritual resources for flourishing in contexts of violence, pain and chronic depression. In a final chapter, I attempt to bring together all these strands in terms of a theology of reconciliation and what this means for a spiritual journey both personal and for the lived faith of Christian community.

I THE DYNAMICS OF THE RWANDAN GENOCIDE

Its Implications for a Theology of Re-Membering

> You may kill as many people as you want, but you cannot kill their memory. Memory is the most invisible and resistant material you can find on earth. You cannot cut it like a diamond, you cannot shoot at it because you cannot see it; nevertheless it is everywhere, all around you, in the silence, unspoken suffering, whispers and absent looks.
>
> *Philippe Gaillard* [1]

For many years we have been aware that 'memory' is crucial for liberation theology in all geographical areas, as it is for the lived reality of any Christian spirituality. The memory of who you once were, an identity that you may have lost, the 'dangerous memory' of both suffering and freedom, fuels resistance and determination not to give way to what seems like the inevitability or impasse of the present situation of suffering. In many contexts and cultures there may be a suppressed or subjugated past. There may be silenced voices only dimly remembered. For example, in my own family history there were few traces of remembering the Irish famine, part of our family story since my great-great-grandmother had emigrated from Mayo (south-west Ireland) to the north-east of England because of it. I often wondered why we asked so few questions about the tragic famine deaths and England's part in it, until it was too late. After my mother's death in 1992, during a visit to the west of Ireland I wandered over hillsides and through ruined cottages, abandoned since this time, and mourned the fact that when people died they took their stories with them, and one possibility of remembering is lost to us.

But in Rwanda the theme of dangerous memory was to take on new dimensions for me. It was not until the day after our arrival, when our group had assembled for our first official meeting in the hall of the Presbyterian Centre d'Accueil in Kigali, that the reality of Philippe Gaillard's words as to memory and 'unspoken suffering' began to sink in. In a wonderful reception where we were welcomed by the local church leaders, the group was thanked for coming to 'this traumatised land' where every family bears the wounds and memory of genocide. A poignant moment was to be told that our coming was part of the healing process, a statement that added an unexpected level of gravity to our visit. It also began to teach me that reconciliation was no add-on luxury, no optional extra, but formed the bedrock of possibility of life itself in this country – and maybe in every context, *but often as a buried ethical challenge.* To sit next to someone at supper who informed me in calm tones that he had lost all his family in the genocide, a wife and seven children, of whom the youngest was three, the eldest twenty years old, was an experience I could not have been prepared for. What kind of hope kept this courageous minister going? Listening to these stories would be an often-repeated experience during the following week. Little by little we understood that everyone we would meet had a terrible story to tell of loss, bereavement and continuing trauma. This included those who had to leave, those who had returned, or those who had not even been in the country – all had experienced loss.

And of course there were the many unspoken stories that could not be told to strangers. There were buried stories of complicity in the killing, unspoken levels of betrayal that I would never know and could only guess at. I could only imagine the personal tragedies of murdered loved ones, burnt houses, looted possessions, slaughtered cattle and lost land that lay behind the faces in front of me. But worst of all were the memories of the brutal manner of killing. People – even women and children – were not 'cleanly' killed, but hacked or clubbed to death with machetes, axes and clubs studded with nails. Some people paid money to be shot rather than undergo this terrible death, which was inflicted even on small children and babies. Husbands were forced to kill their Tutsi wives and children. Women and young girls joined in or were forced into the killing. Far from being told to 'remember' it was unbelievable how anyone could possibly forget. Yet the country is now faced with the reality that perpetrators – who have now returned, or been set free from prison – may be living next door to families who know they have murdered some of their dear ones. How is it possible to carry on living with these memories?

WHAT ACTUALLY HAPPENED?

The next shock was to realise that the story of a hundred days of killing a million people, terrible though this is to report, fell far short of the truth and in fact was the tip of the iceberg. This genocide had not been suddenly sparked off by the shooting down of President Habyarimana's plane on 7 April 1994 – it is more that it is convenient to give this precise date as the sparking-off point for the violence. Rather, it had been systematically prepared for by Hutu extremists during decades and had even deeper historical roots. There had been waves of killing of Tutsis since 1959, and 700,000 had already fled in exile to neighbouring countries: this had happened even before Rwanda became independent in 1962. Up till the Arusha Accord of 1993 in Tanzania, there had in fact been a war between the opposing factions. (One of the tragic aspects is that international reactions did not distinguish between the war and the genocide.)

Now our group began to learn the dynamics of genocide, which are to deny the humanity of your 'enemies' long before the killing begins, just as the Nazis had targeted the Jews long before the 'Final Solution' swung into operation. The Tutsis had been insulted as 'cockroaches' (*inyenzi*), even vermin, and, as a proverb went, 'Cockroaches don't give birth to butter-flies.' 'Tutsi' became defined as 'one whose identity is desire for revenge'. *Humanity was destroyed before any killing took place.*

A further chilling jigsaw piece in the plot was the pub-lishing, on 10 December 1990, by a leading propaganda newspaper, *Kangura,* of the 'Hutu 10 commandments'. These stated categorically that any Hutu interacting with Tutsi neighbours was a traitor. Women were particularly targeted: so any Hutu with Tutsi wife, mistress, secretary or dependant was automatically a traitor. It should be remembered in this context that many moderate Hutus protected and tried to save Tutsis, and therefore became prime targets for the extremists. They were frequently the first to be killed. These 'Hutu 10 commandments' further ordered that all educational institu-tions, strategic positions and armed forces should be specifi-cally in the hands of Hutus. This declaration made us all aware of the Christian permeation of Rwandan culture – actually the most Christianised African country – and that genocide had occurred so soon after the Protestant Revival movement:[2] why use this biblical reference point in a country dominantly Christian, with a Roman Catholic majority, unless to influ-ence subtly and undermine cherished faith sources?

What provided a first clue to understanding the hatred provoking the killing (just to mention one motive in the complex situation) was to see how racist myth had been used by both colonisers and missionaries for their own advantage. Colonialism had sowed the seeds for this genocide. For the truth now agreed by historians is that both Rwanda and its neighbour Burundi were probably first inhabited three thou-sand years ago by the Twa forest-dwellers and hunter-gatherers, now marginalised as 'pygmies' as I mentioned.[3] It is not known whether the herding Tutsis (14 per cent) or agricultural Hutus (85 per cent) arrived first into the country. What all the sources agree is that these categories are not ethnic but social: all three groups shared a language (Kinyarwanda), traditions, territory, culture and clans. What happened was that the nineteenth-century racist myths of anthropologists and ethnographers were exploited by the colonisers (first German, then Belgian after 1919), and these acquired a self-propagating power: they argued persuasively that the physical appearances of Tutsis (tall and thin, and supposedly with a more Hamitic, Caucasian origin) and Hutus (shorter, with broader noses and supposedly more Negroid and indigenous) meant that Tutsis were intellectually and culturally superior. It was said that the Tutsis were Christianised in Ethiopia and therefore more open to re-evangelisation: 'First the German, then the Belgian colonisers developed this theory, delegating power and privilege to the minority Tutsis in classic divide-and-rule colonial tactics.'[4]

Privileging the Tutsis in education and prestigious administrative positions – a process in which the Belgian Catholic Church also participated, by establishing church schools for young Tutsis, the children of the elite professionals – sowed and fomented Hutu resentment that began to boil over when Rwanda became independent in 1962. (Both the Belgians and the Church – in a strategic move, as the Hutu power movement grew – switched allegiance from Tutsi to Hutu just before the Belgians handed over the reigns of government.) *The reality of the dynamic was that ethnic difference had been transformed into racial prejudice.*[5] To make such sharp distinctions between Hutu and Tutsi also made little sense when families had been intermarrying for generations.

All these factors would still not have culminated in genocide without the growth of the Hutu Power movement that was able to manipulate the peoples' fear of the Tutsi domination of colonial days returning, and systematically to orchestrate the killing.

The slaughter of Tutsis had begun already in 1959, as did the process of fleeing in terror to neighbouring countries, as well as that of *Hutu* exiles returning and living in camps in the south of the country, because in Burundi the situation was reversed, as Tutsis held power in this country. The leader of the RPF – who would eventually become Vice-President, and is currently President of Rwanda, Paul Kagame – had fled as a 3-year-old child to Uganda with his parents. Rwandan refugees suffered terribly under former President Obote, and this was one of the reasons that young Rwandans, like Kagame, joined the anti-Amin army of Museveni, and would eventually lead the liberating army into Kigali and end the genocide. It is said that from this point – in 1962 – not only did Rwandan society become increasingly militarised, but that Tutsi families lived in permanent fear.[6]

The killing of the Rwandan genocide has been so well documented that it would be unhelpful to create fresh wounds by engaging in a complete retelling of those frenzied days.[7] But I cannot run away from the questions that emerge. First, I asked myself, what did it mean for my own spiritual journey, and the Christian groups I belonged to at home, to be confronted by a people whose depth of suffering I would never be able to fathom, and who were courageously trying to move on? I had not expected to be faced with this moral challenge: I had come to Rwanda assuming that the violence was a tragic event but over, finished ten years ago, to deliver a paper on the 'Integrity of Creation' as a contribution to the document to be written as part of the World Council of Churches' Decade against Violence.[8] Now I found the legacy of violence a turbulent reality of the present from which I could not stand aside. I also found myself part of the tragedy in the sense that the world had stood aside from this killing,[9] and I realised that if you prioritise justice as a value within spirituality, then you must always seek a deeper understanding of a specific conflict and be willing to accept an appropriate degree of accountability and respond accordingly.

Secondly, how should I react to the knowledge of the Church's complicity? Was this another replay of the many crises of loyalty to the Church that have dogged my life? Starting with my struggles with Oxford philosophy in the 1960s, when the rationality of religious belief lacking empirical proof had been challenged by such logical positivists as Professor Alfred J. Ayer (author of *Language, Truth and Logic*[10]), to the dilemmas presented by feminism that had seemed to question the very integrity of Christian tradition because of its treatment of women, would this be the *coup de grâce* that would finally defeat me?

MEMORY AND SPIRITUALITY

The only way to begin to answer these questions in Kigali was to respect the re-membering process of those who had survived the genocide experience – starting with those who now welcomed us so graciously – and to try to understand their hopes. Although the process of re-membering is such a vital tool in the journey to reconciliation it is not clear how it can work, given the degree of anguish suffered. ('Remembering the victims' was the title of the working group I joined during the Kigali consultation.)

First, I had to reflect what I meant by memory and re-membering as part of my own spiritual journey. As with most human beings, there are distinctive memories I treasure from childhood. Some evoked what now would be called transcendent moments – but then I was ignorant of both word and concept. In the Roman Catholic world of north-east England, our family lived in a small mining town (the mine has long since gone), where the most personal aspect of faith experience was offered through 'devotions', now mostly vanished after the reforms of the Second Vatican Council (with the exception of the Rosary). We children – I am the eldest of seven – were initiated into the 'Nine Fridays' to the Sacred Heart of Jesus, the Novena to Our Lady of Perpetual Succour and even the Nine Tuesdays to St Anthony. Sadly, preparation for First Holy Communion lacked the theological depth and community focus it consists of today. My own memory is that I was so frightened by the story (told to us by Irish Sisters of Mercy) of Blessed Imelda who died of joy at her First Communion that my own prayer on this occasion consisted of begging God not to let me die – even of joy!

But even if the devotions were mostly boring, as were – for small children – the public liturgical celebrations, yet they presented a multi-coloured tapestry by which I perceived the world and I am grateful for the efforts my parents made to hand on a faith they treasured. I loved this small town, its fields and hills and the freedom we children then had to roam them. Somehow the very toughness of the devotions offered cherished moments and memories: there were times when we were encouraged during Advent to attend daily Mass on the way to school. For my sisters and I this involved getting up very early in the dark, a mixture of walking and taking a bus to church (then a long bus journey to school afterwards) – where we listened to the words of Isaiah about the coming of the Kingdom. The mixture of light and dark in Advent liturgies and the inspiration of prophetic texts has stayed with me since. Our parents also gave us special memories of the Celtic and Anglo-Saxon saints who had founded many of the abbeys and churches around us. Holidays on the Holy Island of Lindisfarne brought their memories alive for us and we were given a sense of privilege because we lived in Northumberland and Durham, 'the cradle of the faith'. At that point I hadn't heard of the part that Iona played, but I was very aware of the rivalry between the Roman and Celtic traditions!

My mother soon awakened a dimension of social justice in us children. One December I discovered her in tears while reading a Christmas letter from the late Archbishop Denis Hurley of Durban, South Africa. That was how we first learnt about racism and apartheid. But my first experience of real poverty came later, when as a university student from Oxford I worked in a shanty town near Paris as part of a charity founded by the Abbé Pierre, *Aide à toute Détresse*. As a volunteer I soon realised that any good I might be doing was more for my own level of awareness than for the benefit of the Algerian families of the camp. The priest who directed the shanty town, Père Joseph Wresinski, wrote at the bottom of a report I had written, 'En souvenir d'une vraie misère' ('in memory of genuine affliction'), and it is this act of re-membering that would become the heart of a spirituality that inspired me.

This kind of 'memory of affliction' brings an entry point to what liberation theology means by 'dangerous memory'. The concept was first introduced by the German political theologian Jean-Baptist Metz, who identified both the *memoria passionis*, the memory of suffering, and the *memoria libertationis*, the memory of freedom.[11] When this is related to Christ's suffering and redemptive action in the past, the process of dangerously re-membering can become part of redemptive action in the present.[12] Feminist theology was quick to develop the importance of this in different ways. Women, it was realised, have been absent or erased from official texts, from understandings of human subjectivity and sexuality, and from widely held cultural memories. Or they have been present in subordinated roles. So the process of re-membering has been a vital 'hermeneutics of retrieval', or of recovering the contributions of women to church, scholarship and justice movements. In so doing there has sometimes been a tendency either to reverse male domination by female superiority, or romantically to imagine a Golden Age of egalitarian relationships before the onset of historical patriarchy. (Elisabeth Schüssler Fiorenza's ground-breaking study of Christian origins, *In Memory of Her*, has sometimes been misunderstood in this way.[13])

Yet in the last twenty years it must be admitted that a remarkable recovery has been achieved both in western contexts and in the families of liberation theologies springing up in the Two-Thirds World. Women have discovered a genealogy of foremothers – mystics, saints, biblical leaders, founders of congregations, scholars – even if only a minority have been included in church structures. Goddess feminists recall times when the sacredness of the female body was affirmed through the power of the ancient goddesses in all ancient religions, indigenous to Europe, as well as in Egypt, Greece, Canaan, Asian and African religions and so on. The activity of 'dangerously remembering' these historical periods has become empowering for many women today, as Carol Christ so evocatively relates.[14] Mercy Amba Oduyoye, the Ghanaian Christian theologian, while admitting that many creation myths and traditional African legends are disempowering to women, searches for cultural memories that affirm the humanity of women, sometimes re-working matrilineal myths that offer an alternative.[15] The novels of both African, African American and Asian women are vital participants in the healing process of recovering fragmented and painful memories so as to enable a positive future. Toni Morrison's great work *Beloved* evocatively depicts the *dangerous* nature of re-membering, as Sethe, the central character, who escaped from slavery and murdered her baby daughter in order for her not to be recaptured by the traders, can only dare to recall small fragments of her story, so anguished its nature, so painful its recall.[16]

But what kinds of re-membering are evoked by a genocide situation? How are those involved – either as victims, counsellors or ministers – supposed to break the silence and the denial as to what happened? The cultures of silence in the wake of genocide, whether this be victims of the Holocaust, or the Bosnian or Armenian massacres, are a far cry from the silent contemplation of the mystery of God which is at the heart of ancient faiths. Here what is meant is the tragedy of enforced silences of individuals, groups and whole peoples traumatised and rendered powerless. In our discussion group in Kigali we sought to highlight some examples of cultures of silences enforced on individuals, groups and countries.[17]

First, we acknowledged that many centuries of patriarchy have left a legacy of disordered, frequently unjust power relations between men, women and children. In many societies we remembered victims of rape and domestic violence who were silenced, through trauma, shame and dishonour, and even because the victims themselves are made to feel guilty and responsible for the offence. We acknowledged that in many churches women and children have suffered and are still victims of sexual violence inflicted by some ministers of the church, and are even forbidden to talk about it. Silence here may also be due to the internalising of shame and oppression.

But we also recalled another kind of silence: people are silenced through unspeakable pain and trauma. Sometimes years of distancing were needed before this pain could be expressed. This was certainly true after the Jewish Holocaust, and I had discovered it was true of the Irish famine. Fear of re-victimisation, fear of being accused of participation in the crime as well as fear of standing for the truth are all connected with this. In addition, our group wanted to name specifically the phenomenon of *structural amnesia,* where the context for remembering is deliberately made impossible. For example, the massacre that took place during the Korean war was silenced by anti-communist propaganda and the national security law. Painfully, we admitted the contemporary forms of silenced voices emerging in many countries around the situation of refugees, migrant workers, asylum-seekers and part-time workers; these silences, we knew, were partly due to language constraints, to racism and the lack of status granted to different groups, who fall frequently into the category of 'the despised other'. We noted other important societal groups such as persons of disability or sexual minorities, silenced by the excluding strategies of the dominant discourse. These silences are often maintained because they serve racist and colonial interests, as well as the vested interests of people remaining silent because of their involvement in acts of violence, injustice and corruption. Where injustice and impunity prevail and remain unaddressed, repetitive violence will occur. Yet another silence undergirds much of this – silence over the damage and exploitation done to the earth as part of war and ethnic violence.

How to break open the silence of injustice and many-layered oppressions is the question I have to face. Surely there can be a positive re-membering of Christian and Jewish faith traditions? At least two dimensions of this are crucial building blocks for spirituality. To re-member the anguish of the fragmented past is not only to piece together the broken fragments and reclaim a healed identity; it is to trust that humanity need not succumb to an endless spiral of repetitive violence. As Maya Angelou wrote on the occasion of the inauguration of President Clinton:

> History, despite its wrenching pain
> Cannot be unlived, but if faced
> With courage, need not be lived again.[18]

Secondly, what both Christians and Jews rely on in our respective theologies of remembering is both the discipline of repenting and the vision of the peaceable Kingdom, recognising that both the repenting and the envisioning take very different forms in each faith. Imagining a situation where justice and peace will reign, where the most vulnerable and

victimised will be healed and relations will be based on respect
and equitable sharing of land and resources – these are well-
known dimensions of the vision of the peaceable Kingdom. In
this book I want to put reconciliation at the heart of the justice
struggle and working for the Kingdom, and use an image of
the former President of Ireland, Mary Robinson, to do so.
She, from her Christian vision for reconciliation in that
troubled country, invoked the ancient symbol of the fifth
province:

> as everyone knows, there are only four geographical pro-
> vinces on this island. The Fifth Province is not anywhere
> here or there ... It is a place within each of us, that place
> that is open to the other, that swinging door which allows
> us to venture out and others to venture in ... While Tara
> was the political centre of Ireland, tradition has it that this
> Fifth province acted as a second centre, a necessary balance.
> If I am a symbol of anything I would like to be a symbol of
> this reconciling, healing Fifth province.[19]

With this symbol of the Fifth province as symbol of reconciliation to inspire the process of remembering the peaceable
Kingdom, how could that have any relevance for the situation
that Rwanda has to face? This is the question to be explored. I
take heart, too, that despite the fact that religions are often
cited as the cause of conflicts, yet they can still offer a precious
quality – the resources to build trust. Stories of genocide have
emphasised implacable hatred based on lack of trust, hatred
with specific roots in histories of violence, colonial exploitation and victimisation, as the story of Rwanda illustrates. The
level of trauma resulting on both sides would seem to make
trust impossible. But, sometimes it can happen that 'into the
lives of these victimised people come religious outsiders, who
in varying ways convey a sense of understanding and empathy
for their fears and who have established reputations for honesty, discretion and integrity'.[20]

Without the kind of trust Archbishop Tutu was able to inspire in South Africa, there would have been no possibility of even listening, day by day, to the unfolding of painful stories in the Truth and Reconciliation Commission. And in addition, religions offer disciplines for personal transformation. They do not separate political from social and personal transformation but at their best offer an integrated notion. The late Thomas Merton, a Trappist monk, and still an inspiration for the peace movement today, wrote:

> The rush and pressure of modern life are a form, perhaps the most common form, of its innate violence . . . The frenzy of the activist neutralises his work for peace. It destroys his own inner capacity for peace. It destroys the fruitfulness of his own work because it kills the root of inner wisdom which makes work fruitful.[21]

Feminist spirituality has always stressed these interconnections between personal, political, psychological and spiritual – and these dimensions will be explored in Chapter 6. But in Rwanda the Church itself was compromised by the events of the genocide and leading up to it. With such a background, how could the Church now move into a healing, reconciling role?

RE-MEMBERING INTO THE FUTURE

How to move out of this impasse? This question has haunted me since leaving Kigali. I clung on to the intuition that God never leaves us without hope; that even in the worst of impasses, God sustains and holds us, if we have the depth of faith to believe and trust, as the mystics who survive the Dark Night of abandonment keep telling us. As I write today, the news has broken out that the IRA has made a statement that it is disengaging from the armed struggle and will now participate in the political process. While it is impossible to predict what will happen, and there is much cynicism from some parties, from others there is still a great sense of jubilation that the process has come so far, given the bitterness both of the immediate history of rebellion and conflict since 1916, and the longer roots of colonisation going back to the thirteenth century. But is it too facile to make a comparison with Rwanda?

I then reread the poignant work of Dr Tharcisse Gatwa, a Presbyterian theologian from Rwanda (who was an invaluable participant and guide at the Kigali consultation), and was struck by the comparison he made between Rwanda and Northern Ireland. As with Rwanda, the Churches have been deeply involved in the struggles of Northern Ireland. Again, as with Rwanda there is both a recent conflict and deeper roots in colonial history. Yet movements for peace and reconciliation in 1995 numbered more than 120 – and Dr Gatwa visited many of them personally. Describing the efforts to achieve the Good Friday agreement and citing Tony Blair's speech on that occasion, Tharcisse Gatwa sees a similarity in the way that moral unity and the credibility of the message of the political parties were sacrificed by their divisions. He pointed to the culpability of the Churches:

> Having tarnished their images, they [the churches of N. Ireland] have compromised their power to proclaim the truth, because they did not put in place any mechanism for ecumenical dialogue that would permit the transcending of doctrinaire frontiers.[22]

This was of course written before the more recent developments – whose outcome is far from clear – and it would be presumptuous to make facile predictions. But the comparison does throw up interesting questions for a theology of memory, the theme of this chapter. The Church of England priest Nicholas Frayling, now Dean of Chichester Cathedral, has for years been deeply committed to understanding the complexities of the different communities in Ireland, North and South.[23] His insights reach further than the Irish situation: aware of the need for liberation from falsehood in the way that we remember, and the content of memory, he grieves that at the core of the problem is that memories of the different groups are held in isolation from each other. In his poignant book he pleads for healing spaces where two opposing peoples, from both sides of the border, can relate memories of suffering and oppression – and begin a process of sharing memories of love of the same land, in a tentative beginning to share a history.[24] This would be a process that moves from recognising the other as threatening and hostile, to the possibility of two opposed groups becoming once again neighbours. As Miroslav Volf told us, neighbours like the Serbs and Croats do not turn into enemies overnight.[25] For the last few years, I have been trying to support Donald Reeves, a Church of England priest and founder of the 'Soul of Europe', in his groundbreaking and reconciling work of trying not only to rebuild the mosque of Ferhadija, destroyed in the Bosnian war in the city of Banja Luka, but to construct a memorial of a massacre on the site of a steel factory – owned by the steel giant, Mr Mittal – near Banja Luka. So the question of how to re-member is crucial here in yet another genocide site.[26]

The achievement of the South African Truth and Reconciliation Commission addressed exactly this point: that the two sides should listen to each others' memories and acknowledge their truth. Again, for that to be a reality, safe spaces were needed, enabling the possibility of trust. Surely, if at the heart of Christian theology is the sacred act of remembering God's redemptive deeds, then the Churches should be able to offer these places of safety and trust and facilitate the healing process? The eucharistic liturgy for the Catholic Church is the occasion par excellence for this great act of remembering God's saving act in Christ. But what happens if the Church betrays this trust, as happened in the Rwandan genocide, when, in all the Churches, there was a degree of collusion with the killing? This is the task to be explored in Chapter 4.

I want to stay with the problem of respecting the painful memories of a wronged national group, or, in the case of Ireland, Bosnia and Rwanda, at least two groups who feel they have legitimate grievances. Liberation theology has always honoured the process of dangerous memory that allows an oppressed people to remember their origins. Once they knew themselves as proud and free, God's people, with a faith, culture and identity – this is the experience of, for example, indigenous Indians in Canada and the United States, the aboriginal peoples in Australia and New Zealand. But these complex contexts of reconciliation discussed here are dealing with at least two different peoples both of whom feel they have been wronged. Just how many stories of violence and de-humanising brutality can anyone bear to listen to, without collapsing into despair, losing focus and disrupting any fragile hopes of moving forward? This was what the Truth and Reconciliation Commission faced in South Africa. Even people who wanted to forgive said they did not know whom to forgive. In Guatemala this was also the hope: that in the Recovery of Historical Memory Project (REMHI) the truth-telling of memories of the killings would enable healing. Yet still a people waits for healing to be a reality, as even the murderer of Bishop Gerardi has not been identified and brought to justice.

Two points may bring hope. The first is, as feminist liberation theologians urge, that remembering is exactly that: *re-membering*. It is putting together the painful fragments in a new way, a way that makes just and healed relationship possible. And this is hard work. As Adrienne Rich writes:

> Freedom. It isn't once, to walk out
> under the Milky Way, feeling the rivers

of light, the fields of dark –
Freedom is daily, prose-bound, routine
remembering. Putting together, inch by inch
the starry worlds. From all the lost collections.[27]

The second point is the challenge as to whether those of us who have been part of colonial history, or any form of oppression, are ready to be part of the journey of repentance, to hear the stories that implicate us in the shame of the past, or the responsibility for unjust systems of the present: are we prepared to take any action in response? Re-membering in this case is painful in a different way because it involves coping with the claims of guilt, the need to make restoration where this is possible. Earlier I referred to this as *metanoic* memory, a re-membering that needs humility and a willingness to bear witness to the truth.[28] Women need also to face up to the truth that we have not always been the innocent victims of history. Even in Rwanda, where women suffered so horribly in the genocide, there were women who joined in the killing. Of course some were coerced, but others, including political and local leaders, were enthusiastically encouraging the murders even of neighbours and friends.[29] Now, a worrying thought is nagging my mind: is the dominant paradigm of liberation theology's understanding of memory now adequate to bear the weight of all this?

Liberation theology has been enormously influenced by the Exodus paradigm, still so central for Judaism. That God heard the cries of the Hebrew slaves in Egypt, raised up the prophet Moses as leader, and led them out of slavery to the desert and eventually the promised land, has echoed through the ages as the central liberating paradigm, and the *central content of what we remember*. In the Christian Liturgy of the Vigil of the Resurrection, it is this story of God's liberating action that is remembered as the context of Jesus' Last Supper and redeeming actions through his death and resurrection. In

South Africa, the call for a new Moses to lead black Africa out of slavery was a powerful strategy in the process of ending apartheid. But how helpful is this central image in Palestine today, where two groups of people claim possession of the same land? How helpful is it in Bosnia and in Rwanda? In Kosovo the dangerous memory of 1389 when the Serbian Prince Lazar was defeated by the Turks still sears the inmost being of Serbians, and its memory is still carried into the present in the lullabies sung to Serbian babies. But the truth is that these different religious and ethnic groups must somehow learn to share the country, to accept that there are different experiences and conflicting memories of history. So, what religious sources and images could be helpful in such situations?

The solution seemed simpler when searching for helpful images in the context of the oppressive free-market systems.[30] There, the sense of being in captivity to unjust, dominating systems is symbolised by the imagery of Babylon. Not only can one make a comparison between the Jews in Babylon, captive to the power of empire, and the greed of Nebuchadnezzar, as illustrated by Isaiah, but it is clear that links can be made with John's apocalyptic imagery of the Beast, and the pessimistic depictions of Babylon.

Even a feminist spirituality of re-membering that privileges the subjugated memories is not necessarily helpful here, if it presumes some glorious past that can be reclaimed as a resource for the present. Clearly this is a vital tool where women's subjectivity has been denied, self-esteem made impossible, but here we are seeking something more complex. Can the *theological* theme of re-membering that everyone is precious in God's eyes, created in God's image, that God cares for all creatures as precious vines in a vineyard (Isaiah 5 and John 15), enable the movement beyond privileging only one's own ethnic group into an esteem for the other, even the hated and demonised other? Remembering that we are loved and precious in God's sight, remembering that God's Spirit was poured out at Pentecost in a multi-racial context that privileged no race in particular – can this be the kind of remembering that stimulates repentance and moving forward? Before answering this question my search takes me to ask in greater depth what the complicity of the Churches means in terms of a spirituality of reconciliation.

2 THE GENOCIDE, THE CHURCHES AND THE BETRAYAL OF SACRED SPACE

Seeking a Feminist Spirituality of Reconciliation beyond the Distortion of Sacrifice

I get out and follow Frank across the open ground in front of the Church ... There is a child who has been decapitated and there are three other corpses splayed on the ground ... Inside the gate the trail continues. The dead lie on either side of the pathway ... I must walk on, stepping over the corpse of a tall man who lies directly across the path, and, feeling the grass brush against my legs, I look down to my left and see a child who had been hacked almost into two pieces ... I begin to pray to myself. 'Our Father who art in heaven ...' These are prayers I have not said since my childhood but I need them now.

Fergal Keane, at the massacre of Nyarubuye[1]

Not all sacrifice is victimisation. Conscious self-sacrifice, which is related to resistance, embodies the hope of redemption, and may even bring joy to the one who does the 'letting-go'.

Mercy Amba Oduyoye[2]

The question of the Church's complicity in genocide took a more tangible and tragic tone for all of us when visiting some of the genocide sites in Rwanda. Again, little could have prepared the group for the impact of the visit to the Catholic Chapel of Ntarama, almost two hours' drive out of Kigali. Travelling along the earthen roads of strikingly red soil, what struck me again was the fertility of the land. Banana-laden trees, coffee plantations, trees dripping with avocados were a stunning contrast with the poverty of vegetation of the desert state of Rajasthan in N. W. India, where, as I mentioned earlier, I travel regularly. As a newcomer I did not notice the sinister signs – the lack of houses in banana plantations, for example. (Banana plantations should always have farmers living there to tend the plants.) Nor did I then know of the desperate struggle to sell Rwandan coffee on the world market.

The exterior of Ntarama Catholic Chapel – a dignified, ribbon-streamered enclosure with tall trees and a garden planted with flowers – gave no clue as to what the interior contained. Step inside the church and what greets the visitor are stacked rows of skulls and bones, washed cleanly. By the walls are more sacks of bones. We were asked to be careful about walking in the church, as what is preserved here are the remains of 5,000 men, women and children, massacred on 15 April 1994.

It is difficult to describe the effect on the group of seeing children's shoes, Rosary beads, feeding spoons and rags of frayed clothing, all left as they had been on the day of the massacre. Among the stacked rows of skulls, pathetically, was a cross placed on the skull. In grief? In forgiveness? In protest? As we stood, stunned, numbed, two survivors appeared, together with the caretaker of the church. One of these, a woman, Dancilla Nyirabazungu told her story.[3] What was heartbreaking was to learn that the people of the surrounding countryside had taken refuge in the church (as they had already done previously in 1959). The house of God as sanctuary. As a place people could trust, where they had been baptised and received First Communion. It was the militia that had told them to gather people from the neighbourhood 'so that we can protect you'.

That's how there came to be so many in the church. *It was a Catholic priest who had informed the militia of the presence of so many people.* The women were making porridge for the children outside the church when the *Interahamwe* (or the young militia trained by the Presidential party, the MRND[4]) arrived with their guns, clubs with nails in them, and machetes. No one was spared, not even the small children. Only a few escaped to the surrounding reeds and grasses where they hid until the RPF (army of the Rwandan Patriotic Front) arrived in May and began to take over the country. Most of Dancilla's own children hid with her, but she lost the rest of her extended family and one child. Now she is paid a small amount to look after the church. *And here is where a story of tragedy carries the seeds of a story of hope of reconciliation.* As she told us:

> This place is important to me and to all Rwandans – and to the world as a whole. There are people who deny all this and if they came and saw the bones and the corpses, they would have to believe it. If we have to maintain the place, the genocide might be forgotten.

The fact that the Church let the people down, that they found it a trap instead of being a sanctuary, and that they were betrayed by the priest, continued to haunt our group and haunts me still. Ntarama was not the only site of a massacre – there were many others. Fergal Keane relates the story of 7,000 murdered at Nyarubuye, where, later, he even spoke to the killers.[5] Five thousand were murdered in the church at

Ntamata. Yes, there were heroic priests who gave their lives for the people and were killed with them, but there were many who were silent through fear, and others who were 'roving ambassadors for the *génocidaires*', as the journalist Tom Ndahiro told us in Kigali. Other church leaders played a more direct role and were active members of the Habyarimana regime, which organised the slaughter of their own church leaders, or justified it. For example, in June 1994, the Anglican Archbishop Nshamihigo refused to condemn the perpetrators of the genocide – the *Interahamwe* and other Presidential Guards and the state machinery. There is also evidence of incidents of martyrdom, heroic self-sacrifice and courage shown by some Rwandan priests, lay people, as well as foreign missionaries.

THE ROLE OF THE CHURCH CANNOT BE IGNORED

One Anglican bishop spoke graphically to Christian Aid. I cite his report in full because of the full and vivid picture he gave:

> The role of the church is very visible, traceable and real in the making of the genocide. It cannot be ignored. The church was too much mingled in politics. In colonial times, we were called tribes by our masters. The church could have refused this. They could have said: 'No, this is crip-pling, it is creating a problem which is non-existent.' They are implicated.
>
> In the 1958 so-called revolution, tracts were printed in the church press [often the only presses available], inciting people to kill and burn houses. Churches were manipulated to do the work of colonial masters and pre-colonial native masters ... [and were] ... exploited and employed by these evil policies and plans. They surrendered. They had no prophetic muscle to challenge.

I can tell you [names of] bishops . . . heads of churches . . . who planned the genocide; they blessed it. They were digging ditches in every place for dead bodies. They were ordering machetes from China to do it. They knew.

If we are to create a nation, we must speak the truth. Some churches' leaders have confessed and asked forgiveness, like the Presbyterians . . . I wish that all churches would do this. No church can be let off the hook . . . they should apologise to this country. We owe people honesty.

Now, I think the church has taken the lead in reconciliation. Hutu and Tutsi are mingled together in churches. The church is seeing their failure to go deeper in their analysis. So they have taken the lead in helping to get people to be open and apologise and seek forgiveness. I think the church is becoming more realistic. Not only in reconciling people, but in reconciling itself to its calling. Most churches have carried out programmes in peace and reconciliation. But we must be careful; if everyone does not play his part, we are likely to brew violence again.[6]

Just as the story of the Church's degree of complicity with the Nazi party in the Second World War is complex, so is the story of Church–State relations in Rwanda. The task of reconciliation cannot be furthered without the truth being faced. But first I want to widen the issue to ask, what are the issues about reconciliation that feminist spirituality avoids, and are there ways to meet these difficulties and to bridge what seems an impossible impasse?

'IT IS NOT UP TO YOU TO USE THIS WORD . . .'

I begin the exploration by recalling a personal story. I was invited by the Women's Commission of EATWOT (Ecumenical Association of Third World Theologians) to gather a small team of European women theologians to participate, in December 1994, in an intercontinental dialogue at Costa Rica on the theme of 'Women Struggling Against Global Violence: A Spirituality for Life'.[7] So, just before Christmas 1994, women theologians gathered from Africa, Latin America, Asia and other nations from the South: as a northern delegation, we were joined by North Americans, a white South African woman and a Japanese woman theologian. The black American womanist theologians were in strong solidarity with their African and Hispanic-Latin American colleagues. It became rapidly clear that the unresolved issues between us were political and historical divisions, and mistrust based on the lasting experiences of deep-seated oppressions. The bitter legacy of imperialism and colonialism emerged in attitudes and outbursts of deep resentment and anger. This was for me a humiliating experience: the myth of global sisterhood vanished. Any European suffering was considered a mere drop in the ocean compared with the profundity of oppressions these women had experienced. When, in an unconsidered moment, I expressed my hopes for reconciliation in a discussion, the retort flashed back: 'It is not for you to use words like reconciliation: *we* will choose the time and the place.'

Despite its painful nature, I learnt so much from this event: that trust cannot be presumed but must be worked for; that the possibility for reconciliation is inseparable from justice for those who are wronged; that even if my European colleagues and I imagined we were full of good will, good intentions are insufficient grounds for dialogue and real understanding: historically and politically we could not claim innocence, because we are still involved with the legacy of imperialism and colonialism. And, third, affirming the inseparability of reconciliation and justice does not guarantee a credible commitment to either. After thirty years of struggle for an agreement between the IRA and the Unionists in Northern Ireland, the British government well knows what this means.[8]

But when we begin to tackle these concepts, what is striking is the lack of agreement as to what they really mean, and the ambiguity and areas of un-truth that surround them. There is an oft-quoted sentence of a Caledonian (Scottish) chieftain from a conflict two thousand years ago against the Romans that is still relevant now in the contemporary context of the violence and instability of Iraq: 'They create a desolation and they call it peace.'

Thus Tacitus's Caledonian chieftain declaimed before battle. We know this was a critique of the Roman regime that was the historian's own.[9] Indeed, crying peace when there is no peace still seems to be a well-trodden accusation in religious circles – issuing from the prophetic edge to the powers in the centre, from the prophet Jeremiah to Martin Luther, to contemporary figures like Daniel Berrigan. The very word 'reconciliation' can disguise assimilation, forced agreement, imbalance of power, hypocrisy, or imply a mere temporary cessation of arms. All too often in church contexts it is individualised with scant recognition of structural issues. From a Jewish and Palestinian perspective the Jewish theologian Marc Ellis asks, in the context of what he heard as a triumphalist speech of the late Pope John Paul II at Santo Domingo in 1992:

> if the Gospel message has merit, can one simply assert its importance and brush aside the massive destruction it brought along with the command to forgive? I wonder why the penchant for Christian forgiveness is almost always an afterthought to victory, rather than a humility that precedes, indeed may forestall, the conquest.[10]

So, reconciliation may present ostentatious ceremony that is empty of commitment, and show no understanding of the real process that forgiveness entails. It may be an insult to the victim to be asked to forgive some terrible atrocity inflicted on her. The piercing words of Ivan Karamazov from

Dostoevsky's classic frequently come back to haunt us, in their rejection of the possibility of forgiveness in the face of the suffering of innocent children:

> I do not, finally, want the mother to embrace the tormentor who let his dogs tear her son to pieces! She dare not forgive him! Let her forgive him for herself, if she wants to ... but she has no right to forgive the suffering of her child.[11]

The word 'justice' carries equal ambiguities. 'Justice for whom?' we have to ask. Distributive justice? But what does this mean in the context of what President Mugabe of Zimbabwe has been doing with regard to land and to his own people? To what Israel has done in Palestine and Lebanon? To what both Hutus and Tutsis are now experiencing in Rwanda even after the genocide is over? Does justice mean forgiveness and amnesty? But these very concepts seem to compromise justice. After the Jewish Holocaust (or Shoah), one understanding of justice took the form of hounding the perpetrators of crime to the very end, even if they were aged ninety. This seemed to mean never being prepared to forgive, as in the case of Simon Wiesenthal in his hunting down of former Nazi war criminals.

The gravity of our context, in the seemingly intractable situations that surround us – Iraq, Afghanistan, the Middle East, Kashmir, the 'ongoing war against terrorism', Zimbabwe, and so on – almost defeats the attempt to tackle the issue. Conscious of the complexities involved, I explore one possible approach from an area in which I have been struggling for the last twenty years and which has links with the story of Costa Rica told above. This faces head on the question as to how feminist theology and spirituality can make sense of reconciliation and justice and contribute some light to the paradoxes of the contemporary scene.

Let me now tackle the question as to why feminist theology has so many difficulties around the whole area of forgiveness and reconciliation. Of course feminist theologians are not alone: we share these concerns with psychotherapists, peace activists, feminist theorists and all justice-oriented groups. Here I am writing as a Christian feminist with a social justice focus, within what has now become a family of feminist theologies responding to a variety of contexts and interrelated areas of suffering. The many difficulties in this area rest on deeper ones lurking in the background, namely the whole cluster of ideas around sacrifice, atonement and cross-theology – a lot of disputatious ink has flowed in these areas.[12]

Let me give a flavour of the main arguments and then discover a way to move the discussion forward. An immense amount of energy in feminist theology has rightly been focused on what is called 'a passion for justice-making'[13] across a range of issues, and specifically, as regards this particular theme, into a diversity of peace movements and situations of conflict.

I recall the commitment of the women of Greenham Common in Britain in the 1980s who resisted the presence of American cruise missiles; and the work of the Women's Peace Movement in Northern Ireland across the Catholic–Protestant divide and their efforts to create a culture of peace. There are also many active women's interfaith peace groups in the Middle East, even in the teeth of the present bitter conflict – and these attract little media attention. It is even said that after each violent incident, a new peace group is formed.[14] Yet there is still awkwardness and sensitivity around the subject of forgiveness: indeed it is often rejected outright. Of course this sounds shocking when the command of Christ to forgive seventy times seven rings in our ears: we are all too aware that the injunction to forgive is limitless, and that the ministry of reconciliation rightly remains central for Church and authentic Christian discipleship.

So what is going on here? Why should this be such a fraught area? Why are reconciliation and forgiveness seemingly so incompatible with justice? (This issue has already been alluded to in the previous chapter.) The first difficult area is that of domestic violence and sexual abuse against women and children. Despite legal progress in many countries, this is still on the increase in others. Brutal gang rapes accompany military action in many parts of the world. Trafficking in women and small girls is on the increase since the fall of communism. (A contemporary project in Southampton, Hampshire, where a religious congregation is opening a small safe house for rehabilitation of trafficked women makes it very clear that trafficking is on the increase in the UK alone.) In my own work in Wells for India, in the desert of Rajasthan, in an educational project for the children of prostitutes, progress was blocked by the kidnapping of the girls as soon as they were judged old enough to make money. There are vested interests between government, police, truck-drivers and businessmen that keep the sex trade going.[15] This whole area is now well chronicled not only by writers like Susan Thistlethwaite and Marie Fortune of the Centre for Domestic Violence in Seattle, but now by the English National Board of Catholic Women, and Churches in Scotland, Canada and so on.[16]

The relevance to my argument is, first, that for centuries this was tolerated as part of a deeply patriarchal, or *kyriarchal,* status quo, as it is frequently termed.[17] (Here, the word 'kyriarchy' better expresses the interlocking systems of domination – sexism, racism and economic poverty – than does 'patriarchy' that described male domination alone.) Violence against women in the Bible was rarely mentioned. For example, the story of the raped and murdered concubine in Judges 19 was neither remarked upon nor condemned in a public, ecclesial setting. The Church's response to violence against women, via the confessional or even counselling, has been frequently to order the woman to forgive. Her husband, or the perpetrator, 'didn't mean it', 'didn't know any better'. Or, 'she must have provoked it', even 'she must have deserved it' was a suggestion that women have often internalised. It is her role to keep the peace in the family, to keep the family together at all costs. Such is the emphasis on forgiveness that reconciliation without justice in this area became the norm. Shockingly, in some cultures, wife-beating is still an accepted part of the social code: it is even thought necessary for the maintenance of good order. And women can also internalise the practice. A recent piece of research among middle-class, educated women in Chittagaur, in rural Rajasthan and formerly its state capital (N. W. India), shocked me because it revealed that these women actually agreed with wife-beating in order to keep harmony in the extended family unit.[18]

The very same issues – forgiveness with or without justice, denial of human rights and the endurance of cruelty – are not confined to feminist theology: they emerged in Bishop Tutu's own piercing account of the Truth and Reconciliation Commission in South Africa.[19] They emerged for President Aristide in his all too brief seven months leadership in Haiti: would reconciliation mean amnesty, a sweeping under the carpet (the original word in Creole means exactly this), or what degree of justice could be striven for? As the Methodist minister Leslie Griffiths wrote in his biography of Aristide: 'The fiery priest was very clear that there could be no question of accepting "reconciliation" understood as "papering over the cracks of the past" without a clear recognition of the demands of justice.'[20] Yet this, as Griffiths pointed out, would come back to haunt him in the last days of his presidency when he seemed to be asking for precisely that.

The second problematic area is the essentialising of gender roles to keep this dynamic going. Women are supposed to be *essentially* more eirenic, reconciling, sacrificing, geared to smooth over injustices for the sake of family order. Justice does not even come into it where the issue is holding family unity together, whatever the abuse of power within it. A huge amount of criticism is heaped on women who leave a marriage because of the level of injustice within it. It simply does not fit the stereotype of fidelity, whatever the cost, and women are often accused of being 'radical feminists' who put self-interest before the good of husband, children and family unity. (As if this was the correct understanding of radical feminism!)

The third issue is the way that suffering and endurance are justified in the name of stability and the preservation of the status quo. Enduring suffering and renunciation of personal happiness – so the argument goes – means becoming increasingly Christ-like and earning a reward in the next world. *Another jewel in the crown. Without suffering there is no maturity in holiness.* No pain, no gain. Readers are probably familiar with these arguments, which were certainly part of my childhood faith upbringing, described in Chapter 1. Traditional theology of the cross often persuades women, and any victim group, that enduring suffering never mind its unjust origins, is identifying with Jesus on the cross, and obtaining a reward in heaven. In this line of thought, the path to holiness is the path of endurance, suffering and sacrifice. It is part of atoning, expiating the sins of the world for which Jesus died. This argument has even been used against the ordination of women to the priesthood – still an area of struggle and exclusion in the Roman Catholic Church. The poet and novelist Charles Williams (one of 'the Inklings', together with C. S. Lewis and J. R. Tolkien) wrote:

> Well are women warned from serving the altar;
> Who, *by nature of their creature* ...
> share with the Sacrifice the victimisation of blood.[21]

Behind all of this, and most worryingly of all for a believing Christian, is the image of God who appears to sanction the logic of violence in sending Jesus, the obedient son, to a violent death. An extreme following-up on this line of thought would be Rita Nakashima Brock's argument that, in delivering up Jesus, the Divine child, to a violent death, God the Father is a sadist and a sanctioner of child abuse.[22] While I find this idea both repugnant and unacceptable, it is important to consider what it points to: somehow we have to be able to uncover the roots of what has been described as the logic of sacrifice, forever sweeping under the carpet huge areas of injustice and misery not only for women, but also for undervalued groups of people. There are many mythic echoes of the sacrifice of the young, pre-pubertal girl-child, such as Iphigeneia in Greece, or Psyche, sacrificed on the mountain top. All in the name of some supposed greater ideal, like military conquest, progress or the hidden hand of the market, in a secular context, or participating in the unfinished work of atonement in a religious one.

How, then, to begin to unravel this nexus of ideas? The conflict for women of faith seems insuperable, as desire for God and commitment to discipleship of Christ appear to conflict with demands of justice and human rights. I begin by going to the heart of the problem and asking, why did Jesus have to suffer and die on the cross to save the world? Could he not have simply left us a message of love and compassion? Second, I will ask if Jesus actually preached total forgiveness and reconciliation in a way that disregarded the demands of justice.

WHY DID JESUS DIE?

The Gospels tell us that Jesus himself chose the moment to turn towards Jerusalem: 'When the days drew near for him to be received up, he set his face to go to Jerusalem' (Luke 9.51). From the beginning of his ministry Jesus was in conflict with power unjustly exercised. He protested against the way the Sabbath law lacked compassion for animals, and he reached out to rejected categories of people – to women, Samaritans and lepers. He preached endless compassion, giving without limit and deliberately focused on the poorest and most vulnerable people. There is also no doubt that Jesus of Nazareth was familiar with crucifixions. He would have grown up all too aware of the humiliation, degradation and brutality of the way the Romans despatched their many victims. Yet, deliberately he set his face to Jerusalem, to confront power at power's source. His first act in the city was the overturning of the tables of the money-changers (Mark 11.15–18): the sense that he was inaugurating a new order where money ceases to predominate is strong. And this was the beginning of a week of conflict whose seeds were already sown in the Galilean ministry.

I see Jesus' great work of reconciliation not through an anti-Judaistic lens, but in continuity with the mission of the Jewish prophets. This is where reconciliation and justice are inextricably interwoven. In the prophet Isaiah's vision, when people return to God in repentance, the desert blossoms, water flows in the wilderness, the blind see, the lame walk (Isaiah 35.1–10). In another famous passage, fasting and doing penance for sin are coupled with just action:

> Is this not the fast that I choose:
> To loose the bonds of wickedness,
> To undo the thongs of the yoke,
> To let the oppressed go free ...
> Is it not to share your bread with the hungry,
> And bring the homeless poor into your house ...
> Then shall your light break forth like the dawn,
> And your healing shall spring up speedily;
> Your righteousness shall go before you. (Isaiah 58.6–8)

The young Jesus of Nazareth would have grown up nourished by the poet-prophet Isaiah's dreams. Luke saw him in this way, when he pictures Jesus proclaiming the text of Isaiah in the synagogue at the start of his Galilean ministry (Luke 4.18–30). Matthew, too, makes the link, where John's disciples come to Jesus, asking, 'Are you he who is to come or shall we look for another?' Jesus replies: 'Go and tell John what you hear and see: the blind receive their sight, and the lame walk, lepers are cleansed, and the deaf hear, and the dead are raised up and the poor have the good news preached to them' (Matthew 11.3–5).

Feminist Christologies of justice see this as the Christic pattern of right relation, of earth and humanity held together in a vision of mutual flourishing, only possible where hearts are turned and committed to the justice and peace that is the authenticity of the Kingdom of God, or kin-dom, kinship of right relations. If this kin-ship of right relations is what Jesus is proclaiming, then sin is to be seen as 'going against the relational grain of existence'.[23] This can be deepened to mean 'going against the connections with all life-systems, blocking, denying and destroying the life-giving connections'. So restoring the possibility of reconnecting and restoring the life-giving connections must be what redemption is all about.

So, when Jesus urged his followers, 'Take up your cross', what then could he have meant? Not the full-blown ecological meaning of 'cross' that I now want it to signify. Cross as symbolic of the four arms of the universe. Cross as Tree of Life. Cross sinking its roots deep into the earth – and comprehending all the ecological imagery of trees developed through the centuries, for example the haunting voice in the mediaeval poem *Dream of the Rood*. Trees have both a richness and ambiguity of symbolic reference, and are caught up in symbolising pain and oppression, as Larry Rasmussen points out with great insight. He quotes Toni Morrison's great character Sethe, from the novel *Beloved* (cited in Chapter 1), escaping the slavery and savage beatings of Sweet Home, the slave farm. The white girl Amy, who aids her in her flight and the birth of her baby, discovers to her horror the wounds on Sethe's back – like a tree,

> A chokecherry tree. See, here's the trunk – it's red and split wide open, full of sap, and this here's the parting for the branches. You got a mighty lot of branches. Leaves, too, look like and dern if these ain't blossoms. Your back got a whole tree on it. In bloom. What God have in mind, I wonder.[24]

The tree as map of cruelty and sorrow is etched into the slave woman's back. Yet the tree is also a symbol of compassion in Buddhism: for example, the willow tree bending its branches in compassion to the water is a symbol of the Buddhist goddess Kuan Yin.

But for Jesus, growing up in the first century CE, the cross was the symbol-to-hand of degradation and suffering. As a child he would have witnessed thousands of humiliating crucifixions along the roadside. And he had no doubt as to where the chosen path of resistance would lead him. The meaning I hold central is that amidst the affirming of the patterns of right relations and justice in a context of broken-ness, the unity of Jesus with God and their mutual love is revealed through a passionate commitment to the restoration of justice, through their mutual sharing of the yearning for the world's healing. In the Jewish mysticism of Isaac Luria this is referred to as *tikkun olam*, the healing of the world. Obedience in this context then does not mean the conformity – either conscious willing or unthinking – to a pre-arranged script that must end in violent death, in order to fulfil Scripture and to satisfy the wounded honour of God (again, I see this as a distortion of Anselm's theory of atonement). Rather, healing the fractured body of creation demands restorative justice, restoring the relational grain of existence in the concrete restoration of fertility of land, enabling the right functioning of wounded bodies, hungry and broken through poverty, and spirits crushed with loss of hope; and all of this within a movement of turning to God, the source of life, right relation, love and healing.

It is within this vision of structural justice of right relation that forgiveness finds meaning. David Jenkins argued that forgiveness should never be seen apart from the broader theological issues, or without any realisation of the necessary mediating processes that have to go on in relating these personal categories to structures and institutions.[25] That Jesus was very aware of unjust power structures can also be seen by the fact that the forgiveness parables and injunctions are always from powerful to less powerful people, and not the other way round. There is no urging that the battered woman must forgive her abuser or that land-hungry peasants must forgive rapacious landlords. I think of the woman from the town (Luke 7) who is forgiven because she has loved much. Even Peter's famous question as to how often we have to forgive (Matthew 18) is answered by Jesus in terms of the parable of the unjust servant, where the forgiveness/debt cancellation went from the powerful king to the powerless servant and not vice versa. This goes some way in reconciling the call to forgive with the emphasis on justice. Thirdly, the initiative for reconciliation must come from the wronged person, the victim: to utter words on someone's behalf is to sow seeds for more injustice, as I was reminded in Costa Rica. As Haddon Wilmer wrote:

> In forgiveness the initiative lies with them. The suffering of the oppressed may weld them together into a force capable of breaking powerful regimes. But their real power or powerlessness becomes apparent after their victory: is it the power to reconstruct or to make a society new?[26]

But, finally, there is a gratuitousness in forgiving that must lie in the generosity and graciousness of God.[27] A recent initiative called 'The Forgiveness Project' has collected stories from all over the world of people from appalling contexts of murder, war and bereavement, including Rwanda, who have been given courage and strength not to sink into bitterness and desire for revenge and who have created positive movements for peace and healing from the depths of their sorrow.[28] In England in 2005 the country was astounded by the family of the young woman Abigail Wychalls, who was left paralysed after an attempted murder as she returned home after collecting her 2-year-old son from nursery school. The whole family forgave her attacker who committed suicide, seemingly in remorse.

So within this understanding of reconciliation as the vision of the structural healing of the world, and forgiveness as a step on the way to this, is it possible that feminist spirituality may recover a positive theology of sacrifice?

SACRIFICE AND THE PATH TO JUSTICE

This is the core of the difficulty: what feminist theology and all liberation theologies are working towards is this restoration of right relation; this is what reconciliation means. To reconcile, in Greek καταλλάσσειν (*katallassein*), belongs in a group of meanings that denotes 'the action by which peace is made between personal enemies', the work of mediator whose office is 'to make hostility cease', to 'lead to peace'. When it is applied to divine–human relations, it does not mean a change of feelings, writes Ralph Martin, but, 'an objective change in the relations between God and humanity, and more particularly, a change in humanity itself.'[29]

Even from the 'broken web' of the world becoming healed, creation is possible. But it is only achievable on the basis of restorative justice that demands a level of wholehearted, sustained commitment from both individuals and institutions. In the context of globalised, unregulated capitalism the only alternative lifestyle in the face of structural injustice – for the sake of eliminating the massive suffering of impoverished communities of the Two-Thirds World – is a culture of simplicity and voluntary austerity on the part of the affluent countries.

To refuse this is to ignore the fact that massive over-consumption of resources such as water and fossil fuels affects global warming, for which the Two-Thirds World pays a heavy price in terms of drought and flooding.[30] Developing a culture of simplicity – could this be sacrifice by another name? This was the message of Rodolfo Cardenal (a liberation theologian from El Salvador) in a Liberation Theology Summer School, Southampton 1996. Using Jon Sobrino's concept of the cross, referring not merely to Christ, but to the crucified peoples of El Salvador, he called for a culture of austerity in their name:

> The crucified peoples offer values that are not found any-where else. The poor have a great humanising potential because they offer community instead of individualism, service instead of egoism, simplicity instead of opulence, creativity instead of cultural mimicry, openness to trans-cendence instead of positivism and crass positivism.[31]

The crucified peoples, he says, themselves the victims, show openness to pardon, forgiveness and reparation:

> They open their arms to those who offer help, they accept them, and so, without their knowing it, forgive them. They make it possible for the world of the oppressor to recognise that it is sinful, but also to know itself forgiven. So the crucified people introduce a humanising but a very absent reality, grace, whereby one becomes not only through what one achieves, but through what is unexpectedly, unde-servedly and gratuitously given to one.[32]

The Genocide, the Churches and the Betrayal of Sacred Space   39

This voluntary culture of simplicity in the name of the crucified peoples of the world is neither world-renouncing nor world-denying. It is a similar commitment to that which Mahatma Gandhi made for over twenty years in his attempt to work for sustainability in Indian villages in a context of nonviolence. He too was inspired partly by the teaching of Jesus and the ethics of the Sermon on the Mount. Another contemporary voice in the context of modern greed and consumerism is Ernst Schumacher and his alternative economics.[33] This is also the lifestyle willingly adopted by thousands of aid workers, often in alliances and coalitions with secular groups, by missionary movements, lay or congregational religious dedicated to eradicating poverty and structural injustice. (I think both of the life and recent violent death of Margaret Hassan in Iraq, and the murder of Sister Dorothy Stang in Brazil, killed specifically because she had tried to save the rain forest.) The coalitions of Jubilee 2000, of Trade Justice and the Live Aid concerts, as well as actions to limit global warming, are witnesses to what this means in practice.

So the focus now is not so much on sacrifice, asceticism, renunciation (even if these are part and parcel of what follows), but the deliberate adoption of a gospel-orientated, simpler lifestyle that does not depend on exploiting poor communities. Sacrifice is probably the wrong word, because the outstanding hallmarks of this lifestyle are, first, that it is not purely altruistic: people want to do this. It is part of a joyous affirmation of life for all. Some readers will remember the words of the young lay woman Jean Donovan, who was raped and murdered by the military in El Salvador, along with three other Maryknoll missionaries. When writing to her parents in Ireland, in the context of increasing danger, she said how happy she was in El Salvador: 'Why, there are even roses in December!'[34] The same spirit emerges from Arundati Roy's powerful text *The Cost of Living*, written as protest against the Narmada Dam scheme in India. A mystical appeal to other

To Rwanda and Back

kinds of truth, other kinds of dreams than the dominating ones, rings out:

> To love. To be loved. To never forget your own significance. To never get used to the unspeakable violence and the vulgar disparity of life around you. To seek joy in the saddest places. To pursue beauty to its lair. To never simplify what is complicated or complicate what is simple. To respect strength, never power. To try to understand. To never look away. And never, never forget.[35]

Following on from this, it is a life-stance that actually brings happiness and flourishing, because it is in truth one that enables survival and peaceful co-existence, over against the dominant global order based on bringing excessive wealth to a small minority. The emphasis on truth is clearly highlighted in Gandhi's teaching. While Arundhati Roy is not explicitly Gandhian, her impassioned plea is based on a conviction that the realistic facing of the power of truth is the only starting point. As a contemporary Gandhian argues in an article, 'Is Gandhi still relevant?', a new theory of revolution is needed. The concept of *satyagraha,* the power of truth, he writes, defines this revolution:

> it presupposed a deeper sense of shared humanity to give meaning and energy to its sense of justice. The sense of humanity consisted in the recognition of the fundamental ontological fact that humanity was indivisible, that human beings grew and fell together, and that in degrading and brutalising others, they degraded and brutalised themselves.[36]

This deeper sense of shared humanity is what I mean by the power of right relation and the power that drives to justice and reconciliation. It is what Korean theologian Anselm Min means by 'a theology of the solidarity *of* others', based on our shared humanity in the power of the Spirit.[37] In Gandhi's teaching the *satyagrahi* or enlightened one, like the Buddhist *bodhisattva*, takes upon himself or herself the burden of corporate evil and sustains this by the power of suffering love. The power that *satyagraha* relies on is soul-force, not the power of military force, the power of persuasion rather than coercion, as Gandhi's numerous hunger strikes demonstrate. The *satyagrahi's* endurance of prison sentences is also witness to this power of self-sacrifice.

Gandhi's ideas of truth emerged from the early text *Hind Swaraj*, written in 1909 on the ship taking him back to India after his South African experiences.[38] Although they underwent a considerable evolution, from the beginning they included social as well as personal transformation. *Swaraj* first meant discipline. Then Gandhi developed it to mean freedom and liberation and this is linked with the idea of freedom as the inherent possession of human beings. Freedom means the 'capacity to or power to' act – but always out of the interiorisation of obligations to others. (In feminist theory this would be seen as 'the self-in-relation'.) Freedom and truth belong together, grounded in the concrete struggle of the poor for humanity. 'I cannot find God apart from humanity,' he continually said. But this would develop into a much richer notion of God as truth: 'Where there is God there is truth, and where there is truth, there is God.'[39]

Truth is attainable in every heart, it is discoverable in the great religions, and it is reflected in the moral order of justice governing the universe. Later he would say, 'Truth is God'. It is no surprise that the telling of the truth was the highest aim of the South African Truth and Reconciliation Commission. But the pain of allowing the truth to be told meant, said Archbishop Tutu, that the 'requirements of justice, accountability, stability, peace and reconciliation' had to be balanced.[40]

What I have tried to show here is the inseparability of justice-making from truth and that these are embodied in a lifestyle of suffering love and in shared struggle. In this struggle

To Rwanda and Back

what gives strength is the power of truth, the heart already reconciled to this truth. Hence the focus of this book – spirituality, justice and reconciliation – tries to convey the ongoing process of both personal and structural aspects of reconciliation.

This is exactly what makes the link with Jesus setting his face to Jerusalem. His was the freely chosen path of suffering love, emerging from a being totally reconciled with the power and source of life and justice. 'If anyone is in Christ, he is a new creation. All this is from God, who through Christ reconciled us to himself and gave us the ministry of reconciliation' (2 Corinthians 5.17).

But feminist Christology also stresses the community dimension of Christ's setting his face to confront the power of the system. Christ-and-community embodied the struggle for truth and justice. The struggle that appeared to end with crucifixion was a protest against all crucifixions, against the necessity of the violent putting to death of the innocent, poor and vulnerable. As Beverley Harrison wrote in a widely quoted passage:

> Jesus' death on a cross, his sacrifice, was no abstract exercise in moral virtue. His death was the price he paid for refusing to abandon the radical activity of love . . . Sacrifice, I submit, is not a central moral goal or virtue in the Christian life. Radical acts of love . . . are the central virtues of the Christian moral life . . .
>
> Like Jesus, we are called to a radical activity of love, to a way of being in the world that deepens relation, embodies and extends community, passes on the gift of life . . .
>
> . . . To be sure, Jesus was faithful unto death. He stayed with his cause and he died for it. He *accepted* sacrifice. But his sacrifice was *for* the cause of radical love, to make relationship and to sustain it, and, above all, to *righting* wrong relationship, which is what we call 'doing justice'.[41]

In a similar way, Rodolfo Cardenal quoted his Jesuit colleague Ignacio Ellacuria, murdered by the government soldiers, as saying, 'To liberate means to take the crucified people down from the Cross. But the world of oppression and sin cannot tolerate that the people be taken down from the Cross.'[42]

Those women who stood steadfast at the cross of Christ in the presence of the violence and brutality of the soldiers were ready to receive the empowerment of resurrection morning. The fact that these women had already experienced forgiveness and reconciliation within the community of those who struggled in suffering love for a new order of living – this is crucial to the argument. They had already accepted a ministry of reconciliation. As such, their resistance to the established order was made possible because it was empowered by a vision of a world graced with reconciliation. The task now is to explore how this works today and what its relevance is to the genocidal tragedy with which I began.

TO STRUGGLE WITH A RECONCILING HEART

Reconciliation is both a symbol of healed creation, a vision that enables and inspires action for a future state of being, and something that one already tastes and lives from now. It is something that touches our deepest yearnings. Originally the phrase 'to struggle with reconciled hearts' came from the Taizé community in south-west France. It seemed to sum up the commitment to reconciliation this community has practised since it was founded by the late Brother Roger Schutz after the Second World War. My changing of the word 'reconciled' to a more active 'reconciling' symbolises the dynamic nature of the process that touches all aspects of our lives. Where violence is experienced culturally, politically, economically, sexually and ecologically, resistance to this can never uncouple the longing for peace and reconciliation from

To Rwanda and Back

the justice of the Kingdom of God and the commitment to the overturning of the order of domination for an order based on right relation between God, all peoples and all creatures of the earth.

In feminist theology's work with victims of abuse and violence, theological and pastoral networks engage with the need for forgiveness through a many-staged process. Forgiveness is a word based on 'letting-go' for the sake of moving on, away from bitterness and hatred to a new way of being. Because it should be based on a mutuality that is seldom present or even possible, many say that forgiveness is only possible for God. *To forgive is Divine* – this is most frequently heard in the context of the genocide of the Jewish people in the Holocaust (or Shoah). Others also use it in the context of massive genocide – not only in Rwanda, but in the ecocide during the colonisation of Latin America and the recent ethnic cleansings in Greater Serbia and Kosovo.

So the deepest level of forgiveness is always the graciousness of God's gift. But how does this help the innocent victim? The point to hang on to is that it is only possible to move towards flourishing and to any concept of a happy life if victims are able to let go of the destructive hatreds that corrode their inmost being. But it is not only bitterness that needs healing but the annihilation of self-worth, the feelings of shame, humiliation and the need to hide from society. In the context of rape and domestic violence, where there is no question of the perpetrator asking for forgiveness, theologian Marie Fortune has proposed a seven-stage process of moving forward. This involves hearing the victim's story, acknowledging its truth, before moving towards what justice and restoration is possible, bearing in mind that full justice is never possible. The crime can never be undone. Yet, she writes, 'forgiveness means acknowledging the humanity of the offender . . . while never condoning what he did'.[43] It will be absolutely vital that the victim experiences some form of justice and restitution. If the offender does not repent, the legal system may prove an expression of justice in holding him accountable. But if not, counsellors, school teachers or, hopefully, someone in pastoral authority whom it is possible to trust. Only where there is a possibility of real repentance, of accountability and healing of the broken trust can there be any hope of genuine reconciliation. Later in this book I will ask the question as to what extent this could happen in Rwanda.

The process of 'struggling with a reconciling heart' touches individuals: but individuals are also persons in communities, with histories, cultures and memories. In contexts like Rwanda, Palestine and Northern Ireland it is important to discover how this could work on the wider level of whole communities separated by centuries of bitterness. First, bearing in mind Marc Ellis's earlier-cited critique of the Catholic Church, I ask if we can mine Christian tradition, looking for deeper insights of prophetic justice, asking if peace and reconciliation with justice – often subversive – has remained a priority for marginal groups, even if lost sight of by the wider Constantinian tradition where military violence calls itself the preserver of peace.

PEACE – A SUBVERSIVE FOUNDATION FOR RECONCILIATION?

Reconciliation in the early Christian communities always involved a double process of expelling in order to welcome back. There was a sure instinct for discerning sins that could not be tolerated because they wounded the community – sins such as idolatry, adultery and killing. But, being deprived of community in order to take the time for repentance was always followed by the welcome back of the penitent into full community. The narthex of the great churches emerging in the fourth century is witness that there was always a place for the community of penitents and catechumens preparing for baptism. Second, the tradition of fidelity to non-violence, the intuition that violence was contrary to the gospel ethic, has a strong witness in Christianity from Irenaeus, Tertullian and Justin Martyr onwards. It was expressed in terms of refusal to bear arms in the emperor's army. This text of Tertullian expresses it eloquently, even if incredible to contemporary ears:

> But now the question is whether the believer can be a soldier and whether the soldier can be admitted to the faith, even if he is only a member of the rank and file who are not required to take part in sacrifices or capital punishments. There can be no compatibility between the divine and human sacrament (= military oath), the standard of Christ and the standard of the devil, the camp of light and the camp of darkness. One soul cannot serve two masters – God and Caesar ... but how will a Christian go to war? Indeed how will he serve in peace-time without a sword which the Lord has taken away? ... the Lord, in subsequently disarming Peter, disarmed every soldier.[44]

Even if it would be too much to claim that this is pacifism in the modern sense, we can still see a community struggling with the tension between the standards of Christian living and the active life of the soldier. (There were similar tensions for Christians with regard to dancing, acting, circus life and being a gladiator.) When it comes to Hippolytus of Rome in the third century, the same prohibition is found, but he is also worried about the idolatry involved as well as the immorality accompanying a soldier's life.[45] Origen, too, who imagined an empire at peace, made a powerful plea that the vocation of Christians was offering prayer to God on behalf of those fighting for a righteous cause.[46]

Tragically, this early idealism was swept away by the Emperor Constantine's need to defend the empire, and then when successive waves of Germanic 'barbarianism' threatened the very existence of the empire itself. Augustine's attempts to put limits on military aggression by the Just War theory are well known,[47] but his conditions are now widely felt to have been superseded by the threat of total annihilation that modern warfare presents. Yet even in the Middle Ages, against the background of the Crusades, the expulsion of both Jew and Muslim, the radicality of the vision of the Kingdom of peace could sometimes be glimpsed. It is seen in certain monastic orders, in the prophetic teaching of non-violence, and in a remarkable movement in central Europe called Peace of God, and the Truce of God which illustrates the focus on justice for the vulnerable.

> The Peace of God was the protection from military violence won by special groups in mediaeval society. These included the clergy and their possessions: the poor; women, peasants and their tools, animals, mills, vineyards, and labour; and later pilgrims and merchants – in short, most of the mediaeval population who neither bore arms nor were entitled to bear them.[48]

This is linked with the preaching of St Francis of Assisi, who not only condemned the military and brought about reconciliation between warring factions in Perugia, but acted out of a love of poverty and simplicity of lifestyle specially in response to a culture of affluence; reconciliation and justice are once more seen as inseparable. In the many examples from the Reformed tradition, such as the inspiration of Quakers and Anabaptists, as well as contemporary movements for reconciliation – Taizé, Corrymeela, Pax Christi, the inspiration of Dorothy Day, Thomas Merton, Coventry Cathedral – I mention two, because they emerge from some of the most painfully violent settings today, where reconciliation seemed an impossible dream. These are the Mennonite tradition of conflict resolution and the work of the community of San Egidio in Rome.

John Paul Lederach, a Mennonite who has mediated between the Sandinistas in Nicaragua and the Yatumas, indigenous peoples of the East coast, declares that reconciliation is based on three paradoxes: it promotes encounters between open expression of a painful past and the search for a long-term viable future. Second, it is a place where justice and peace meet. Third, it recognises the need to give time and place to justice and peace, where redressing wrong is held together with a vision of a connected future.[49] Later, I will return to Lederach's vision for further inspiration. What he offers can be seen as a public and communal version of what feminist theologian Marie Fortune worked out in a more personal context. Another Mennonite, Ronald Kraybill, describes a similar process, where Christianity played a part in mediating the transition of Rhodesia to Zimbabwe. Different denominations brought different gifts: the Catholic Institute of International Relations (CIIR) and the Justice and Peace Commission represented Catholicism, stressing listening to the victims, the voice of moral conscience and negotiation. The Moral Rearmament movement stressed 'absolute love' involving 'listening to God', whereas the Quakers wanted to establish solidarity with all parties through disciplined listening.[50]

But the overwhelming reason why it was felt that religion offers an indispensable quality to the process of mediation and reconciliation is not so much its record on forgiveness and non-violence, but on the quality of trust it may be able to offer. Earlier I cited Joseph Montville's statement that into the midst of dehumanised, raped people 'come religious outsiders, who in varying ways convey a sense of understanding and empathy for their fears, and who have established reputations for honesty, discretion and integrity'.[51] This is exactly the quality that describes the almost miraculous efforts of the

Sant'Egidio community.[52] Ten years ago, in a garden in the hills near Rome, this community managed to facilitate a reconciliation in the context of the bitter civil war in Mozambique. The negotiations were between the Transport Minister of Mozambique (Frelimo) and the guerrilla in charge of the rebel army (Renamo). The founder of Sant'Egidio, Andrea Riccardi, and his companions (including the Archbishop of Beira of Mozambique) had broken through the government's insistence on a ceasefire and the rebel insistence on constitutional changes before laying down weapons. Riccardi invoked their common African heritage, their being Mozambique patriots, and the principle enunciated by Pope John XXIII, 'Let us be concerned with seeking what unites, rather than that which divides.' One breakthrough moment was over the menu. In Mozambique, the head of the table has the right to the head of the fish. But the Italian hosts served up two whole grilled fish so that each could have one! 'It was these two fish which pointed towards the parties' mutual recognition, and the moment when the facilitators became the mediators.'[53]

This is a remarkable story, all the more given the violent background I have been describing of the genocidal wars in Rwanda and Burundi, as well as the conflicts in the Congo and Angola. The lack of institutional support, the appeal to civil society and the ability to create active links with countries genuinely interested in seeking a peaceful solution, were all crucial aspects. This fish story opens up again the crucial dimension of the role of symbols in making reconciliation and justice, as well as the respectful invoking of cultural memories (as discussed in the last chapter). For all parties bring to the struggle – not yet the table – the horror of the memories of atrocities of living memory, and of centuries of violence never to be forgotten. Whereas a prophetic individual – a Mandela, or a Gandhi or a Gordon Wilson, with his young daughter murdered at Enniskillen – all usually people with years of suffering witness behind them, may rise to the heroic and saintly levels of forgiveness, they are not often able to carry a whole nation with them. The question of timing is crucial – the heart may not be ready to reconcile.

John de Gruchy tells a poignant story of this in the South African context.[54] He relates the story of a white South African policeman who wanted to do more than tell his story of murdering the son of a black couple. He wanted to tell the couple personally of his repentance and ask for forgiveness. So he visited them – and apparently the event was videoed. The couple, though moved, said they were not ready to forgive yet, but asked him to return later. Eventually, they said, yes, they would forgive him – and at that moment a flower vase came flying through the air and hit the policeman on the forehead so that he was bleeding heavily. The dead man's younger brother had been watching the video in the next room. In a timely warning of the intergenerational nature of painful memories of atrocities, the message was: his parents might forgive, but he was not ready. Yet through being personally wounded, the policeman felt that somehow he had participated in the suffering of the parents of the murdered man. For me the story's message for spirituality is that if we are committed to reconciliation and justice it means bearing the pain of wounded memories in our own flesh and bone. As the young journalist Antjie Krog wrote, while she covered the Truth and Reconciliation Commission for South African radio, and could only make sense of the process by gathering with her fellow journalists around Archbishop Desmond Tutu each night:

Because of you
This country no longer lies
Between us but within . . .

In the cradle of my skull
It sings, it ignites

My tongue, my inner ear, the cavity of my heart
Shudders towards the outline of intimate clicks and gutturals

Of my soul the retina learns to expand
Daily because of a thousand stories
I was scorched.

A new skin.
I am changed forever. I want to say:
Forgive me
Forgive me
You whom I have wronged, please
Take me
With you.[55]

Struggling with a reconciling heart, this journalist is able to
feel the affliction of the conflict in the fibres of her own body.
So, in societies bent on self-destruction through the urge to
dominate and through violent conflict, our hope lies in
building counter-cultural communities based on gospel-
inspired visions of truth, simplicity and austerity, in the name
of building restored just relations; in so doing we will move, in
Miroslav Wolf's words, from exclusion to embrace. The
inspiration in struggling for reconciling hearts is the biblical
call to reconciliation and forgiveness based on a vision of
justice and flourishing of the most vulnerable people and the
earth herself. Even if that vision eludes fulfilment at the
moment, faith in a God of reconciliation is what holds our
hope firm. As Canon Naim Ateek of Jerusalem writes with
regard to his own context – and he has every reason to despair:
'Ultimately justice will prevail, the occupation will be over,
and the Palestinians, as well as the Israelis, will enjoy freedom
and independence. How do I know this will take place? I
know because I believe in God.'[56]

I write this after just hearing the news of Brother Roger of Taizé's brutal murder in a church service. In a way it provides a link with how this chapter began, namely with the tragic depiction of the massacre in Ntarama Chapel in Rwanda. Again a violation of sacred space. How could the Churches have let people down so horribly? This had been our question. How could reconciliation be possible, given the gravity of the crimes? Yet Brother Roger's life has been an icon of love in search of reconciliation ever since he arrived in the small village of Taizé at the end of the war. Thousands of young people have climbed the mountain to the monastery, heavy-hearted, with lost dreams and dashed hopes. And what did they find? With a warm welcome from the Brothers, candlelit prayer before the icons and the famous Taizé chants that stretched deep into the night, somehow a vision was rekindled. And part of the welcome and abiding inspiration was the sight of the ageing figure of Brother Roger, in his place in the church, always surrounded by a group of children. Over the last fifty years Taizé has inspired journeys to many poor countries, identifying places both of suffering and hope, and has been responsible for a global movement of pilgrimage in search of peace and reconciliation. And the lasting legacy of Brother Roger is to shed light on the meaning of sacrifice for Christian life as voluntary self-giving, within a kingdom vision of reconciliation, right till the end.

Here, I have been discussing the problems that feminist theology shares with other marginalised groups, namely the ideologising of reconciliation and forgiveness without due attention being paid to justice. Problems crystallised especially around the logic of sacrifice, where Jesus being 'handed over' by the Father to a violent death[57] seemed to legitimise papering over the cracks of injustice. Women too often suffer from the violating of sacred space – in this case, not the church but the home itself. But even if Brother Roger was assassinated in his own sacred space, the monastic church, *his life is a shining witness to the fact that the real sacred space is the space of redeeming action*. For Taizé's theology is never to make an idol of church. Even if those of us who journey to the mountain seek and find inspiration to heal our dying visions of Church, the message from the Brothers is always that the place to be is where action of reconciliation and justice is needed.

Thus I have tried to show that in the ministry of Jesus the call to repentance went hand in hand with the claims of justice, and within what feminist Christologies from different parts of the globe see as the vision of restoring broken relation. Could sacrifice be re-envisioned as the willed lifestyle of resistance to domination and oppression, and as the solidarity of suffering and self-giving love? Gandhi's life blazed a trail by showing how vital is the task to tell the truth amidst the deceptions and spinning of culture where truth has become undervalued. Brother Roger of Taizé has taken this a step further in actively seeking the way of peace on the world arena and paid the same price as Jesus and Gandhi.

In stressing the personal and communal dimensions of 'struggling with reconciling hearts' I have shown how Christian tradition reveals riches of subversive resistance to violence, linked with working for justice for the poorest peoples. Feminist theology's task has been to bring the position of poor and oppressed women into this process and in so doing to challenge the foundations of oppression in all their complexity. Perhaps the very resistance to the distorted concept of sacrifice by many feminist theologians is so strong because a purified living out of sacrifice already underpins the daily lives of so many women in positive ways that feminist spirituality would want to uphold. *The reality of many women's lives is the sacrificial quality of suffering love.*

The way forward then lies in looking empathetically at these lives of women who are icons of suffering love, in their commitment to their loved ones, to the community and to the sustaining of life itself. What could they – like Dancilla in Rwanda, who cares for the bones in the chapel of Ntarama – teach the Churches about the lived practice of reconciliation?

3 THE WORLD WAS SILENT — AND ABANDONED RWANDA

Seeking a Spirituality of Care and Compassion

> It has been almost nine years since I left Rwanda, but as I write this, the sounds, smells and colours come flooding back in digital clarity ... For many of these years I have wanted to return to Rwanda and disappear into the blue-green hills with my ghosts. A simple pilgrim seeking forgiveness and pardon. But as I slowly begin to piece my life back together, I know the time has come for me to make a more difficult pilgrimage: to travel back through all the terrible memories and retrieve my soul.
>
> *Colonel Roméo Dallaire*[1]

This chapter begins with another sort of silence. Neither the silent contemplation of God nor the silence of structured amnesia that buries the dangerous memories of oppressed peoples: rather, this is the silence that masked a massive failure of compassion and solidarity on the part of governments, the United Nations and the Churches at the time of the genocide. It was the silence of those who passed by, who closed their ears and hardened their hearts, and left thousands of Rwandans to their fate.

Where was the Church in all the killing? Our group in Kigali continued to ask this. Why did they not try to stop the genocide? Why did the World Council of Churches, the international NGOs and social activists mount global campaigns against apartheid in South Africa, yet fall silent about genocide in Rwanda? There are numerous witnesses still continuing to speak of 'churches blind to genocide'. And of complicity not only because of omission, but of *commission*. It is painful to relate that the time of the genocide coincided with the Synod of African Bishops in Rome (1994), fully reported on in *The Tablet* – but the genocide scarcely merited a mention in the Bishops' proceedings in Rome.[2]

I watched a poignant BBC television documentary about the return to Kigali of the Commander of the United Nations Peace-keeping mission in Rwanda (UNAMIR), General Roméo Dallaire, in 2004, for the tenth anniversary of the genocide. As my opening extract shows, General Dallaire's life has been searingly affected by his Rwandan experience. A man of great courage, he speaks of being sick at heart when, at the height of the killing, expatriates panicked and fled the country, using his all-too-few troops to guarantee their safe passage to the airport. These were troops that he sorely needed to protect the people under attack. Yet the people who had become rich and enjoyed a luxurious lifestyle in Rwanda were now being protected and given an escape route, while many of the country's own people were slaughtered.[3] But apart from the sheer horror of the killing, which eventually destroyed his spirit and almost his mind – for years he suffered from post-traumatic stress disorder and attempted suicide – what broke General Dallaire was his inability to get anyone to give any effective assistance. He relates how continually, on a daily basis, he telephoned and faxed the United Nations, the US government, his own government (Canadian), the Belgians – in fact any government and NGO with whom he could get in contact – begging for help, material or financial, for troops, equipment or permission to take a more proactive role, in his efforts to save the Rwandan people. Even revisiting Rwanda ten years later, this abandonment of Rwanda by the world is one of his greatest sorrows, a fact testified to by other witnesses in the BBC documentary. One of the most striking statements was by Rwanda's president Paul Kagame, who (as was related earlier) led the Rwandan Patriotic Front (RPF) into Kigali, effectively stopping the genocide. Now, eleven years later, viewers of this documentary could observe Kagame telling Dallaire – frankly and chillingly – that he was merely a pawn in the game. This, as anyone could observe, did not remotely help the General, who remains deeply troubled by the fact that he failed to stop the killing.

General Dallaire knows that the real responsibility lay with those Rwandans who 'planned, ordered, and eventually conducted' the genocide. Responsibility also lay with two world powers, France and the United States, both of which lacked the political will to make the Arusha Accords work. If his modest requests for troops and capabilities had been answered he still thinks he could have stopped the killings. But he analyses his own responsibilities more deeply:

> My own *mea culpa* is this: as the person charged with the military leadership of UNAMIR, I was unable to persuade the international community that this tiny, poor, over-populated country and its people were worth saving from the horror of genocide – even when the measures needed for success were relatively small ... at its heart, the Rwandan story is the story of the failure of humanity to heed a call for help from an endangered people.[4]

THE FAILURE OF COMPASSION

How can this massive failure of solidarity and compassion be explained? The question lies at the core of any attempt to mould a spirituality of reconciling justice. In Chapter 1 I focused on re-examining the importance for a spirituality of justice of re-membering, while the previous chapter tried to understand sacrifice in terms of suffering love. Here in this chapter I am trying to discover a new understanding of

To Rwanda and Back

solidarity and compassion as vital components of a liberation spirituality. Of course in the context of the Rwandan genocide, there were many individual acts of compassion which did save lives on both sides of the struggle. But what made the horror so inhuman was the blocking of the normal flow of human kindness between friends, neighbours and even within families themselves.

But, inside the refugee camps that were established just over the borders of Uganda, Tanzania and Zaire (Congo), a remarkable flow of compassion was displayed. This is when the conscience of the world awoke to what had happened and the combined resources of NGOs, Churches and humanitarian organisations poured into Rwanda's borders to confront the oceans of human misery that were forming. By 1995 a quarter of Rwanda's surviving population was still in the camps; 250,000 alone had crossed over the bridge between Rwanda and Tanzania in 24 hours. Hugh McCullum writes: 'The feeding and watering of 330,000 people crowded into 10 square kilometres at Benaco Camp in the arid bush of Northwest Tanzania captured the world's attention.'[5] Mere survival was the first goal: searching for water, for scarce wood for cooking, and joining enormous, chaotic queues for food formed daily rituals:

> Shelter is non-existent, but soon little round huts emerge, later to be covered with blue and green plastic sheeting. It is an impossible situation, but the professionals from UNHCR, ICRC, Oxfam and other relief agencies [like Care International, Caritas, Christian Aid] move quickly to establish order and set up camps along the lines of the same sectors and communes the people are used to at home.[6]

But the tragedy of the camps consisted in more than the struggle for mere survival. Even though, initially, in Tanzania there had been an attempt to confiscate thousands of machetes, in case the *génocidaires* among the refugees would continue to murder Tutsis, there were insufficient resources to apprehend the real killers, and eventually:

> The killers quickly took control over the camps. Some even got work with relief agencies. Because UNHCR had organised the camps along Rwandan administrative lines, power was taken over by the same people who started the genocide inside the country.[7]

The scandal remains not only that many of the killers are still at large, still able to organise armed resistance, but that there were massive reprisal killings by the Rwandan Patriotic Army (RPA – formerly RPF), for example at Goma, where 2 million people streamed to avoid death, as well as at the terrible massacre at Kibeho. Here at least 400,000 people were placed, under supervision of the reorganised UNAMIR and many international humanitarian agencies. And the people did not want to leave the camps, as there was sufficient food and medical care. But the official government argument was that Rwanda was now safe and refugees should return. So another round of killings began in the camps around Kibeho. The policy to force the refugees to return began in earnest. The killing at Kibeho is one of the worst post-genocide stories: estimates of deaths are between 4000 and 8000 people.[8] Most were killed by the RPA, many were crushed to death in the stampede, and some bludgeoned by the *Interahamwe*. Yet still many Hutu extremists escaped to other camps on the borders, meaning that the spirals of violence were able to continue. But the tragic irony of this situation was that the compassion that might have helped to prevent or bring the genocide to an end came tragically too late, poured into the refugee camps, where the aid workers found themselves face to face with the *génocidaires*.[9] Many found this a great crisis of conscience: yet they had no choice but to feed this teeming mass of people – hungry, thirsty, homeless and sick. They were helpless in the

Hutu extremists' project of re-arming and continuing the armed struggle. So, what could all this mean for spirituality?

SPIRITUALITY AND COMPASSION

'Spirituality', Kathy Galloway writes, is 'that which ultimately moves you – the fundamental motivation of your life'.[10] 'Spirituality', says Brian Woodcock, 'is inclusive and holistic. It crosses frontiers and makes connections. It is characterised by sensitivity, gentleness, depth, openness, flow, feeling, quietness, wonder, paradox, being, waiting, acceptance, awareness, healing and inner journey.'[11]

Put in Christian terms this means that the fundamental motivation of the human psyche is longing for God. It is this longing that is transformed into the active practices of faith, be they openness and sensitivity to others, compassion and thirst for justice and peace. All this sounds inspirational, but the sentiments do not seem to make sense in the grim Rwandan situation I have just been describing of the failure of compassion, tenderness and care. Reconciliation needs all of this, but never separated from struggle for justice. So, here I am going to explore what compassion could mean, first, by looking at motherhood, asking what insights are gained for spirituality today, and what could be offered to the Church and the wider community in the dilemmas now being faced.

I have chosen motherhood because it is an easy place to see how essential are care, tenderness and compassion for the sustaining of life. It is also chosen because motherhood is a neglected yet well-attested metaphor for the love of God.[12] Mindful of the diversity of contexts where motherhood is lived out, I am trying to hold before readers' eyes the dilemma between the constraints and burdens of motherhood on the one hand, and yet the crucial importance of the qualities most privileged for contemporary spirituality, such as tenderness and nurture, care and compassion. I also want to bring the lived experience of mothers into reflection on spirituality. The body of the mother – frequently despised or erased from texts – is sometimes idealised by intense devotion to the Virgin Mary. (I will return to and deepen this reflection in Chapter 6.) This focus on motherhood neither attempts to romanticise, nor to describe women's identity as necessarily being about mothering: I will range cross-culturally in this exploration and attempt to show how the care and nurture of mothering need to be interpreted in a far more holistic way.

A PERSONAL STORY

This journey matters to me deeply, not least because motherhood has been part of my life across three generations. I explained that I was the eldest of seven children growing up in north-east England. My parents were teachers at a time when teachers were very badly paid. They relied on my assistance – and that of my sisters – with the newest baby and small children, and with house work, as my mother needed to keep teaching just to help our family survive. So from an early age I struggled to balance study with care of small children. I experienced history repeating itself a generation later, when I began to study theology in Louvain (Belgium), with four small children of my own, the youngest being just two years old. All my examination periods at the university were fraught because of children's illnesses. And now I have a growing number of grandchildren the pattern again repeats itself: one of these children is autistic and his special needs have brought his parents and the extended family into a new awareness of the kind of caring needed by children with such a different experience and perception of life.

All this experience has presented enormous riches, but at the same time quite a cost, even though I have lived in a very privileged environment compared with impoverished Third

World women, mothers in war situations, and young African children forced to be mothers and head households because their parents have died of AIDS. But personal experience for all its limitations is not a bad place to start and to ask, *what are the insights drawn from motherhood for a spirituality of care and compassion?*

LOOKING AT SCRIPTURE AND TRADITION

What I observe, first of all, is that we are in a new situation – at least in the West. For mothers in the North and West, motherhood need not be a permanent identity. At one point in my life, it did provide the entire parameters of my life. But I find now that although I love my children and grandchildren intensely, my energies are also focused on theological education and social activism. At the same time there is a sense that the sands in the hourglass are running out, and time with those I love, especially my husband Nicholas and those closest to me, becomes more precious, as *being* becomes equally as vital as *doing*. It could be argued, on the other hand, that we have many identities and that when we speak about the self, we mean our many selves and the *self-always-in-process*.[13]

By contrast, mothers in the Hebrew Bible had little choice. Valued for the vital task of bearing the children of a small group of people, who knew themselves threatened by larger nations (like Egypt and Babylon), barrenness was experienced as an enormous social stigma. Wives were valued for bearing sons – as they still are in many countries today. In addition, wives and mothers were the property of their husbands, with no legal rights of their own. Like village mothers in Asia and Africa today, the lives of Jewish women were tough, as they coped with the daily tasks of care of the family in an extended family situation (often a multi-generational family), work in fields, olive groves or in vegetable gardens/plots near the household, or mending fishing nets, baking bread and weaving clothes. We have very few studies of women's work in the New Testament – sadly, it is part of the invisibility and silence that surrounds women in the Scriptures.[14]

There are also only relatively few examples of women's leadership or scholarship. Miriam, Esther and Deborah are examples of female leadership, and it is possible that Judith belonged to an ascetic sect and was steeped in learning. With the possible exception of Queen Esther, none of these were mothers. The wives of the patriarchs – Sarah, Hagar, Rebecca, Leah and Rachel – were valued because of the children they bore. Finally – a point highly significant for our times – motherhood in the Hebrew Bible was often fraught with danger. I think of the midwives Shiprah and Puah (from Exodus 1), who rescued the Hebrew babies from Pharaoh's murderous edict, as well as the Holy Innocents killed by Herod after the birth of Jesus. Motherhood has dangerous political implications.

When it comes to the Christian Scriptures, the context is the Roman occupation of Palestine, and the poverty of most of the Jewish families struggling for a living, many of them landless. From the Gospels we gain vital insights: Jesus valorised women *apart* from their role in bearing children: '*Blessed are they who hear the word of God and put it into practice*' (Luke 8.19–21). For him discipleship of the Kingdom was the valued category and he numbered women among his disciples. We know they accompanied him on his journeys (Luke 8.1).

Secondly, the role played by Mary, the mother of Jesus, would become crucial in the history of redemption. As readers are aware, not only has devotion to Mary often been an ecumenical obstacle, but it has been part of the reason why motherhood has been essentialised as the only way to holiness for women. Fortunately, rather than focusing on contested doctrines like the virgin birth, recent theology has stimulated more enriched and historically accurate understandings of

To Rwanda and Back

Mary. In Latin America, Maria Clara Bingemer and Yvone Gebara see her as Mother of the Poor, the prophetic Mary of the Magnificat who raises her voice in the name of all poor, cast-down women.[15] Rosemary Ruether understands Mary as the first redeemed believer, thus a figure of the Church – a mothering role in an ecclesial symbolic sense.

But this does not quite do justice to any role Mary has in redemption specifically as mother. In fact the bodily experience of Mary has been erased. I think it is with Mary, if we can disentangle all unnecessary accretions of devotion around her, that we discover the practice of a profound spirituality of motherhood. (I realise I am influenced by my Roman Catholic background.) The Catholic Church has always stressed the importance of Mary's *fiat*, her obedient assent to God's word. But, sadly, this has served to essentialise the passive obedience of women to superiors, be they father, husband or son, and emphasised obedience as unflinching acceptance of authority.

A very recent study by Elizabeth Johnson, *Truly our Sister*, changes our perspective: she places Mary in her historical context as a young Jewish girl, in the socio-geographical context of Galilee.[16] This means that we have to put aside the famous depictions of Mary from our western traditions, beloved though they may be, of a beautifully dressed Mary, usually in white and blue, who, awaiting Gabriel's message, is discovered reading a book. Here is not the appropriate moment to discuss all the Marian dogmas. I simply want to get at the historical roots of Mary as a poor peasant mother, with all the responsibilities mentioned earlier, probably illiterate, given statistics for peasant communities then and knowing what we know now about illiteracy of women globally in peasant communities. Yet she is a person of deep faith, schooled in Jewish Scriptures, through listening to synagogue prayer and the oral prayer tradition, in addition to her own life of prayer. She is a person able from this faith to be capable of courage and action, and willing to make a risk-taking response to God. As Johnson writes:

> A woman of spirit, she embarks on the task of partnering God in the work of redemption. African-American theologian Diana Hayes describes Mary's action here as one of 'outrageous authority'; standing alone, she had enough faith in herself and in her God to say a powerful and prophetic 'yes'. From a Latin-American viewpoint, Ana Maria Bidegain argues that far from signifying 'self-denial, passivity and submission as the essential attributes of women, Mary's consent is a free act of self-bestowal for the purpose of co-creating a new world.'[17]

Through this lens it is possible to reinterpret many of the scriptural scenes that appear to give Mary a passive role (for example the Marriage Feast at Cana in John 2) and to move the perceptions of motherhood from confinement to the domestic scene – something that in Britain dates only from the nineteenth century – to its wider social context. The responsible role given to mothers in the time of Mary, despite the patriarchal context and the poverty, contests the fact that women were so oppressed. It could also be said of mediaeval Europe – even if this is a huge generalisation – that despite the inferior position of women, if there was no desperate poverty and no war, there was a degree of respect for women as responsible for the intergenerational household. In a similar way there was respect for the women abbesses, who sometimes held responsibility for double monasteries, and exercised the role of spiritual motherhood. I think of Hilda of Whitby, of Hildegard of Bingen and of the wisdom of the anchoress Julian of Norwich, for whom *Jesus was our mother.*

Lest readers think that I am presenting an over-rosy picture, I want to give three examples that point to the difficult area of motherhood and suffering which lead us into what is important for spirituality. I begin with the slave trade that affected both Britain and the United States. African American writers of novels drawn from slave narratives leave us in no doubt as to the anguish experienced by mothers in these situations. Here it was not just a question of lack of freedom and back-breaking work. Vulnerable to the seductions of the slave owner and the cruelty of his wife, despised for producing his child, she had to endure her own children being sold, her own motherhood of no account. In Chapters 1 and 2, I cited Toni Morrison's novel *Beloved*, which poignantly evoked the anguish of the escaped slave woman and mother Sethe, and the horror of Sweet Home, from which she had escaped. But the book's central focus is the fact that in order to save her children from being recaptured by the slave team hunting them down, Sethe tried to kill them, and did manage to kill the baby, *Beloved* (the book's title). Countless other slavery texts recount similar stories of the sorrow of mothers: for the African American women's context, these narratives count as sacred texts.

This points to the fact that motherhood can be exploited, that it is a site of danger, frequently because of women's vulnerable sexuality and role in procreation. *The dangerous memories of motherhood have been overlooked by liberation theology together with the sexual experience on which it is frequently based.* Let me link this example with that of war situations. It is nothing new to say that rape is a concomitant of war, and despite it being punishable there are still numerous horrendous occurrences. Thousands of Bosnian young women, for example, in the Balkans war were raped and forced to bear Serbian babies. In Rwanda, women and mothers were mercilessly targeted by the *génocidaires*. Tutsi mothers were vulnerable to be murdered because they carried the 'seeds of Tutsi life'.

I relate these two examples to indicate the vulnerability of mothers within unjust political regimes and cruel systems like slavery, apartheid and genocide. A third area connects the suffering of mothers with environmental pressures. I know this from my experience in the desert state of Rajasthan, N. W. India. Since women in Asia and Africa are responsible for fetching water and searching for firewood, in a drought situation, coupled with massive deforestation, this has calamitous consequences for mothers trying to sustain the basic fabric of life.

So how do we make theological and spiritual sense of the 'suffering mother'? There can be no justification for the violence I have described through the oppression of war and slavery: what is clear is that in these situations women as mothers are vulnerable and particular targets of humiliation. Their suffering is of no consequence to those in control of the war machine. The third example has a more far-reaching impact, because it points to the suffering and vulnerability of women in the daily sustenance of life, when basic resources are extremely strained. Indeed there are links here with the New Testament situation and with rural women in poor communities everywhere.

Theological reflection – feminist, liberationist, pastoral – has to look at the wider context for suffering, as I attempted in the last chapter, when criticising the logic of sacrifice. The Johannine Christ of the New Testament portrays Jesus saying that a woman has sorrow because her hour has come, but when the child is born, this sorrow turns to joy (John 16.21). This insight of Jesus reveals the link between suffering, sacrifice and the creating of new life.

Putting suffering in this wider context is seeing it as part and parcel not only of bringing children into the world, but of nurturing, rearing and accompanying them through life. It is this that is the background to motherhood being considered as sacrificial, or as the willed giving of life for others. When there is insufficient food, a mother feeds her husband and children. She stands with them whatever trouble they are in. But this involves joy as well as sorrow. It is not a masochistic choice for suffering: it is a choice for well-being and flourishing of family and community. And it brings its own satisfaction. Sally Purvis has argued that mother-love can serve as model for agape, traditionally prized as Christian other-centred love.[18] She is aware of the dangers of romanticising motherhood, and also that mother-love is only *part* of mothering, which involves a wide-ranging set of practices. Mother-love, she says, is 'intensely involved and other regarding. At times there is no clear line between the needs of the lover and the needs of the beloved.'[19]

But the point is that although the mother is responding to the child's needs, her *own* need may be to comfort and feed, rock the child and so on. When the child matures, some would argue that this intense connected love would diminish, and love would be more detached. Purvis argues the opposite: the sense of commitment to the well-being of the child and the intensity of love do not diminish. Thus mother-love is one model for agape, the other-centred love that involves the two persons-in-relationship. What is wrong, as my examples have shown, is the context where mother-love has to be practised and experienced. Through war, sexism, racism and caste-ism, poverty, environmental stress, lack of basic human rights, motherhood is often lived out in situations of flagrant injustice. We need then to revisit this tension between justice and care, for motherhood to be seen as contributing to a spirituality of compassion and caring that has far-reaching implications beyond the experiences of mothers themselves.

The tensions between these two values were first focused on in the early 1980s, in both educational and ethical circles. The discussions between the two educationalists the late Lawrence Kohlberg and Carol Gilligan sparked the debate that still continues. Carol Gilligan questioned the assumptions of Kohlberg's stages of moral development because they were too narrowly based on the development of boys, since girls of equal intelligence were emerging as more immature on his moral scale.[20] From her own research she was able to point out a gender difference: girls appeared less mature on Kohlberg's scale because they were making decisions on a different basis and from different criteria. Whereas boys tended to make judgements on the basis of justice and fairness (often appealing to rules), girls would make a decision on the basis of relationships and caring. This seemed to make them less mature on the Kohlberg scale. Gilligan did not want to make society choose between the two bases for decision-making, but argued that society needs both justice and care/relationality. In the last twenty years much ink has flowed over this issue. Even if both Gilligan and Kohlberg could be accused of massive generalisations, the germ of truth in this debate has been very fruitful. Trying to understand the significance of motherhood for a liberation spirituality, I listen to what Gilligan says:

> As we have listened for centuries to the voices of men and the theories of development that their experience informs, so we have come more recently to notice the silence of women but the difficulty of hearing what they say when they speak. Yet in the different voice of women lies the truth of an ethics of care, the tie between relationship and responsibility, and the origins of aggression in the failure of connection.[21]

Mothering is about the practice of care and nurture – and the reality of it is what makes mothers so vulnerable when caring takes place in contexts of injustice and oppression. So when Christian tradition glorifies the *Stabat Mater,* the *Mater Dolorosa* in art and music, Mary at the foot of the cross of her son, or cradling him in her arms, it is not only the personal grief over her loss that is meaningful and even iconic, even given the fact that her son is unique in significance; it is the sorrow of all mothers mourning the unjust killing of a beloved child. It is a witness, too, of motherhood as caring unto death – and beyond. Here is a mother who courageously followed her son in his ministry, tried to understand him, risked confrontation and passionately believed in his mission to confront unjust power. She is an icon for mothers who resist injustice. I think of the Madres de la Plaza in Argentina, as well as the Women's Peace Movement in Northern Ireland. These present an icon for a spirituality of resistance that goes wider than motherhood. It is this caring-unto-death that is the basis for a spirituality of compassion that I now explore, linking with my intuition that this will contribute to spirituality today as mystical, political and creation-centred.

SPIRITUALITY, CARE AND MOTHERING

First, I will tell a story that illustrates the fundamental nature of care. It is a Roman myth retold by the German philosopher Martin Heidegger:

> Once when 'Care' was crossing a river, she saw some clay; she thoughtfully took up a piece and began to shape it. While she was meditating on what she had made, Jupiter came by. Care asked him to give it 'spirit' and this he gladly granted. But when she wanted her name to be bestowed upon it, he forbade this, and demanded that it be given his name instead. While 'Care' and Jupiter were disputing, Earth rose and desired her own name to be conferred upon the creature, since she had furnished it with part of her

body. They asked Saturn to be their arbiter, and he made the following decision, which seemed a just one: 'Since you, Jupiter, have given its spirit, you shall receive that spirit at its death; and since you, Earth, have given its body, you shall receive its body. But since 'Care' first shaped this creature, she shall possess it as long as it lives. And because there is now a dispute among you as to its name, let it be called *homo*, for it is made out of *humus* (earth).[22]

How striking it is to see here the fundamental priority of care as a necessary precondition for all life on earth. Care-for-life itself, I will call it. (Sadly, Heidegger does not work this out in terms of daily practical living.) This being so, let me now explore motherhood as one model of this care-for-life itself. I do not mean to ignore the importance of fathers, nor to skip over the fact that great changes are taking place in the increasing role that fathers play in child-rearing. But traditionally care for children and the elderly has focused on mothers and I explore what this means for spirituality.

What are the qualities of caring we estimate so highly in mothers? First, let us stress *attentiveness*, being attentive to the needs of others – this has been stressed by many writers, from Simone Weil to Iris Murdoch.[23] It is enabled by the quality of deep listening – the old English word 'hearkening' comes to mind – and empathy, although empathy can be a poisoned chalice, when women find difficulties in keeping clear boundaries between self and other. Listening to the silenced voices has always been a crucial part of a liberation spirituality.

The second quality is that of *responsibility*. This means not only being responsible for the children of one's own family, but interpreting this culturally and politically. Only on the basis of the intuition of a deep sense of connection with others is this possible. Care and compassion are rooted in this mystical sense of connection. The words of Thomas Merton, on a visit to the town of Louisville, remain an inspiration for this:

To Rwanda and Back

> In Louisville ... in the centre of the shopping district, I was
> suddenly overwhelmed by the realisation that I loved all
> those people, that they were mine and I theirs, that we
> could not be alien to one another even though we were
> total strangers. It was like waking from a dream of sepa-
> rateness, of spurious isolation in a special world, the world
> of renunciation and supposed holiness ... I have the
> immense joy of being ... a member of a race in which God
> Himself became incarnate ... There is no way of telling
> people that they are walking round shining like the sun.[24]

Care should never have been considered as an individual
practice, so privatised as to isolate a family in their struggle for
survival in an unjust world. Yet mothers have experienced the
paradox of being isolated in their daily struggles and at the
same time often having that space violated through cruelty and
sexual abuse. Responsibility embraces the whole area of
nurture, nourishment and growth. But care-for-life in its
widest meaning is also care for the environment, the earth, the
context for any human well-being.[25] My earlier example of
the desert of Rajasthan points to the fact that if there had been
sufficient care for the environment, trees would not have been
drastically destroyed, exacerbating the water-stressed situation
and turning the lives of women into drudgery.

The third quality is *competence*, the competence of care-
giving. This is illustrated in the case of mothers' struggles to
feed their children despite all odds. A poignant illustration of
this is Melissa Raphael's account in her book *The Female Face
of Auschwitz*, where mothers in the camps exerted amazing
energies to care for children, for each other, for children other
than their own.[26] They found scraps of bread, knitted warm
scarves from bits of wool, nursed the sick and dying children
and struggled to keep them alive by extraordinary means. On
the level of society, this draws attention to the vital need for
competence in care-giving of those in the so-called caring

professions – nursing, teaching, prison and any form of detention centre. The recent BBC television drama based on the real-life story of Marie Stubbs, the headmistress and successor of Philip Lawrence, the murdered Headmaster of St George's School, London, illustrated clearly this quality of tough, competent caring. This was no emotional lovey-dovey form of care, but competent care, based on an insistence on discipline among staff as well as students, respect for each pupil in their particular difficult circumstances, and sheer determination that it was crucial for the whole community that the school succeeded.

But we do not need to go to the desert of Rajasthan, or the death camps of Nazi Germany to illustrate competence in care. Nearer at home there are many examples. My youngest son is a guardian-ad-litem, following troubled children in court to represent their interests: should they go into care, or be left with their parents? It is specifically his work with mothers that concerns me here: Ben works with their stories, asking them how, despite the dice being loaded against them (in terms of abuse, violence and poverty), they have managed to be relatively competent care-givers.

Joan Tronto writes that the fourth element is that of the *responsiveness* of the care-receiver to the care, taking into account inequality and vulnerability.[27] A balance needs to be created here, between care-giver and receiver. This is very clear in the case of children and elderly people (where inequality and dependency are obvious), but not so clear in terms of the dependency of all strata of society on the humblest forms of work, like street-cleaning and toilet-cleaning. Vulnerability is easily prey to exploitation and forms of domination, as the tragic cases of the trafficking of women show us. It is easy to forget that the earth herself is vulnerable to human overuse and exploitation: yet at the same time the earth is supremely responsive to care-givers, in blossoming forth in fruitfulness.

To Rwanda and Back

All these elements come together in the *integrity of care*, requiring judgements beyond the personal, in social and political contexts.[28] And in the integrity of care are the seeds of a spirituality of compassion.

THE RECOVERY OF COMPASSION

This chapter began with the massive failure of compassion twelve years ago in Rwanda on the part of the entire world. As I write, the world observes another failure, in the wake of hurricane Katrina that swept through the southern tip of the United States from Florida to New Orleans and onwards, completely destroying the city of New Orleans. But whereas for Americans the act of remembering September 11th could focus on deeds of bravery, sacrifice and compassion in the attempt to save lives, it has been very different in the wake of hurricane Katrina. As culture historian Simon Schama wrote, even television networks

> have not flinched from their responsibility to show corpses drifting in the water; lines of the forlorn and abandoned sitting amid piles of garbage outside the Convention Centre's patients from Charity Hospital waiting in the broiling sun in vain for water and medical supplies; helicopters too frightened of armed looters to actually land, but throwing bottles of water down from their 20ft hover.[29]

Thus, he continues, Americans saw, not civilisation, but the brutality, destitution, desperation and chaos of the Third World – in their own land:

> Instead of instinctive solidarity and compassion, they have witnessed a descent into a Hobbesian state of nature; with Leviathan offering fly-by compassion, 30,000ft up, and then once returned to the White House, broadcasting a defensive

laundry list of deliveries, few of which showed up when and where they were needed.[30]

Whether or not Schama is right in seeing this monumental flaw in compassion as sounding the death knell for the Bush regime remains to be seen: but he highlighted for my argument the central place of active compassion as a publicly held value and ethic. Compassion is not the private emotion of the individual, even if this is manifested in heroic deeds. Nor is it a sort of paternalistic pity, but a form of active love. It is the way the state publicly displays its care and respect for its citizens, including the poorest and most vulnerable. Those abandoned citizens of New Orleans were poor and black. Rwanda is one of Africa's poorest countries. India's Dalits (former Untouchables) are not considered as contributing to 'Shining India'.[31] So there is a link between caring publicly manifest as responsibility and competence towards especially the poorer sections of the population, and compassion as the relational mode that inspires this.

Liberation spirituality is grounded in faith in a compassionate God, calling humanity into communities of compassion. The American theologian Wendy Farley defines compassion as both relational mode and power. It includes sympathetic knowledge of another's suffering, and is an enduring disposition, integrating many dimensions into a coherent model of world-engagement, as the whole self becomes a servant of compassion's care for the world.[32] Instead of power relying on force, compassion has the potential to be a transforming power, a power for preservation and a power 'to bring to life what is broken by pain, to bring to justice and redemption what is broken by brutality'.[33] In the spirituality of reconciling justice I am placing compassion as a crucial cornerstone.

How could society recover the power of compassion as default relational mode? I ask myself this at the end of a week that saw the worst atrocities in Iraq since the downfall of Saddam Hussein. News from Iraq almost seems to have lost the power to shock. At the same time we hear how nations are reneging on the promises to Africa they made at the World Summit in July 2005 at Gleneagles, in Scotland. Stories of compassionate individuals are never lacking, but how could they inspire society as a whole? Surely, I mused, faith resources offer hope? Feminist theology has long been sensitive to the fact that the Hebrew word used for the compassion of God is *rehem,* womb-love, metaphor for the mothering love of God.[34] The Greek equivalent, σπλάγχνα, also refers to inner parts, viscera, and metaphorically to the heart as seat of feeling. Still, this seems to limit us to personal emotion. But the Latin 'compassion', suffering with, implies a relational mode, shared suffering, or shared passion for life. The Chief Rabbi Jonathan Sacks, in his recent book *To Heal a Fractured World,* not only sees compassion as a cherished tradition of the Jewish community, but understands it as the loving kindness towards strangers and foreigners, the attitude that enables us to recognise our common humanity across the cultural divide.[35] Not only does he relate a fund of stories about compassion as practised through the ages in Jewish communities, but sees the figure of Ruth as iconic, she who practised fidelity to an older woman from a different race, and in her turn received loving kindness (and marriage) from a stranger. Is it significant that in the English language the word 'ruth', loving-kindness, is now archaic, whereas 'ruthless', its absence and opposite, is a word much relied on?

I began to see the ministry of Jesus with this new lens. In my mind's eye I had frequently imagined the weary figure of Jesus, on a dusty road, meeting some desperate figure (the Samaritan woman, the woman with an issue of blood, the widow of Nain), being moved with the womb-like compassion of God and inspired to perform some miracle. His own parable, the Good Samaritan (Luke 10.25–37), is paradigmatic of the response needed. But looking again at the story of the raising to life of the widow of Nain (Luke 7.11–17), I see there is far more to it. To begin with, Jesus is not alone, but accompanied by his disciples and 'a large crowd'. The context does not seem appropriate for a display of personal emotion. I knew that one of the factors of the story could be that Jesus' own mother was now a widow, and Jesus her only son. But the social position of a poor widow was known to be desperate in Jewish society of this time, as it still remains in many poor countries in Asia, Africa and the Middle East. In India poor widows may be driven to prostitution or become itinerant beggars. Luke was well aware of the position of widows, as we know from chapter 18, verses 1–8, the story of the widow and the unjust judge. It is possible that Luke is aware, but not as concerned as Jesus was, because the point of that story is just as the woman would not give up, but pestered the judge for justice, so Christians are exhorted to persevere in prayer. But with a feminist lens we can recover here a tradition of women's resistance to injustice.[36]

Yet this is not what we see in the story of the poor widow from Nain. Nor is it understood as a story prefiguring the resurrection, as is the raising of Lazarus. Through the compassionate action of Jesus in restoring the son to the grief-stricken mother, I see judgement passed on how societies treat poor widows. Compassion means also judgement. The reaction of the crowd is to see this as a prophetic act: 'A great prophet has arisen among us.' It is directly linked with Divine compassionate care: 'God has shown his care for his people.' And the story now ripples through all parts of Judaea. And so Luke has – perhaps unwittingly – given us a paradigm story of the need for societies to practise structural justice towards poor widows today, relevant too in Rwanda where these head so many households, and where it is almost impossible for them to come to terms with their tragic memories. (That Luke is aware of the needs of widows is shown by Acts 6.1 where deacons are elected partly because (Greek) widows were being neglected in the daily distribution.)

But compassion is also being recovered as a chosen ideal in new communities springing up in contemporary society. Here I give an example of only one of these, because it leads directly to the achieving of peace, reconciliation and conflict resolution that is my focus. In Chapter 2 I told the story of the conflict resolution in Mozambique and the part played by the community of Sant'Egidio. I was so inspired by this story that, some years ago, when I visited Rome for the first time, I sought out the community one evening in the ancient church of Santa Maria di Trastevere, a very old and beautiful part of the city. The prayer was just beginning as I entered the packed church. I was immediately taken up into a world where the prayer – both like and unlike that of Taizé – focused on both love of the poor and longing for peace. Like Taizé there was an atmosphere similar to the Orthodox Church with many candles, icons and chants. Like Taizé, too, the community holds great attraction here for young people, but here it was actually founded by young people (Andrea Riccardi is known as the founder), a group of students originally concerned for migrant families who were forced to live in Rome's shanty towns:[37]

> At night they roomed in basements in the Trastevere, to establish solidarity with the immigrants, the unemployed, the elderly and the lonely. Every day they prayed together, meeting in churches to read the gospel ... Piazza Sant' Egidio became a meeting place, a place for discussion of what it meant to be a church present among – and hearing the Good News from – the poor.[38]

From these humble beginnings the community now numbers over 40,000 members in 60 countries – including Antwerp, New York, Buenos Aires, Havana. Members are all lay people – although they have now a bishop and a few priests – who put prayer and friendship with the poor at the forefront of their lives. But what is very striking is the way that the charism of reconciliation is at the heart of the community. The community is a clear icon of what I have searched for in this chapter: through putting care, compassion and simple friendship at the heart of community values, peace with justice becomes a real possibility:

> The community's model for peacemaking is the famous story of St Francis taming the wolf of Gubbio. Like St Francis, the community comes to conflicts without any agenda or vested interest except peace with justice; like St Francis, they come unarmed, their weakness being their strength. Like St Francis they start from the assumption that no one can be defined as barbarian or evil so as not to deserve even a word; and they embark on a dialogue that some would regard ... as madness and possibly treason.[39]

The community's involvement with the Mozambique peace process was followed by an involvement in Algeria, then the Guatemala Peace Accords of 1996, and then in many other parts of the world, such as Lebanon, El Salvador, Columbia, the Ivory Coast and the Sudan. But it should be stressed that Sant'Egidio is not an unofficial arm of Vatican diplomacy. It is more that their charism of friendship and compassion has been steadily developing into a means of reconciling opposed ideologies, a means to prevent the world from accepting the inevitability of the clash of civilisations.

This is the link I have been seeking. Compassion, seen as a longing for structural justice, rooted in the shared vulnerability of humanity and all creatures, is a bedrock for a spirituality of reconciliation. What is lived out by the suffering love of poor mothers in many situations is an inspiring icon of the response needed to break the deadlock of hatred and the conspiracies of silence. But how can this function as a path for the Churches, still locked in the guilt and memories of complicity in genocide? It is to this that I now turn.

To Rwanda and Back

4 FRAGILE BRIDGES OVER
TROUBLED WATERS

Building Communities of Reconciliation

One way to understand cycles of violence and protracted conflict is to visualise them as a narrative broken. A people's story is marginalized, or, worse, destroyed by the dominant culture, and by this act meaning, identity and a place in history are lost. This is the deeper challenge of peace-building: how to reconstitute, or re-story, the narrative and thereby restore the people's place in history . . .

When deep narrative is broken, the journey towards the past that lies before us is marginalized, truncated. We lose more than just the thoughts of a few old people. We lose our bearings. We lose the capacity to find our place in this world. And we lose the capacity to find our way back to humanity.

Jean Paul Lederach[1]

Inspired by the story of the Sant'Egidio community as an example of the praxis of compassion leading to conflict-resolution, let us now explore ways forward for communities of reconciliation to become a wider and more powerful reality. I begin by looking again at the stumbling block of church complicity in the Rwandan genocide; then look at five models or tasks for the Church proposed by Dr Tharcisse Gatwa. I then meditate more personally on biblical sources for reconciliation. But in the end I appeal to resources from feminist theology and contemporary Quaker witness to point the way towards a non-violent society.

The picture our group was given in Rwanda in December 2004 was of a country that was desperate for reconciliation and peace. Yet the world is aware that the official Arusha Trials of the *génocidaires* in Tanzania were conducted in a manner both painful and slow. By 1996 only 6 per cent of the perpetrators had been tried. By the end of 1998 only one condemnation had been pronounced, against the former Prime Minister, Jean Kambanda, who had 'supervised' the genocide. Many perpetrators have been freed, including Fr Wenceslas Munyashyaka, the curate of the Holy Family (Roman Catholic) Church, Kigali, who played a terrible role in the genocide and now lives free as a priest in France. Although the church of the Holy Family had sheltered 8000 refugees, Fr Wenceslas provided the militia with lists of those sympathetic to the Rwandan Patriotic Front, and agreed to let them come and pick out those they wanted:

> Wearing a flak jacket and toting a pistol during the massacres, he fled to Goma during the interim government and was one of the twenty seven who wrote to the pope defending the Rwandan army and blaming the RPF for the massacres.[2]

Although, as I wrote earlier, there were priests and bishops who made heroic sacrifices to save lives and died for it, some even dying with the people they had tried to rescue, this does not explain or exonerate the enormous degree of church complicity with the genocide before, during and after. Mamdani gives a figure of 105 priests and 120 nuns who were killed, and cites certain evidence from the UN Centre for Human Rights that about a dozen priests actually killed, while others supervised the gangs of young killers.[3] (This could be a conservative estimate.) As I indicated earlier, the hierarchy was also implicated: more than two months into the genocide, in June 1994, the Anglican Archbishop Nshamihigo categorically refused to condemn the genocide and the Catholic Archbishop even moved with the interim government from Kigali to Gitarama.

But it was not only churches that were changed from sacred spaces into sites of massacres, but schools and hospitals too, places that should nurture and protect life, turned into places where life was threatened and destroyed: '*Médicins sans Frontières* . . . pulled out of the University Hospital in Kigali after its patients began disappearing.'[4] Doctors began to refuse to treat Tutsis, asking patients for their identity cards. One doctor directed the militia into the hospital in Kibeho, shutting off the power supply so that the massacre could take place in darkness. Even newborn babies were not spared. Some of the most experienced and respected surgeons, hospital administrators and gynaecologists participated in the killing of their own colleagues, families and refugees. The story is repeated in the context of teachers and even human rights activists.

A particularly ambiguous part of church complicity in the genocide is the part played by some religious sisters. In particular, the story of Gertrude Mukangango, Mother Superior in the convent of the Benedictine monastery of Sovu, Butare, and another sister in the convent, Sister Julienne Kizito, has become notorious.[5] Because thousands of refugees had forced their way into the convent, the prevailing story goes that Sister Gertrude (calling them 'dirt' who should not sully a sacred place) brought armed soldiers to force them out. Even little hungry children pleading for grains of rice were not spared. Many refugees were killed immediately after they left, including Tutsi relatives of sisters in the convent. Sister Julienne is accused of working directly with the killers, 'standing in their midst while they massacred refugees, handing out jerrycans of petrol which were used in her presence to burn people alive'.[6]

African Rights Watch quotes many 'eye witnesses' that seem to make it impossible for this story to be denied. Afterwards, some Tutsi sisters of the convent were themselves killed. The other sisters left Rwanda and went to Belgium via France. After the war Sisters Gertrude and Julienne remained in Maredret, Belgium, protected by their congregation until 2001, when they were tried and convicted. Sister Gertrude was sentenced to fifteen years in prison and Sister Julienne to thirteen. Yet Martin Neyt of the Catholic University of Louvain is convinced that the sisters neither had a fair trial nor were they guilty of violence: they simply did what they could in desperate circumstances.[7]

The slowness of the Arusha Trials and the ambiguities of their outcome made it urgent that there were other sources for bringing those involved in genocide to justice. Another area which would evoke great concern were the prisons in Rwanda which were overflowing, their inmates suffering – even dying – in appalling conditions. So the traditional system of justice, known as the *gacaca* courts (*gacaca* = grass courts, and is an adapted traditional community justice system), now operates at village level. It is estimated that there are about 12,000 *gacaca* courts. This means that prisoners are brought face to face with the very villagers they have tried to wipe out, whose families they have murdered, and creates possibilities of public confession, repentance and forgiveness. That is the best scenario. The villagers know exactly who killed whom and are able to recite the crimes in gruesome detail. Even today *gacaca* operates every week and businesses are closed to allow people to attend. Estimates for the total number of people imprisoned for crimes relating to genocide vary from 100,000 to 150,000: 'These people – of which the chief prosecutor earlier estimated 20 per cent were falsely accused – were detained in appalling prison conditions waiting trial,' according to the OECD.[8]

This raises the issue, so far only hinted at, of the failure of the present Rwandan government and RPA to deal with their own crimes of revenge against Hutus. The *gacaca* courts deal with crimes against Tutsis and not vice versa, as the following story shows. It is the story of a Hutu, Robert, and tragically illustrates the plight of moderate Hutus, the first to be forced into the genocidal killings, after 7 April, and against whom were some of the worst reprisals:

> On the night before the genocide, we were all called out onto the streets. The *Interahamwe* told us that we must kill Tutsis. But I was not given a rifle, and I managed not to kill people. I escaped to Kigali because I knew a military officer. Three months later, I returned to my home town. I found work in a multinational company. But there was a woman working there who knew me. She was Tutsi, a bit extremist. She was full of hate; I suppose you could understand that. She told me it was out of the question that I work there. 'This is a different age,' she said. Maybe I understand that. But then she accused me of being Interahamwe, and she accused me of trying to kill her. She had cousins in the military. When I went to work, she told her cousins to come and arrest me. On my arrest warrant was written 'Attempted Murder'. And then later they added the word 'genocide'. Like other people in prison, I had an empty dossier, because there was no evidence against me. Justice officials sometimes came to the prison. I kept saying there was no truth and no proof. But it made no difference. They just go away, and you stay. They don't do anything about it.
>
> I was in prison for seven years. It was very difficult. We were allocated a 20cm-wide space to sleep in. Sometimes we went three days without eating because the stocks were empty, or there was no firewood for cooking, or the government fell out with the Red Cross suppliers. I heard that after I left, people could even go one week without eating. Others had people who brought them food; I had no-one.

Perhaps the only thing I had was the determination to survive.

In prison, you risk being killed. Fellow prisoners are your guards, they are called brigadiers or captains. They make the law. They are the intermediary with the 'outside', the prison director and the administration, who use them to promote and tax lucrative businesses like cannabis and locally brewed alcohol, food, cigarettes and sex. There were various gangs in the prison, and violence when the brigadiers stole the prison food supplies.

After seven years, I was taken to my *colline* (hill, or neighbourhood) to confront the survivors of the genocide in the *gacaca* courts. Nobody accused me. Absolutely no-one said that I was *Interahamwe*. They said: 'We know of nothing bad that he could have done.' I had spent seven years in prison without having done anything. This government had promised a programme for rehabilitation. But they lie a lot; there was nothing. This was the experimental phase of *gacaca;* we will be obliged to go back. But I am not afraid of that. I am 100 per cent innocent, I have done nothing. I have done seven years of prison for doing nothing.

I have serious problems. My family were massacred in the war. I have no land, no house. I live with friends, awaiting a stable situation, but it is difficult to find a job with this record. I have no future.[9]

I cite this story in full, not trying to soften the horror of genocidal crimes against Tutsis, but to illustrate the complexity of the current situation. The same Christian Aid report relates an estimate that 87,000 people are currently in detention, following government pardons and *gacaca*-related releases over the last two years. *Gacaca,* we are told, inevitably faces numerous difficulties, including the slow pace of dealing with huge numbers of people, intimidation of witnesses, little incentive for communities to attend and relive their trauma, fresh accusations (with the danger of overfilling the prisons), and donor caution at funding a process which could not possibly try such a huge number of people with standards compatible with international human rights. Another problem occurs when perpetrators are freed and they return to their own villages: it is very hard for victims' families to live with them again in the old way. Families feel vulnerable to renewed attacks.

The basis on which the RPF government refuses to permit its own – admitted – human rights abuses to be tried under the *gacaca* system is the argument that RPF abuses cannot be compared with genocidal crimes. However, the same government is willing to release 'genocide survivor' funds to Tutsis who were outside the country at the time of the genocide: 'There is a clear inconsistency here; genocide must either have been suffered only by Tutsis inside Rwanda in 1994, as is generally accepted, or it extends to other groups. The criteria cannot be changed to suit government priorities.'[10]

Another tragic example of one-sidedness of the justice system is the recent persecution and arrest of the Catholic missionary priest, and noted human rights activist, Fr Guy Theunis (a White Father), whose 'crime' appears to be that he has fought for justice for both Tutsi and Hutu.[11] Fr Theunis was hauled before the *gacaca* tribunal on 11 September 2005 and accused of planning the 1994 genocide. He was convicted as a Category 1 criminal. Yet many of the hundreds of people who attended the tribunal knew him as a fearless human rights campaigner who fought for the safety of both sides of the struggle. In fact he had helped to found the first human rights association in Rwanda, ADL (Association pour le Défense des Droits et de la personne humaine), and was managing director of the magazine *Dialogue,* which kept the world informed of political events in Rwanda through publishing a press review and translating into French articles from the local press – including extremist media. But this fact is now being used against him. He was also the local correspondent for *Reporters without Borders*. Despite the fact that Fr Theunis has dedicated his life to peace in Rwanda, he now faces the possibility of the death penalty, or at the very least a long wait in prison before any justice is meted out.

So even though the official line is that 'we are all Rwandans', that there is no Tutsi/Hutu divide, but 'we are a country committed to reconciliation', the reality is very ambiguous as I have tried to show. The problem goes to the very heart of the integrity of the Church today. Even if 'reconciliation' is the buzz word everywhere in Rwanda, there is little attempt to grasp the profundity of the processes needed. Only the Presbyterian Church has made a full apology for its actions during the genocide.

RECONCILIATION AND THE CHURCHES: SEEKING A NEW ECCLESIOLOGY

The honest approach of the Anglican Archbishop talking to Christian Aid (already cited in Chapter 2) introduces a fresh look at processes of reconciliation. But I want to explore this more widely than simply in the Rwandan situation, conscious of ecclesial failure in other contexts, and recognising wider responsibilities in the collapse of global solidarity and compassion. Through this method I want to link with the commitments of all people trying to live a spirituality of justice and peace. I am also conscious that these questions haunt my own faith commitment, as I hinted in Chapter 1.

I begin by looking at the suggestions for the Church to move forward offered by the Rwandan journalist and theologian Tharcisse Gatwa (cited in the previous chapter). As Secretary General of the Presbyterian Church in Rwanda from 1983 to 1987, and Director of the Bible Society in Rwanda from 1988 to 1994, his is an invaluable theological reflection on the situation. Tharcisse Gatwa has shown clearly how the Churches failed to prevent the genocide (acknowledging that it is not only the Churches that are responsible). He depicts *all* the Churches as being too closely allied with Hutu power and privilege.

As regards the Catholic Church in particular, there are wounds still left unhealed by the Belgian Catholic Church having given privileges to the Tutsis, thus educating a professional Tutsi elite and fomenting deep-seated Hutu resentment. The picture of self-criticism in the Church immediately before the genocide is very mixed. Of the prophetic word, writes Gatwa, *the picture is of too little, too late*.[12] There are a few examples of self-criticism, of individual action and even parish attempts at reconciliation. In the Diocese of Kabgayi there was an initiative on the part of the new bishop, Monsignor Thaddée Nsengiyumva (not be confused with his namesake in Kigali, Archbishop Vincent Nsengiyumva, who was heavily implicated, and remained close to President Habyarimana). This new bishop signed a revolutionary document in the name of the presbyterate of his diocese, affirming that the Church was sick, sick through lying, sick from working in the shadow of state power, sick from working without transparency.[13] Analysing the current problems, the document called for radical solutions. The Bishop demanded that the Church be freed from alliances that compromised Christ and that it become engaged in seeking and speaking the truth. There was a mixed reception to this initiative, some church leaders following him, but some enemies were created. Indeed his relations with the Archbishop were soured: both men were to die from the bullet of an RPF commando in June 1994, near Kabgayi.

Moving to the period after the genocide, in 1996, a memorandum of 36 pages was addressed to the Pope by 24 people from different professions, accusing the Catholic Church of not only being the vehicle of ethnic ideology, but for denying that the genocide took place.[14] From hindsight the tragedy seems to have been that as the outbreak of genocide moved closer, so did the protest movements for peace: indeed 1994 was designated the 'Year of Peace'. Looking more deeply, the blame is not only on the churches being aligned with power, but on a lack of prophetic leadership, itself based on the lack of a theology to deal with violence. *What was needed was to develop a theology of structural justice leading to awareness that reconciliation is the vocation of the whole Church.*

Revd André Karamaga, now of the African desk at the World Council of Churches in Geneva, who is a key witness to events, and who had himself lost many members of his family, now speaks of the dominating image of the Church of Rwanda as the 'dry bones' of the book of Ezekiel (chapter 37). How can these dry bones be brought to life? How can people trust the Church again? These were his questions to us in Kigali. They introduce a reflection on the kind of ecclesiology needed. I begin with the five models suggested by Tharcisse Gatwa, none of which need exclude the other.

● *Total reintegration*

First, Dr Gatwa cites A. Dumas's examples of three biblical stories of reintegration in the case of murders between families.[15] The third example from the story of Joseph makes the guilty party (meaning Joseph's brothers) become 'the bearers of a new revolution'. No longer will they be a means of eliminating or excluding the other: instead, the 'new revolution' will be a strength bringing responsibility for brotherhood and national cooperation with those who were at the basis of the separation.[16] Gatwa finds this inspirational for Rwanda, seeing that what is problematic is the danger that each generation will repeat the crimes of the previous one, without due process of moving forward. Donald Shriver writes that 'the stones of the past weigh heavily on the present:

the burden of history is one of the chains that is carried, and each category of responsibility adds its weight'.[17]

In Chapter 1 I explored how the activity of remembering was an essential prerequisite for a spirituality of reconciliation, for perpetrator even more than for the victim, who cannot in any case forget. Lederach, at the beginning of this chapter, cited the awesome consequences when the narrative strand is broken. Meg Guillebaud, in her biographical book of her family's missionary activity in Rwanda, *Rwanda: The Land God Forgot? Revival, Genocide and Hope* (cited earlier), sees an urgent need for Rwandans – and not only Rwandans – to develop a better understanding that sin has consequences, and that unresolved injustice in one generation will come back to haunt the next.[18]

Gatwa suggests that the Hutu community take the lead in confession and repentance, an initiative that should be accompanied by political will and moral strength. In this context he appeals to the speech of Richard Weizsäcker, a former President of Germany, to his fellow citizens, where the legacy of the Nazis could be applied to the Rwandan situation. Weizäcker appealed to every German to witness that their fellow Jews have suffered and asked, in view of this fact, who could be innocent? This message together with others from Archbishop Tutu and Nelson Mandela show how moral and political forces can be harnessed for repentance. When a political or moral figure starts to say he has changed by seeing the suffering of the other, a channel is opened for people to change attitude and behaviour. Gatwa feels that an authentic mediation between the Rwandan people would help our children to move beyond ethnic hatred, to a universe where the priorities are 'Rwandan-ness', meaning solidarity between humans and the sanctity of life. A re-evaluation of ancient values would get Rwandans to question orders before blindly executing them. Others have also suggested that a church climate of obeying orders had removed peoples' traditional judgement as to the immorality of the orders to murder so brutally their neighbours, families and friends, even inducing amnesia as to ancient African values of decency and morality. He suggests building on the *gacaca* system that has emerged since the genocide, so that it would culminate regularly in a National Conference, as one of the best ways of enabling a dialogue that restores 'the word' to the people of Rwanda.

● *Tell the stories of suffering*

This is Tharcisse Gatwa's second suggestion. Stories need to be told for the healing of memories, again a theme touched on in Chapter 1, where I called for safe spaces of trust to enable this to take place. (This is a method much practised in feminist healing spiritualities in contexts of domestic violence and abuse.) The new revolution referred to in Gatwa's first model depends on a process of socialisation where the telling of the stories of suffering can take place. But is this happening in Rwanda – as it happened in South Africa? Gatwa relates that a Rwandan, now become a French citizen, J. Kagabo, returned to the country and became convinced that nothing was being done for the victims on both sides of the divide to tell their story. He became convinced that the tragedy could repeat itself.

The idea of the *space for experience* – a space of safety for assembling 'the residue' of the sediments of the past, which could still engender fear, anticipation and projections, has been proposed by the philosopher Paul Ricoeur. Through confession, consciousness of culpability is brought to the level of speech and the penitents linked to the spoken word by the experience of suffering and anguish. Like the Truth and Reconciliation Commission in South Africa this model encourages the recital of stories also on the part of the perpetrator and not only from the victim's perspective. Yet it must be said that this has happened from time to time in

Rwanda. For example, Père Masinzo, himself a genocide survivor, has acted as a pioneer for the process of listening to the stories and introduced the process into the Catholic parish of Karama, in the Diocese of Butare. Bringing together widows and women with husbands in prison, knowing that they were deeply wounded in their heart of hearts, he asked them to listen to his own story for five minutes, before requesting them to listen to each other and learn of the suffering of the other. A dialogue began and, amazingly, the first questions to emerge were: 'What can God dare to say to us now? Does He still have something to say to us?' Only after they had spoken of their traumas, with the aid of a psychologist, could they begin to speak of their material needs.[19] So, only through such a process of listening to both survivors and the incriminated community can the healing of society be achieved.

But the case for using this model is even stronger. Telling stories is at the heart of narrative theology, at the heart of recovery of an identity that is threatened through conflict. People are broken because they have lost their story. So they have also lost their link with the past. As Jean Paul Lederach says, in his profound book cited earlier, the need is always for *re-storying*, in order to enable broken people to recover their own proper space and place in the world, and to restore them to their own memories and relationship with time.[20]

• Stop the cumulative build-up and cycle of violence

It cannot be enough to listen to the stories of the recent killings, however vital this is, if what is really going on is the build-up of cumulative violence, since 1959, with deeper roots in the colonial period. As I mentioned earlier, citing Meg Guillebaud, unredeemed evil and the unresolved sin of one generation may come back to haunt the next, especially within a political and juridical community that protects the impunity of those in power. Rwandans have so many personal histories of loved ones brutally murdered: memories cannot heal because they are part of a cycle of repetitive violence. Another blockage to reconciliation is the fact that many people were not only murdered, but denied any form of human death and dignity in the manner of killing, for example being left for wild animals to devour or thrown into latrines. Furthermore, not everyone was allowed the dignity of a proper burial. The Catholic Church indeed opposed an initiative in 1995 to exhume remains of genocide victims and give them decent burial.[21] Gatwa calls for liturgies of mourning and purification to restore dignity to human life and reinstall creation in its primordial role as Divine gratuitous action. He cites the example of the South African Council of Churches, which has worked on such a liturgy, consisting in the purification of the different elements such as water, vegetation, air, people and animals. People are then recalled to that unity and cohesion of creation liturgically represented by the sacraments.

But he also points out that to destroy the logic and cycle of violence means rethinking the theology and ecclesiology of Christian Church, and that is exactly what feminist Christian spirituality is calling for in its questioning of the logic of sacrifice (discussed in Chapter 2). For Tharcisse Gatwa it means reopening a theology based on human rights, where this rehabilitates African values and liberates Africans from oppression, including a western paternalist Christianity, badly articulated and assimilated. But not only Africa needs such a theology: the world is crying out for a return to the gospel of love.

● *The model of justice and human rights*

This goes to the heart of things. The emphasis is on the fact that there can be no reconciliation without justice, a dimension stressed throughout this book – and stressed also by Pastor Bizimungu, the post-genocide President of Rwanda. This same urgent need is attested to in all genocide occurrences – in Armenia, Bosnia, Germany and so on. But the justice called for has to be many-faceted, and tempered with mercy, pardon and a universal love. For this, our model of Church must change, as Gatwa keeps repeating.

● *Interpret the suffering*

In the story related above, in the parish of Karama, Père Masinzo found himself confronted with the question of the agency of God in the genocide. This is a question that continues to trouble Rwandans, as it troubles all believers confronted as we are with what seems like a never-ending series of tsunamis and earthquakes (it was an immense question and faith crisis after the Holocaust). Did God suffer with the people, or did God have better things to do? asks Gatwa; he then turns the question around to challenge everyone concerned in the situation. What position did we take? Did we turn away? How were we involved in the killing? Are we open or closed to the process of repentance? On the one hand, Gatwa reflects on the suffering of Job as entering the mystery of God's relation to suffering; on the other hand, he calls on the Rwandan people to name their own suffering, inflicted by centuries of repetitive violence, slavery and colonialism. Only this could encourage Rwandans to struggle for a theology of resistance to suffering, for rehabilitation and reconstruction so as to inspire other Africans.

For this an *attentive* ecclesiology is essential, a church that emerges from below rather than from the powerful elite. Such a church will exercise authority in dialogue, argues Gatwa, the hierarchy not assuming that it is the sole dispenser of truth. Inspired by three sources – Word, sacrament and charity – clergy and laity together confront evil and dehumanising forces; together they keep alive the light of hope.[22] I can give my heart and hope to this . . .

In response to these five models, which all have a vital role in the challenge of reconciliation, the first crucial step is to build on the suggestions of the need to recognise the truth of the other. For this a suspension of one's own (supposed) unique right to be right is needed. How impossible this sounds. It involves the process of self-emptying or *kenosis*,[23] an almost paradoxical concept. Johnston McMaster (of the Irish Ecumenical Institute), speaking at a consultation of the World Council of Churches at Oslo, 2005,[24] in his presentation on Northern Ireland, stressed the need to realise the praxis of *kenosis* as the key to a shared future. If power is exercised or abused according to each person's capacity, there can never be peace. What is important, he argued, is to develop an attitude that is sensitive to the needs of the other and affirms plurality over privilege. To that extent, recognition of mutual vulnerability is crucial. McMaster then went on to discern the form and functions of the Church in situations of brokenness. He said that the Holy Spirit holds the broader responsibility for the transformation of the world: '*Pneumatology* is about social justice and there is no *koinonia* [= true community] without the creation of the spirit, without solidarity with the poor and the vulnerable.'

Therefore, the *koinonia* of *ecclesia* needs to be viewed as a site of radical partnerships and as a potentially revolutionary site of social transformation. In a way highly relevant to the Rwandan situation, he spoke also about the need to cultivate a culture of active non-violence. Violence always delays justice and also destroys it. Does the experience of the apostle Paul ring in our ears? It was Paul who discovered in his Christic experience that the heart of God, the ultimate mystery, was characterised by *cruciform vulnerability*. He added:

The Damascus road meant that the person of violence discovered that *the antidote to sacred violence is identification with the victim*. The body of Christ has no option but to live a theology of public responsibility, a life of embodied *kenosis*, and *koinonia* as the culture of community in radical contrast to sacred violence.

His words *embodied kenosis* ring in my ears, and already I suspect there is more to this idea than he has unpacked. What is striking, however, is that Gatwa, McMaster and feminist Christian spirituality are calling for a radically different ecclesiology, an *attentive ecclesiology*, that embodies a different ethic from that of violence. All appeal to a biblical witness that stands in judgement over any church that colludes with unjust power and violence. How could the witness of the New Testament be heard anew as part of this attentive ecclesiology?

A NEW HEARING — THE GOSPEL'S MESSAGE OF NON-VIOLENCE

On a stormy, windy morning in England, when hurricanes lash the coast of Florida, and earthquake victims in Kashmir still await rescue, I ponder the meaning of following Christ in today's violent world. Up till now I have understood Jesus as 'the embodiment or pattern of right relation'. This was also a way for feminist theology to overcome the exclusive stress on Jesus as male that seemed to eliminate women from a redemptive schema, giving men a privileged place in authority and leadership of the Church. But I know that does not do full justice to the issues I now wrestle with. There must be a way to live, inspired by a spirituality with a Christology of peace at its heart, particularly as an alternative to the traditional western Christologies so frequently associated with Christian triumphalism and colonialist expansion. In Chapter 2 I suggested looking at the death of Jesus as God's act of suffering love, which is at the core of the meaning of sacrifice. I want to hold on to that. And to the vocation of all Christians as bearers of Christ in the world, in so far as they respond and witness to the ministry of suffering love. But it is the death of Jesus that tradition calls redemptive and is at the heart of the reality of reconciliation. It is still this idea that a brutal death can be redemptive that makes so many recoil. How would it help or explain the murdered victims of the genocide to call their deaths redemptive? Would not that be insulting and worsen the trauma for survivors?

When I think of those inspired by Jesus' ethics of non-violence, like Gandhi, it is far more his attitude of non-retaliation, his ability to reach out to the marginalised and his command to love the enemy, that are particularly exemplary. Here I want to evoke a very special figure, the nearest to Gandhi that I – and those I work with in Wells for India – will ever get. This is the Gandhian leader, the late Laxmi Tyagi (known to family and colleagues as Tyagiji) who died in the summer of 2005, aged 60. He was a loyal Hindu, but like Gandhi, was open to the truth and wisdom of other faiths. I think of him as someone who truly practised the way of *kenosis*, of cruciform vulnerability in the service of radical transformation – the path called for by Johnson McMaster in the passage cited above. Disciples and co-workers recognised this – as too did strangers. At his funeral in Jodhpur (western Rajasthan), more than 8000 people followed the procession to the cremation site. Poor people – even children – came from remote areas of the desert, hiring buses, jeeps, camels, anything they could. Bystanders and strangers marvelled, asking, 'Who could this man be?' Yes, the words of the gospel echoed in my ears: 'What manner of man is this?'

Ever since his student days, Tyagiji was inspired by Gandhian thought and wanted to work in the rural areas. This inspiration led him to join the *Sarvodaya* movement,[25] and then to become a volunteer in the famine-relief programme of Jaya Prakash Narayan, an eminent social activist and politician, in drought-stricken areas of rural Bihar. Later, he joined the *Bhoodan* (land-gift) movement of Vinoba Bhave, the spiritual heir of Mahatma Gandhi. It was this experience that left an indelible impression on him. When he came to found his own NGO, Gravis, in 1983 in the Thar desert,[26] with his wife Shashi, the inspiration of Gandhi, Vinoba Bhave and Jaya Prakash Narayan – whose pictures now hang on the walls of every Gravis Field Centre – was embodied in a life of service to the rural poor and vulnerable. In this movement women and disadvantaged groups were privileged, and all were caught up in a wider struggle for a non-violent society. This was based on a life of prayer. Daily life in the ashrams begins for the whole community with prayer, centring on the Hindu prayer for peace, *Om shanti, shanti shanti*. Tyagiji, like Gandhi, was deeply inspired by the ministry of Jesus in the New Testament. During our visits, when it came to the time of teaching within the morning prayer, he unfailingly requested the teachings of Jesus. It never ceased to amaze us how extraordinarily relevant to this desert community, committed to the well-being of the rural poor, was the core of the gospel message, especially in its longing for peace and justice.

But it is particularly the way Tyagiji and his wife were able to practise forgiveness as part of the struggle for justice that is the reason for bringing his voice into the present discussion. When they first arrived in the Thar Desert and began to put the poor, low-caste people at the heart of their programmes, the reaction of the rich upper-caste people was so violent that they burnt their entire office buildings down and the Tyagis lost many cherished personal possessions. From the burning rooftops they tried to persuade the people that their whole philosophy was wrong. Like Gandhi they believed that people will choose good if given a proper chance and that wrong education lies behind violent protest against social change. So they persuaded the police not to prosecute the rioters – and now these same people are their devoted disciples. Again, when it came to the marriage of their daughter, they tried to break down caste barriers. But 80 per cent of their family refused the wedding invitation because they had 'broken caste'. Again, with gospel echoes of the unresponsive guests of the wedding feast in my ears, I saw that the Tyagis had indeed gone into the highways and byways to bring in the village people and children to the celebration. It was an unforgettable occasion.

Despite his principles of non-violence and work for a transformed society, Tyagiji did not die a violent death. He died in August 2005, totally worn out, after a failed kidney transplant.[27] He had never had a holiday in thirty years. His whole life was literally poured out for the poor communities of the desert. The kenotic witness of his life inspires me to hear the message, the life and ministry of Jesus anew, seeking a message of peace, non-violence and reconciliation in a way that gives new hope.

Christians understand the theology of reconciliation as framed initially through the words of Paul. The word itself is not mentioned in the Gospels. But Paul tells us:

> When anyone is united to Christ, there is a new world; the old order has gone and a new order has already begun. From first to last this has been the work of God. He has reconciled us ... to himself through Christ, and he has enlisted us in this service of reconciliation. What I mean is, that God was in Christ reconciling the world to himself, no longer holding men's misdeeds against them, and that he has entrusted us with the message of reconciliation. (2 Corinthians 5.17–19, NEB)

These inspiring words seem to put reconciliation at the centre of the meaning of Jesus' ministry. Here his death is not specifically mentioned. What I am riveted by, and have not

always noticed, is that Paul speaks of the 'service' of reconciliation, and the word he uses is the Greek διακονία,
diaconia. If we bring this out of the context where reconciliation is understood as reversing the Fall of the Garden of
Eden (and it is true that Paul does speak elsewhere speak of
Jesus' death in these terms), and see it more as the responsibility of mutual caring for others beyond our families and tribal
groups, then the heart of faith is a call to that caring and
compassion that brings about peace and conflict resolution.

Of course it can be argued that to put peace-making at the
heart of Jesus' ministry is to ignore the ambiguity of his say-
ings. For example:

> I came not to bring peace but a sword. I have come to set a
> man against his father, a daughter against her mother, a son's
> wife against her mother-in-law; and a man will find enemies
> under his own roof. (Matthew 10.34–35)

I would argue that this injunction is in the context of the
absolute priority of the Kingdom ethics and the need for this
commitment to be the central one in the life of all disciples. It
should not be seen as a call to violence. But if we listen to the
words of the risen Jesus in John's Gospel, 'My peace I give
you' (John 20.19–20), a gift that goes hand in hand with the
gift of the Spirit, then we take this together with the great
Farewell Discourse spoken before Jesus' death (but written
after it, especially John 14.27–28), I believe we are given the
three vital ingredients as to the meaning of reconciliation: it
means the gift of peace, the presence of the Holy Spirit and
being entrusted with the work of forgiveness. For, the risen
Jesus in the same passage continues: 'Whose sins you forgive
shall be forgiven: whose sins you retain shall be retained' (John
20.22–23). Too often this passage is reduced to its hierarchical
meaning as the power of the ordained priest to forgive sins,
and split from the gift of peace and the bestowal of the Spirit. I
believe we should link this gift of peace and the Spirit with

Jesus' earlier words in the same Gospel, 'I came that your life might be full' (John 10.10). Living out of the peace that Christ gives is living out of the fullness of life. The second point that this gift of peace means is that forgiving sin is part of a process. Not for nothing is the command added, 'Whose sins you retain shall be retained.' So, the process of forgiveness cannot be set in motion without some movement of repentance, willingness to change and commitment to achieving justice.

John-Paul Lederach (cited earlier) tells a poignant story about the complexity and sensitivities of peacemaking, here in the context of conflict-resolution in Tajikistan at the end of a brutal civil war. One of the warlords, a commander mullah, was blocking the peace process between rival chieftains. He was refusing to come down the mountain to join the peace talks. So a learned professor, Professor Abdul, volunteered to climb the mountain and talk to him. But he did not talk about war and peace, but about Sufi mysticism, a passion that he shared with the mullah. And in Sufi mysticism there is a tra-dition that discussions have no end. So Professor Abdul kept going back for months, and at last, after all this time, enough trust to speak the truth emerged. At the end of a fortnight the mullah offered to descend the mountain with the professor to confront his rivals, 'but only if you can guarantee my safety'. Sadly, the professor confessed that he was unable to do this, but, he said, 'I can guarantee this. I will go with you, side by side. And if you die, I will die.' So, a few weeks later, they left the mountain together and when they met the others, the mullah said: 'I have not come because of your government. I have come for honour and respect of this professor.'[28] Thus peace was made in Tajikistan without further bloodshed. I tell the story to show that peace involved a commitment to a person's life and to the values he held dear. Also, as Lederach makes clear, conflict resolution depends on the 'serendipitous appearance of the moral imagination'.[29] It also means taking risks and making oneself vulnerable for the sake of reconciliation.

Here we are given a clue to Paul's contrast between worldly power and the power of the cross, which he calls power in weakness.[30] 'Weakness' is the translation of the Greek *asthenes*, ἀσθενές. There appears to be no Greek equivalent of 'vulnerability' a word with a Latin root, *vulnus*, wound. But suppose Paul's meaning was more that Jesus' stance was 'cruciform vulnerability', in the sense of a willingness to take risks, and make himself open to death, for the sake of his love of fullness of life for all, and empathy with people trapped in poverty, debt, sickness and the unjust structures causing all of these. This would put the emphasis not on the cross as sacrifice and expiation but as symbol of identity in love, and a readiness to share the same vulnerability that afflicted the people he loved.

That this could be so is also attested to by the fact that the cross did not become the central Christian symbol until after Constantine's conquest (AD 312). Before this time symbols of the fullness of life that the risen Christ bestows were far more central.[31] Eucharistic symbols of bread, wine, grapes and fish appeared in mosaics and on tombstones. In Ravenna the early frescoes show Christ as Good Shepherd in a caring role. For the early Christian, baptism was made tangible through the symbolism of Paradise (as feminist theologian Rita Nakashima Brock writes), meaning the sense of renewed life on this earth:

> Paradise was depicted by various scenes: the four rivers of Eden and Jordan. Flower-dotted hills, emerald meadows, fruit-laden trees, vineyards, and dolphins and fish frolicking in crystalline waters. Serene sheep often stood for apostles, while deer and doves symbolized souls of the risen dead. Clouds of white, red and blue streaked across golden skies. Sometimes, saints, martyrs, virgins and the heavenly cities of Jerusalem and Bethlehem stood in paradisiacal landscapes.[32]

It seems that the focus was more on the fullness of life on this earth that the risen Christ brings – and as I showed, this came with the gift of peace and the grace of forgiveness. The peace of Christ, which Paul fleshes out as given with the Spirit, means also kindness, love, joy and goodness (Galatians 5.22). Psalm 130 describes the experience of the peace of God as the restful state of the weaned child on its mother's breast. But to show that this should not be individualised and reduced merely to an inner private state, and that struggling with a reconciling heart embraces many dimensions, I now tell the story of the Quaker theologian and minister David Nyonzima of Burundi, a powerful witness to all I have been saying, and who himself had been with the group in Kigali.

'UNLOCKING HORNS':[33] RECONCILIATION IN ACTION

Burundi's story represents the other side of the coin to Rwanda, because the dominant government was Tutsi, who inflicted terrible slaughter on Hutus. The title for David Nyonzima's powerful story of reconciliation comes from the symbolic weight put on the fact of Burundi's cows having heavy horns, making it difficult for the animals to get though the narrow gate into their pen. Once inside, their horns become entangled:

> Because of this experience with the cattle locking their horns, there is a saying, '*Ntazibana-zidaku – bitana ama-hembe*,' meaning, 'The cows that live together will lock their horns' ... What the owner would hear before he went to sleep would be the sound of the locking and unlocking of their horns.[34]

Unlocking horns becomes a powerful metaphor for reconciliation for David Nyonzima. He shows us that Burundi,

To Rwanda and Back

Rwanda's neighbour, has a similar story to Rwanda, and that the roots of violence lie deep in history and the colonial regimes. His own hope is partly based on peacemaking traditions of Burundi's own culture. It is this fact that makes him deny that the communities of Burundi have always lived in violence. David Nyonzima's family became Christian through the Quaker missionaries, Arthur and Edna Chilson and their daughter Rachel, so the boy David himself grew up in a deeply Christian home, from where he made his own personal commitment in 1976.

Like Rwanda, Burundi endured many decades of killings. David Nyonzima himself was in danger of being murdered in 1993, following the assassination of Burundi's President, Melchior Ndadaye, apparently by Tutsi soldiers. On 25 October, four days later, Tutsi soldiers – on a mission to kill Hutus – arrived at the school where David Nyonzima was teaching. At the firing of guns the students all scattered. Although David managed to escape after hiding in a workshop, and eventually in his father's house, many students were murdered, as was his father's brother and many friends. However, grief-stricken and horrified by the killings though he was, he experienced a God-given call to forgive the killers. Meeting one of the leaders, Filbert, in the town later, he shook his hand and told him that, by God's power, he forgave him for his part in the killings. The killer was thunderstruck (although he did not confess), but for David Nyonzima this became a turning point in his life, which now became dedicated to peace and reconciliation.[35]

But it should not be thought that his ministry of reconciliation was directed only to individuals. This would be to undervalue the Quaker tradition within which Nyonzima stands firm. First, it is a reconciling faith based on service and action. It is addressed to both rich and poor, to the powerful and the powerless. And, most significantly, it is based on an understanding of the peace that Christ gives as one breaking down barriers between divided groups (Ephesians 2.13–17), and recognising the vulnerability and woundedness of both. Nyonzima's ministry was able to take on another dimension when, because of death threats in 1996, he and his wife Felicity left Burundi temporarily for Kenya. Here he was able not only to lecture widely on conflict-resolution and leadership training for peace, but to make many materials available in the language of the people, *kirundi*, instead of in French. The witness of his life is not only to the crucial need for forgiveness and repentance, but for the peace of Christ to take root in hearts, minds and whole communities. He and his colleagues in Burundi are under no illusion that the longed-for reconciliation is also dependent on a vision of justice and flourishing for all. So it is to the need for structural justice to go hand in hand with forgiveness that I now inevitably turn.

MEDITATION

'Fragile Bridges over Troubled Waters' has trodden a thorny path. Before moving on, I reflect on what this has meant for a spirituality with reconciliation at its heart. Coming to terms with both church complicity in violence (or in any form of oppression, like sexual abuse) challenges faith and hope. I feel sick at heart. Integrity remains compromised. I face too my own inadequate response to the tragedies that continue to unfurl around me. I belong to this Church and cannot off-load all responsibility on to church leaders. A culture of blame, I realise, nurtures hatred and prevents renewal and social repentance.

I realise, by the running waters of the small river outside where I live, that for the flow of church life to continue, structural sin and social repentance must be taken far more seriously, with ongoing acts of repentance as part of ecclesial life, and the developing of an attentive ecclesiology. Have I learnt anything at all from this attempt to face church complicity? Are the bridges too fragile to hold? As I walk across the small wooden bridge over the river, I wonder at the fact that this small crossing has been effective for hundreds of years.[36] Even before the bridge existed, drovers came with carts and forded the river at this point. The idea that dawns on me is that what is needed is not grand plans and mighty resources to uphold fragile bridges. It takes the small acts of courage of many people, people who take risks in the name of peace and reconciliation. Reconciliation is work and service, as I learnt from looking again at Paul's words. Sacred work with which we have been entrusted.

Yes, it is about taking risks and about resistance. But it is not about making resistance the core value of a spirituality. As the Swedish feminist theologian Karin Sporre writes, it is not 'I resist therefore I am, *but I am*, therefore I resist and create'.[37] This prioritises the bodily reality of *being* over political strategy. It means resistance is always in the service of a higher vision of flourishing for all. Thirdly, putting bodily reality at the heart of reconciliation is recognising the suffering of bodies in a context of violence. Johnson McMaster's words, *embodied kenosis*, are still ringing in my ears. I have emphasised the praxis of *kenosis* in the context of listening to the needs of the other. But surely there is a more positive and life-giving dimension of this if looked at from a feminist perspective? Earlier I looked at motherhood as an example of a spirituality of care. But we could take this further and look at giving birth as a metaphor for *kenosis*.[38] *Kenosis* has always been seen from the Christic paradigm of leaving glory behind in order to take the form of a slave (Philippians 2). In other words, in negative, sacrificial terms. But if we focus on the actual female experience of giving birth there is a literal self-emptying that is also a positive growth process. There is pain but joy in the creation of something new as Jesus himself said (John 16.20–21). How could Christian experience have missed out on this self-evident truth for all these years? Filled with new hope with this idea, to which I will return in Chapter 6, I turn to the area of structural justice as companion to and component of forgiveness.

5 LISTEN TO THE CRYING OF
THE EARTH

*Poverty, Structural Justice and Reconciliation with
Non-Human Creation*

How then will this martyr church in this ecological and
cosmic era love nature? Passionately, persistently and per-
vasively. We Christians will be a voice for the voiceless, for
the sake of all the creatures who have no voice in human
affairs. We will listen to the plaintive cries of the whales and
hear the groaning of the rain forests, and we will be their
advocates in the village square and in the courts of power by
the grace of God. All the more we will hear the bitter
wailing of the little children who live on the trash mountains of this world and who wear clothes washed in streams
overflowing with heinous poisons and who sometimes
drink those very waters ... With comic beauty or with dead
seriousness this martyr church will also raise its voice in holy
rage against the plundering of this planet's God-given
bounty ... We will be a martyr church, witnessing in word.
But not words only. We will also love nature and all the
little ones of this earth in deed.

Paul Santmire[1]

The earth dries up and withers,
The whole world withers and grows sick;
The earth's high places sicken,
And earth herself is desecrated by the feet of those who live
   in it,
Because they have broken the laws, disobeyed the statutes

And violated the eternal covenant.
For this curse has devoured the earth
And its inhabitants stand aghast.

Isaiah 24.4–6

STRUCTURAL JUSTICE: THE PATH TO RECONCILIATION

How could anyone argue that structural justice should not be an integral part of the processes of peace-building and reconciliation? I will start with this assumption. Reflecting on what I have written, I know everything points to this. It is the hope of every Truth and Reconciliation Commission, from South Africa to East Timor to Guatemala, even if the achieving of it may lie beyond the Commission's power. But it is not so easy to define what *kind* of struggle for justice should be part of a spirituality with reconciliation at its core. So many pathways have been tried and failed. Over-focus on resistance and the fight for justice can lead to burn-out and compassion fatigue. Christian NGOs are doing sterling work in fashioning a prophetic spirituality of justice and everything I write is in support of this. Liberation theologians have also been creating inspirational contextual spiritualities of justice, and, again, I want to build on these. In the Catholic Church, conscientisation as to societal forms of oppression has been steadily growing, fostered in an official way by over a hundred years of papal social encyclicals condemning structural injustice, which have tried to influence public policy. Many consider these as a precious but under-used resource. This has much to do with the fact that encyclicals are simply not written in a language that touches the hearts of ordinary people and are frequently perceived to be 'top–down' documents displaying – with a few exceptions – little pastoral sensitivity.

To Rwanda and Back

But why have all these resources not been more far-reaching in achieving structural justice, or at least putting it as a high priority for every person? The answer is complex: sadly, following the long development of individualism in western society (so that people now think of themselves as separated units), the breakdown of traditional communities, including faith communities, and the permeation of globalising market forces where unstoppable consumerism frequently triumphs over more ancient spiritual habits – these are all causes.[2]

So I am trying a different approach. One hugely neglected area is structural justice and reconciliation with the earth herself. Devastation of the earth, as Isaiah reminds us in the passage cited above, is an area of structural injustice that is directly consequent on human wrongdoing and hard-heartedness. Because the well-being and flourishing of people and earth are held together by the interdependent functioning of ecosystems, when one is damaged, all are affected. Yet there is a lukewarm attitude at best to the urgency of ecological justice, and an attitude of total denial at worst, even in the face of the seriousness of climate change.

James Lovelock, in his latest book *The Revenge of Gaia*, describes the level of this crisis as terminal.[3] In chilling terms he foresees rises in sea levels, storms of unprecedented severity, cities rendered uninhabitable and their citizens reduced to becoming refugees. The level of denial (to which I shall return) as to what is happening to the planet results in justice for the earth never claiming attention comparable with hunger, child abuse or cancer research, despite the fact that it concerns the urgency of sustaining life itself. Statistics about extinction of species, devastation of the rain forest, increasing desertification and melting of the ice cap overwhelm us every day, yet seem only to increase a deep-seated inertia. Indeed, entrepreneurs are already taking advantage of warmer temperatures in the Arctic to set up money-making enterprises.

There is no scene of global conflict where ecological justice is not an underlying issue, even if frequently overlooked. This is certainly true of Rwanda: as I mentioned in my introduction, 90 per cent of Rwanda's population is rural-based and heavily dependent on agriculture. With no minerals, coffee, introduced by German missionaries in 1904, is the only lucrative export crop. (Tea is also exported.) In fact, Rwanda is the ninth largest producer of *Arabaica* coffee, and of course Rwanda suffered terribly, as did other African countries, when prices of coffee dropped on the world market. But, in reality, Rwanda suffered more because the world has never been interested in her problems, as the refusal of help during the genocide illustrated. There is considerable evidence to show that a decade before the genocide people were struggling to find a piece of cultivable land 'from a relatively stagnant pool'.[4] At this time average land holdings had shrunk by 12 per cent between 1984 and 1989. 'Another evaluation, this one following the genocide, pointed out that 57 per cent of rural households were already having to farm less than one hectare of land in 1984, while 25 per cent of these had less than half a hectare. At the same time, these shrinking land parcels had to feed an average family of five people.[5]

Because inheritance patterns demanded that the land be divided between all sons, plots were both fragmented and diminished, pointing to land scarcity as a source of rivalry and conflict. (This certainly suggests similarities with Ireland at the time of the potato famine in the nineteenth century.) Food production had also decreased, dropping from 2,055 kilo-calories per person per day to 1,509 in the period 1984–91. This is the underlying background to genocide, but how seriously it should be regarded as a crucial cause is disputed. Yet the situation was critical, merely awaiting ignition, some could say.[6] What is beyond dispute is that the genocide itself ensured that agricultural production decreased further and that hunger and starvation became widespread.

The same link between the suffering of people and

exploitation of the earth is observed in many contexts. The destruction of the Amazonian rainforests in Brazil and of tribal forests in India has destroyed the livelihood of many thousands of people. Removal of forest cover affects rain patterns so that drought ruins the very possibility of a life of dignity: failure of rains brings ruin of agriculture with starvation looming for people and animals alike. Global warming is already wreaking havoc, as witnessed, for example, by the unusual number and severity of hurricanes and tornadoes affecting the Caribbean and the United States in the summer of 2005. One friend from Trinidad told me that there was no dry season in 2005/6 in Trinidad – Christmas Day itself was marked by a heavy storm. In fact, the proportion of hurricanes reaching categories 4 or 5 increased from 20 per cent in the 1970s to 35 per cent over the past decade.[7]

It is not merely on the macro level of disasters that the effects of climate change have been felt. The same phenomenon occurs on a personal level. Environmental factors, *caused by ourselves*, could be responsible for between 60 and 80 per cent of cancers, yet mostly the deaths are treated as purely personal tragedies. This massive denial as to the severity of damage we are inflicting on the earth is at first sight hard to comprehend.

Churches have not been completely silent as to the suffering of the earth. There are landmark moments of awakening and awareness. The late Pope John Paul II in many of his writings provided some of these, and took important initiatives when he called for peace that brought reconciliation with the whole earth on World Peace Day, 1 January, 1990. Again, in his speech at the symposium on the environment he emphasised the fundamental moral character of the environmental crisis, laying particular emphasis on the value and respect for life and the integrity of the created order. Pope John Paul did not separate issues of justice from those of reconciliation, calling for all to make a commitment 'to the equal distribution of this earth's goods, to respect for the life of the neighbour in trouble or on the fringe, to development of volunteer agencies'.[8]

Sadly, the former Pope's leadership has not trickled down or spread throughout the Church at leadership level, with few exceptions. But there are signs at last that this is changing. Mary Colwell, writing recently in *The Tablet*, reports that New Zealand's bishops are urging Catholics to change lifestyles, use less energy, and so on.[9] At the end of 2006 CAFOD launched a national programme in Britain, 'Live Simply', with a similar intent. Yet, at an ecumenical level, there had already been a breakthrough, since the Earth Summit in Rio de Janeiro in 1992. Following the Earth Summit, the famous *Letter to the Churches* was promulgated:

> We dare not deny our role as Churches in the crisis which now overwhelms us. We have not spoken the prophetic word ourselves. Indeed, we did not even hear it when it was spoken by others of late, including a number of scientists. Much less did we hear the cries of indigenous peoples who have told us for centuries that modernity would foul its own nest and even devour its own children. We need to mourn and repent ... We plead for forgiveness and pray for a profound change of heart.[10]

In liberation circles this had enormous impact (that is, among people already committed to the struggle for justice). Leonardo Boff led the way to making the connections between the suffering of poor communities and the exploitation of the earth in a way that liberation theology could not ignore.[11] But it is disappointing to relate that the European Ecumenical Assembly in Graz, Austria, in 1997 took no huge steps forward, although I do not underestimate the energy, commitments and actions of the many small groups who were present. I saw this personally. This is how two participants, Donald Bruce and David Pickering, evaluated the event:

Sadly, the Graz theme of reconciliation was not an ideal motif for raising contemporary environmental issues, so major topics such as transport and genetic engineering were covered only peripherally, and some like waste and water were hardly touched ... The Team (that is, the drafting team) seemed out of touch with both the experts and the delegate working groups ... Their failure to work with the experts also produced sweeping theological statements which, had it not been noticed at the last minute, would have set the Assembly in opposition to all genetic engineering, and most genetic research, without discussion, and in opposition to the carefully researched positions of many member churches.[12]

This conclusion that 'reconciliation' was not an ideal motif to raise contemporary environmental issues flags up the problem this chapter faces: the gulf between the perceived issues around reconciliation (repentance, forgiveness and reparation), all areas that concern *churches as churches,* and areas of justice that are considered to be about advocacy and political lobbying, often thought to be only marginal as church issues, together with the way all these issues are embraced by spirituality. In 1998 a new initiative tried to stir up the flagging energies, through the *kairos* movement, now focusing on Europe, as *Kairos Europa.* Although the primary focus was not on the environment,[13] but on the economic systems spawning injustice, the environment was an important part of its agenda:

> We call upon the churches not to avoid conflict with power and money. Reconciliation can only be real and can only grow on the basis of truth and justice, if the real conflicts of interests are tackled and not avoided. In particular, it cannot grow where lies, semi-truths and repression are commonplace. *The fundamental decision today of prophetic theology: life for all instead of money for a few.*[14] (my italics)

Many church initiatives carry on, and are well intentioned. The process 'Justice, Peace and Integrity of Creation', an initiative of the World Council of Churches, seems to have lost some of the energy of its initial years, although in some cases the initiative has been picked up by local churches. But in the UK it never really gained momentum. Yet, as I mentioned earlier, the purpose of my visit to Rwanda was to address the subject of the integrity of creation (as part of a group organised by the WCC's Faith and Order Commission), and the context with its history of violence had been deliberately chosen. My hunch is that the chasm referred to earlier is part of the problem – the barriers between ecclesial issues of repentance and forgiveness, the political activities of lobbying and advocacy and the lack of a thought-through ecological spirituality with justice at its heart. The editor of *Vocation for Justice* (published by the Columban Fathers) hinted at the same problem recently in his final editorial for the journal:

> I have come to believe that the community of believers has a specifically different contribution to make in the struggle for a more just world, and that presently we are distracted from even beginning to identify it, much less from acting out of it, because of overemphasis on political lobbying and corporate campaigning. I do not believe that even if the power of 'all the king's horses and all the king's men' was put into advocacy and lobbying alone that we would achieve the transformations we desire.[15]

Eamon O'Brien is not trying to underrate political lobbying. He suggests that the power of transformed lifestyles within believing communities is the missing ingredient. But it could also be that social transformation also needs transformed consciousness, and a new symbol system that inspires different way of relating to the earth, and that ecological ethics needs to be built on this.

A more hopeful note, and an inspiring example of leadership, has been offered recently by the Australian Catholic Bishops. For example, *The Gift of Water*, a report on the water situation by Catholic Earthcare Australia, was endorsed by the bishops of the Murray Darling Basin on 4 October 2004.[16] There are also now many examples from the Catholic Bishops' Conferences in the United States and in the Philippines, to mention only a few. These give signs of hope: but a more radical response in terms of theology, spirituality and ethics is called for. Lovelock himself calls for a new Sermon on the Mount that sets out constraints for living decently within the Earth, and which sets out rules for its achievement.[17]

ECOLOGICAL SPIRITUALITY AND THE PATH TO RECONCILIATION

A surprising witness that these two dimensions can be combined, indeed that they belong together, is discovered in Dostoevsky's novel *The Brothers Karamazov*. This passage comes at a crucial moment in the life of the young monk Alyosha. Father Zossima, his beloved mentor, famed for his holiness, had just died, and Alyosha, in meditating by his coffin on the scriptural story of the marriage feast of Cana,[18] had just received a revelation of his presence in heaven at the Great Messianic Wedding Feast. His reaction is to seek an experience of his own presence within with the great cosmic mystery of creation:

> Alyosha did not stop on the steps either, but went down rapidly, His soul, overflowing with rapture, was craving for freedom and unlimited space. The vault of heaven, studded with softly shining stars, stretched wide and vast over him. The Milky Way ran in two pale streams, from the zenith to the horizon. The fresh, motionless, still night enfolded the

earth ... The silence of the earth seemed to merge with the silence of the heavens, the mystery of earth was one with the mystery of the stars ... Alyosha stood, gazed, and suddenly he threw himself flat upon the earth, He did not know why he was embracing it ... It was as though the threads from all those innumerable worlds of God met all at once in his soul ... He had fallen upon the earth a weak youth, but he rose from it a resolute fighter for the rest of his life, he realised and felt it suddenly at the very moment of his rapture.[19]

He would never forget this visionary moment for the rest of his life. With it came the strength to carry on his mission, to leave the monastery and to 'sojourn in the world' – effectively to carry on the troubled work for reconciliation between his brothers and all with whom they were involved. This is Alyosha's message to us: *peace with the earth and peace with justice between humans are intrinsically interwoven.*

But an ecological spirituality with reconciliation at its heart, that also honours structural justice, has to find its way through many pitfalls. First, many individuals remain trapped in a very privatised notion of salvation: if it is still hard to embrace an inclusive community dimension, how much harder to envision the involvement of the non-human community. Second, Churches themselves have frequently become comfortable with the logic of market economies promising progress that is harmful to the earth – even if, at last, things have begun to change with action addressing climate change and the consequences of global warming.

Digging deeper, our heritage of philosophical dualisms still make us reluctant to admit our dependence on and vulnerability to nature's graciousness as well as her ferocity and her limits. We still suffer from the impact of the spiritualising, *body-denying* strand of western Christianity and the heritage of a spirituality where the spirit is identified with the real person, the body experienced as an inferior tool, eventually to be discarded. In fact the true home for the human spirit is still most frequently deemed to be beyond the earth, in Paradise, the Garden re-created for us in the New Jerusalem. This can encourage us to believe that the earth, in the last resort, is expendable. As eco-theologian Catherine Keller has written, as if to the spoilt child who takes no care of his toys: 'Waste. Spend. It matters not. Destroy this earth: Daddy will give you a new one!'[20] If the earth is ultimately expendable it is far easier to justify ecocidal policies. Small wonder that we urgently need to re-imagine our views on heaven in a way that includes the survival and well-being of the planet. So many aspects of contemporary culture, such as the current fascination with the manufacture of GM food, the cloning of animals, even human beings, and the ability of the computer to assume numerous human functions, all foster the illusion that the greater the cultural advance, the further *Homo sapiens* moves away from being nature-dependent. Virtual reality is preferred to embodied relationships.

Yet so many of the ancient myths warn us against this *hubris*, this arrogance in trying to reach for the heavens – the Greek story of Prometheus stealing fire from the gods, Icarus with his waxen wings who died from flying too close to the sun, for example. We carry, too, the consequences of Christianity's total rejection of paganism. Nature has been dismissed as the abode of specifically pagan deities, animistic sprites, and as the place of the idolatry of trees and of Druidic rites. Lovelock notes with irony that his first attempt to describe Gaia as a living organism – an attempt initially ridiculed by the scientific community – coincided with New Age rediscovery of the Goddess as earth mother, a move criticised by Christian Churches. Nature religions are assumed to be opposed to Judaism and Christianity. It is no coincidence that the early spread of Christianity was in the cities, while pagans, *pagani*, were literally the country-dwellers. I am not advocating the total reversal of these attitudes, but calling at the very least for a reconsideration of certain dimensions of nature religions that honoured the earth and her rhythms and were consequently more in a position to develop an earth-respecting ethic.

Associated with this rejection of nature is the negative attitude to women, particularly female sexuality, a well-defined strand in Christian tradition: 'Nature is to culture as woman is to man.'[21] This expresses the dualistic split that associates women with nature. It is not only that both are associated with embodied existence, where this was deemed inferior to eternal, disembodied life, but both can be idealised, so that the actual suffering of either women or nature can be ignored. Another important area is that ongoing military violence anaesthetises us as to the suffering and woundedness inflicted on nature. Continuing war in Iraq, Afghanistan and the Sudan means that farmers who should be sowing seeds are forced into military action. There can be no harvest here. In Palestine, the great wall built by the Israelis has confiscated the land of Palestinian farmers and separated them from their olive trees and fruit orchards, a vital and often the sole source of income.

Finally, *anthropocentric* thinking keeps 'man' at the top of the Ladder of the Great Chain of Being. All creation exists for him. He is expected to be a wise steward: but ultimately, all created and living things exist for his usage. (Usually the verse from Genesis 2.20 is cited here, where Adam is given the task of naming the creatures.) When asking what blocks awareness, acceptance of a humbler place in creation, and effective action, it is well known that anthropocentrism, or *anthroposolism*,[22] a focus on humanity's importance and well-being alone, is a huge obstacle to an effective ethic and spirituality that enables reconciliation between people and earth alike.

So a spirituality of reconciliation must move away from this presumption of human superiority, and instead must stress responsibility, accountability and commitment to ecological justice. Seeking to understand why theology and the Churches have been so apathetic, it becomes clear that it is not statistics of doom and gloom that change people, such as an endless litany of how many species of plant and bird die each day, but when our capacity for awe and wonder, our levels of compassion, sensitivities and our caring abilities are all touched, as were Alyosha's – this is when transformation occurs. If our desires can be uprooted from endless craving for material satisfaction and re-rooted in nature's rhythms (which elsewhere I called 'sacred longings'[23]), the seeds of reconciliation are sown.

But if the process of turning away from the earth has taken hundreds of years (at least for us in the West), reconversion will not be accomplished with a few brief gestures and shallow commitments. Reconversion will be on many levels and will involve changing all our vital points of reference. In the first place, it will seek a new way of *seeing* the earth. One reason for the wanton destruction of nature is precisely because of the insensitive way we perceive the earth and all earthly dimensions. Our seeing is always through different metaphors, or lenses. It is probable that all of us look at the world in many widely disparate ways, as a field of conquest, for example, as battle ground, as a commodity to be bought and sold, as wilderness, as gift, as friend, or as self, deeply connected with us. If through spiritual practice and discipline we were able to see the world differently, as gracious gift that we hold in trust but do not own, what difference could this make? This is the practice that Sallie McFague calls 'seeing with the loving eye'.[24]

From awareness of our connectedness and deep affinity with the earth, from valuing these connections, and through compassion for all life forms, the roots of an earth-honouring spirituality are planted. As Susan Griffin wrote:

> We know ourselves to be made from this earth. We know this earth is made from our bodies. For we see ourselves.

And we are nature. We are nature seeing nature. We are nature with a concept of nature. Nature weeping. Nature speaking of nature to nature.[25]

Shug, a key character in Alice Walker's novel *The Colour Purple*, discovered this connectedness and cried, 'I knew that if I cut a tree my arm would bleed.'[26] John Seed expressed this connectedness through his experience in the rainforest: 'I am the rain-forest,' he said. Martin Buber's discovery of the 'I and Thou' relationship included the *thou-ness* between people and nature. He spoke of being seized by the thou-ness of the Tree.[27] From the experience of connectedness, a new seeing and awareness arises.

Secondly, given this new way of seeing and awareness of connectedness, our spirituality will spring from this earth-rooted authenticity, in our relatedness with the whole of creation and its Creator. As our lived and practised faith, it becomes the yeast, our daily bread, prompting how we will put flesh on the bones of our beliefs. This will have both practical and ordinary expressions, yet will be permeated too with our dreams and longings and expressed in myriad ways, in every aspect of our lifestyles, by what we eat and buy, how we respect fair trade and organic living;[28] how we heat our houses and resolve the fossil fuel and carbon emissions dilemma; how we travel and how our music, art and patterns of relationships honour and respect creation.

Let us start with the conviction that the earth is suffering, perhaps even irreparably damaged – as Lovelock argues – due to human exploitation. Let us see faith communities as the space where eco-spiritualities reverencing the earth can be created and lived out, and that this spirituality cannot be split from justice-making. So an eco-spirituality of reconciling with the earth begins with awareness of the poverty of poor communities, whose very survival is intricately bound up with environmental well-being, and with the ability to grasp the structural causes of these realities. As Yvone Gebara wrote, describing the roots of her ecofeminist spirituality in the grim realities of Brazilian shanty towns:

> I see that ecofeminism is born of daily life, of day-to-day sharing among people, of enduring together garbage in the streets, bad smells, the absence of sewers, and safe drinking water, poor nutrition and adequate health care. The eco-feminism I see is born of the lack of municipal garbage collection, of the multiplication of rats, cockroaches, and mosquitoes, and of the sores of children's skins.[29]

In the water-stressed villages of Rajasthan, vulnerable people – especially women and girls – find it almost impossible to climb out of the vicious poverty trap, with poor health, diet, failure of agriculture, illiteracy and the harshness of traditional patriarchy and caste-based discrimination forming the contours of their lives.

With this grounding and just two examples, we can revisit the insights of previous chapters to incorporate these now in an ecological context. Chapter 1 focused on re-membering as crucial for reconciliation. But re-membering embraces how a community's land has suffered exploitation in the course of history; remembering how, in the rapacious conquests of colonialism, land has been robbed from poor communities, forests stripped, and subsistence agriculture replaced by the production of cash crops. Tharcisse Gatwa related how the South African Churches have created liturgies lamenting what has been done to the earth, and calling for this to happen in Rwanda.[30] Lament is a neglected liturgical experience within our churches: but it will sink to mere emotionalism unless part of structured repentance and genuine movement towards reconciliation. In Chapter 2 the focus was on rethinking sacrifice from within an ethic of suffering love. The same difficulties reappear in connection with the earth. As with the low value put on women, so the earth's limits and rhythms have been ignored, in the interests of profit and extravagant lifestyles.

In Chapter 3 the failure of compassion was looked at, especially *social* compassion, and a spirituality of care was developed, whereas Chapter 4 looked at new models of Church needing to be developed in response to this failure. But if the core of what the gathering together we call Church is all about, is its ministry of caring or *diaconia*, in the context of being called to practise the diaconia of reconciliation, then Church as the cosmic body of Christ means becoming a community conscious of dwelling on this earth. It means taking responsibility for the bio-region and integrating sustainable living into the heart of a vibrant, re-imaged Christian identity. We have scarcely begun to imagine a 'diaconia of responsibility for the earth'.

Becoming community in any real sense begins with responsibility for where we dwell. And we dwell on planet Earth, in city, soulless suburb, village, desert, mountain, forest and lakeside – as a small part of a very ancient story, earth-story. And a late-comer at that – the last five minutes, as cosmologists like Thomas Berry and Brian Swimme would say. We dwell in bio-regions with specific giftedness and vulnerability to human need and greed. We do not just depend on the earth, but as Susan Griffin put it in the citation above, we are the earth, breathing in her air, treading her soil lightly or heavily, depending on what demands we make on the bio-region.

Practising the diaconia of reconciliation embraces all dimensions of spirituality, mindful of the insight gleaned from Dostoevsky's Alyosha. In its prophetic dimension, it will take three forms. The first is critique, meaning the need to denounce ecological sin specifically as structural injustice. This is the first step in the lifelong journey of repentance/metanoia as both personal and community response. Part of this journey is the commitment to resist injustice. Resistance as the core of a prophetic spirituality means never allowing oneself to accept the unjust status quo as the final reality. Roger Gottlieb writes that in acts of resistance we 'can feel a deep connection beyond the boundaries of the isolated ego'.[31] The second dimension is that of prophetic vision – of the redeemed and reconciled creation. Imagining or dreaming has become a lost dimension of Christianity. Deborah Bird Rose writes of aboriginal indigenous peoples in Australia who still live out of 'dream time'.[32] A high value is placed on memory in the context of competing land claims and 'forgetting' is seen as a form of capitulation, as giving the last word to the conqueror. Dreaming is not an optional extra, but a way of keeping identity and hope alive. Third, lamenting – grieving and mourning for what is lost, *in community liturgical space* – is an integral part of prophetic spirituality.

Together with this prophetic core, the sacramental, the Sabbath and the mystical traditions form vital reference points for ecological spirituality. Another major reference point for Christians is the rereading of Scripture from a penitential, earth-friendly perspective. We begin to ask ourselves: 'Who are we, reading Scripture?' What is our context, faith, lifestyle? What are we looking for? Mindful of the current crisis of global warming and our own responsibility, as well as of globalisation and the privatisation of water, the patenting of seeds, and so on, we seek a different interpretation of Scripture. We are reading not through the lens of hierarchical ordering, domination, dominion: this is a *penitential reading*, recognising that we are all part of the problem, part of the exploitation, and taking to our own hearts the prophetic critique, where people are urged again and again to change their hearts. Ecologically responsible Christians read Scripture, seeking a view beyond anthropocentrism, for clues to value all living organisms in the web of life; looking to promote *eco-kinship*, or kinship in the web of life. The view sought penetrates beyond romanticism. Accepting no cosy view of nature, we pray for the courage that admits all dimensions of *tragedy/excess/terror and beauty, of majesty/particularity/sorrow and ambiguity*. We endeavour to inhabit a world view admitting the double dynamic of celebration and lament.

With my students I have long tried to suggest a new beginning to the way we read Scripture. Instead of starting with the book of Genesis, which lands us automatically with the problematic of the seeming superiority of the human race and the command to subdue, I suggest we begin with prophetic texts like Isaiah and Jeremiah, for example the text with which this chapter began. Thus justice for the earth is seen as central, belonging with the well-being of humans. Both Jeremiah and Isaiah associate drought and desertification with turning away from God, and redemption of earth and people alike with conversion and reconciliation. But other starting points are inspirational, such as Wisdom literature and the feast of creation's fullness (for example, Proverbs 9), as well as the wonderful creation theology of the book of Job.

Another approach to this diaconia of reconciliation, for example that of Rosemary Ruether in *Gaia and God*,[33] has been to reclaim major strands from the tradition and re-envision them to respond to the crisis. Ruether suggests the sacramental, the covenant and the prophetic. I have added the mystical and the Sabbath tradition of blessing: the vital point is to reclaim these traditions of honouring the earth while factoring in the current devastation and the associated suffering of women and poor communities. For example, discovering the sacredness of water in all religious traditions could inspire another practice,[34] as Vandana Shiva suggests in *Water Wars*.[35]

This morning, as I try to articulate this diaconia of reconciliation with the earth, I am looking out at turbulent waves, in Brittany on a stormy day, when Lovelock's predictions certainly seem to have a ring of truth. On this same sea, Celtic monks in the sixth century, coming from distant Wales, struggled through the waves in frail coracles to found monasteries on the shores and live out ascetic lives as witness to the gospel simplicity. Yet, in the Abbey church of the market town of St Gildas today, where the theologian Peter Abelard was once Abbot – for a brief and unhappy period[36] – there is little tangibility as to their witness. And witness is exactly what is sought, as Santmire's words (cited at the beginning of this chapter) expressed so eloquently. How will the prophetic church live out its witness?

While all approaches I cited are important, and I hold on to the insight that new seeing and vision inspire a lifestyle of reconciliation, a tougher approach is still required, an effective language that the World Bank, the World Trade Organisation, and all institutions who make vital decisions, will listen to. It is the toughness and radicality of the lifestyles of Gildas and his Celtic fellow saints, together with the vision that inspired them, that must be rediscovered. So, I will try once more, and look now also for a sound ethical basis, a set of principles for turning to the earth, mindful that the above-named approaches are based on a specifically religious perspective. And that is what we cannot always presume in the current debates.

SEEKING A NEW BEGINNING FOR ETHICS

Let us hold onto the need for a new way to behold and perceive nature, through the discipline of seeing with a 'loving eye', mentioned earlier, in order to transform practices of control and domination. In the context of changed perception, Anglican theologian Michael Northcott invokes Maurice Merleau-Ponty (1906–61), the French phenomenologist and philosopher. Northcott understands the problem of global warming and climate change as caught up with the disembodied, over-rational thinking of liberalism. Solutions emerging from this framework – like carbon trading – simply promote individualism, and are rooted in a diminished notion of the Common Good. Merleau-Ponty's work, surprisingly, prefigured more recent (ecofeminist and ecological) attempts at seeing consciousness as embodied, and spoke of 'the lived body' or flesh, rooted in the flesh of the world. Northcott shows how our familiar notions of progress and development that frame the current discussions of climate change emerged from a disembodied consciousness.[37] But, operating from a changed model of consciousness means, according to Northcott, changing our understanding of time, and giving attention to narratives, the way stories reflect a community's attitude to earth and their relation to time. The poet Denise Levertov observes that time is not included in the Genesis account of creation:

> The hand that inscribed Genesis left out
> the creation of Time. Dividing
> darkness from light, God paused to reach
> into the substance of Eternity,
> teased out a strand of it,
> and wound its arabesques throughout
> the workshops of creation, looping it through
> the arches of newmade days and nights.[38]

If we could only move away from our rigid dividing of time between past, present and future, would we gain greater understanding of the power that re-membering plays in current conflicts? Could appreciating time as connecting with earth's rhythms bring wisdom as to the depth of commitment needed to allow the earth to heal from longstanding ecocidal policies? What I propose is trying to live out of a deepening embodied consciousness, as part of the diaconia of reconciliation. A second move is to strengthen this approach with a new ecopsychology, thus moving away from standard models of humanistic psychology. This is suggested by Andy Fisher, in *Radical Ecopsychology*. He declares that 'The essence of humanity lies in discovering commonality with nature'.[39]

What this adds is the conviction that embodying our consciousness in 'the flesh of the world' (Merleau-Ponty), we are not only enabled to practise more eco-friendly lifestyles, but actually discover more about what it means to be human. (This is not meant to encourage creeping anthropocentrism!) With this commonality as part of the way we perceive and feel, from within deepening embodied consciousness, we are enabled to reread Scripture and other sacred texts with a new lens – as described above. It then becomes possible to rethink liturgy as a place of ethical commitment, and sacrifice as a community act of solidarity with the suffering earth/suffering people. Liturgy becomes the place of awareness and revelation; the place where memory/anamnesis becomes remembering what we were once, what we have been, what we can now never be, given so much destruction. A place for the recovery of prophetic lament and grief for all that has disappeared, and the glory of God that can never be, because of what has been destroyed, what we are still destroying. A place where we commit ourselves concretely to lifestyles geared to the flourishing and survival of threatened peoples and wounded earth.

In this quest to live responsibly with the earth we are not alone. Gildas and his fellow Celtic (and Anglo-Saxon) saints are not alive, yet the inspiration of Celtic spirituality is their thriving legacy. The witness of St Francis, of Gandhi, of communities like Taizé, Iona and Lindisfarne are journey companions. The green movements, the eco-warriors, the deep ecologists all have prophetic figures, some even practising the asceticism of an earlier monastic age. Specifically Christian lifestyle movements, such as Christian Ecology Link, and those religious communities – like the Benedictines – who reclaim their charism of caring for the earth in these threatened times offer great sources for hope.

My own personal source of inspiration has been that we are given a new revelation of the mystery of God, in the midst of the crisis, the Spirit as the Green Face of God, the wounded face of God in creation.[40] The paradox is that if the face of God is revealed in all the ravages of creation, yet, as healing Spirit, as life breath of all that is created, there is still hope for renewal and rebirth, as I will explore in Chapter 6.

Mindful of all these changed reference points, realising that the ecological footprints of the communities of Isaiah, Jesus or Gildas were infinitely smaller than ours, I now search for a new ethical basis for the current crisis. When seeking an ethical basis for attitudes to the environment, in my own work in Wells for India, solutions to the water crisis range from grand interlinking of river schemes (bring the water from elsewhere), to desalination, to proper water management at a local level, using ancient systems (the traditional wisdom of the desert peoples) – the latter being Wells for India's preferred solution. But in this chapter I seek to discover what are the ethical principles and systems that enable the kinds of decisions that will promote earth justice comprehensively across the many areas of need.

Another approach is to change attitudes of ownership to land, water and trees – the idea that, for example, water belongs to the common good. Vandana Shiva, in an attempt to cross the barriers of race and religion, proposes that water be accepted as a 'commons'. She offers ten principles towards establishing a water democracy, ranging from recognising water as nature's gift, as essential to life, and as a common good to which everyone has a right. Selling water for profit violates this inherent right.[41]

The difficulty here is, what is the basis, indeed the authority, for speaking about 'inherent right', 'duty' and 'principle'? I alluded to Michael Northcott's conviction as to the difficulty of the idea of the Common Good in the framework of liberalism. The 'Common Good' is exactly what we have lost. Part of the difficulty is that we can appeal to no sound tradition of environmental ethics, indeed as a discipline this has only been developed in the last twenty years. So what options do we have? But, while exploring these, I want to hold onto the hope of recovery of the 'Common Good'.

The problem is that our long history of exploiting and dominating nature has made it almost impossible to develop an environmental ethic that is authoritative for all nations. There is a general assumption that ethics is about moral principles that human beings invoke to shape their common life. The earth and her resources are included only as backcloth to human endeavour, although recently the attitude of 'responsible stewardship' has become more prominent. The hundred and ten years of Roman Catholic encyclicals on social justice – from *Rerum Novarum* onwards – offer very few starting points for an environmental ethic. The background to this is of course a dualistic philosophy, built on the superiority of the human being – ultimately relating back to Aristotle, who took it as written into the universe's laws that humanity was superior to nature:[42] this would develop later in Enlightenment philosophy, to the conviction that 'man' is the centre of the universe, coupled with a post-Cartesian rationalism that led increasingly to the competitive individualism, referred to above, that is a major factor in the globalisation discourse.[43] *Nature as sacred* as core value gradually disappeared with the growth of the market economy and the process of commodification of nature itself. Then, given the seriousness of the denial of the crisis, the challenge is how to factor in the environment into the ethical framework?

A first possible approach is to *replace anthropocentric ethics with an ecocentric, biocentric or organic model*. This emerges both from deep ecology and from Gaian theory – associated with the scientist, James Lovelock, mentioned above, and with ecofeminist theologian Anne Primavesi.[44] What is common to these approaches is the notion of the universe as an organic whole, with its own agency. Freed from human interference, Gaia, or planet earth, is a holistic organism with its own self-correcting mechanisms. Deep ecologists believe that the entire web of life has its own inherent value, agency and subjectivity. As Thomas Berry frequently says, 'The universe is a communion of subjects.'[45] My own view is that, while the idea of Gaia seen as interlinked, interdependent, organic ecosystems is attractive and convincing, the idea of the interventionist agency of Gaia in the teeth of the crisis of climate change is not. So I want to search further.

I suggest the preferred goal should be *an ethical framework where human beings take responsibility for the earth, not merely for the sake of our own well-being and flourishing, but caring for the well-being of animals, plants, trees and the earth's resources.* This is an ethic of responsibility proposed by a variety of voices, for example Sallie McFague, and the German philosopher Hans Jonas[46] who advocated the principle: 'Act so that the effects of your action are compatible with the permanence of genuine human life.' The strength of this principle is that it is consonant with a changed definition of nature that cuts through the opposition between humanity/nature/culture, allowing a proper measure of respect for nature in different cultural expressions and recognising our mutual dependence. It would mean an appropriate measure of respect for the earth's organisms in accordance with their form of life and being. Such an approach would take seriously Vandana Shiva's suggestion of water as a commons belonging to all, not a commodity to be sold for people. It would open up a way for a water ethic within a framework of structural justice.

How do my other discussion partners value this ethic of responsibility? Michael Northcott, in his *Environmental Ethics*, starts from a different point. Fully aware of the damage caused by mechanistic science, he bases his approach on the land ethic of Aldo Leopold:

Leopold localised his land ethic in an ecological understanding that viewed ecology in terms of energy flows and nutritional cycles between different members of a holistic ecological community. For him all parts of the community are worthy of respect, they are all valued as citizens.[47]

This sounds like Gaian theory again! But, not so: Northcott distances himself from a totally holistic ethic like Lovelock's and deep ecology. For him moral value has biblical roots and must be linked with moral and social order. Like many other ethicists, he places himself between the anthropocentric and biocentric poles. This is where an ethic of responsibility can emerge.

An interesting contribution is made by Robin Attfield: worried that the idea of ecological communities would have a narrowing effect, he stresses that the real need is to see ethical obligations in a wider way, namely, rooted in any agent or community, either individually or corporately. However, he does admit to 'the idea that non-human nature has moral standing, which means . . . that it has a good of its own, even if it does not have moral significance.'[48] This type of argument is termed *cosmopolitanism*, and there are different versions of this. For Laura Westra the principle of *integrity* is central: this is essentially 'the injunction to respect the integrity of ecological and biological processes (save for the purposes of self-defence)'.[49] She then develops a virtue-ethics approach related to this principle of integrity. All three – Northcott, Attfield and Westra – offer approaches that are helpful in the context of the wider discussion, where a faith perspective cannot be presumed.

A more nuanced virtue-ethics approach based on Thomas Aquinas has been developed by the eco-theologian Celia Deane-Drummond, and I would like to show the steps by which the argument moves. The first step is to widen the idea of natural law. (Northcott had already argued for this, to take into account the common ground between human and non-human.) As she states, the first principle of natural law is that good needs to be sought and evil avoided. Of course Aquinas is thinking of human beings, and his idea of reason is not the vastly reductionist understanding of Descartes, but set within a theological understanding. The suggestion of Deane-Drummond is that this could be extended to non-human creatures.

The second level of natural law refers to natural tendencies and inclinations and the third refers to basic activities like self-preservation, rearing of young and reasoning. Of course I cannot argue for an ethic for the whole of nature *directly* from this, but Deane-Drummond is suggesting that from natural law we could infer 'a dynamic movement of all creation towards flourishing and the good'.[50] This is very helpful.

The second step is to integrate this within a virtue-centred approach. In the Catholic tradition the virtues concerned are *prudence, justice, fortitude* and *temperance*. Although many others refer to this approach, the question is how far it can be useful for practical action. Deane-Drummond rejects the precautionary principle accepted by many ecologists. (The precautionary principle means that where there are threats of serious or irreversible damage, lack of full scientific certainty should not be used as a reason for postponing measures to prevent environmental degradation.) Many feel it is inadequate for decision-making in complex cases, since it is directed simply by the worst imagined scenario. Rather, we need to include different facets of *prudence*.[51] By prudence Deane-Drummond means the facet of deliberation, capacity to make decisions in emergency situations, to take advice from others, to have foresight in a way that accurately anticipates the future in so far as it is feasible to do so – all dimensions relevant in environmental contexts. Yet Lovelock, who does accept the precautionary principle, gives an example that is very close to the virtue of prudence that Deane-Drummond evokes. He cites the example of the British retreat at Dunkirk in the Second World War, considering it as an honourable retreat from an unsustainable place, calling forth courage and generosity from numerous people:

> We need the people of the world to sense the real and present danger so that they will spontaneously mobilise and unstintingly bring about an orderly and sustainable with-drawal to a world where we try to live in harmony with Gaia.[52]

This seems to me very similar to the way Deane-Drummond invokes the aspect of wisdom including practical prudential knowledge. (Fortitude and temperance can easily be included in the scheme but more attention is given to the other two virtues.)

Third, justice can be developed to include a web of inter-acting, overlapping cultural diversity embracing belonging to both local and global communities. In Aquinas's ability to link individual, community and global justice Deane-Drummond finds a way forward, specifically through adapting the second level of natural law, to include the self-preservation of all life forms. Justice for non-human life *in kinship* – rather than by analogy – with the human is her suggestion.

The advantage of all these approaches is that they take human responsibility seriously. The special attraction of Deane-Drummond's approach is that we can reclaim resources from a much-respected tradition and refashion them for the current situation.

Before strengthening this case I need to give attention to approaches arising from liberation theology. I have suggested that the strong Roman Catholic social justice tradition is flawed in this context because of its almost total focus on the human person, human rights, the dignity of human work and so on. Frequently in my journeys to Rajasthan, a pitiable sight is the number of donkeys, burdened by panniers of bricks, struggling in the hot sun for the entire day, often being whipped to keep them going. Even more distressing are the 'dancing bears' of Agra. Even though this activity is illegal, it perseveres in some places: the so-called 'dancing' means that the bear is reacting in anguish to a rope being pulled through its nostrils. These are just two examples of human insensitivity to the pain of animals.

Hence the concern over the anthropocentric mindset of social justice encyclicals. For example, in *Gaudium et Spes*, the famous Constitution on the Church in the World of the Second Vatican Council, it is clearly said, 'God intended the earth and everything contained in it for the use of all peoples.'[53] Despite this anthropocentric mindset, there are three ways that the social justice encyclicals can still be developed towards a usable environmental ethic. The first is the critique of economic systems, right from *Rerum Novarum* onwards, and more specifically with more recent works like *Sollicitudo Rei Socialis* (1987) and *Centesimus Annus* (1991), which discussed the encyclicals' critique of global economic systems in the context of structural sin, naming specifically desire for profit and thirst for power. Although earlier documents maintain a traditional anthropocentric approach, *Centesimus Annus* states explicitly:

> Humanity, which discovers its capacity to transform and in a certain sense, creates the world through its work, forgets that this is always based on God's prior and original gift of the things that are. The human race thinks that it can make arbitrary use of the earth, subjecting it without restraint to its will, as though the earth did not have its own requisites and a prior God-given purpose, which human beings can indeed develop but must not betray.[54]

This offers a clear breakthrough, because it recognises the earth and her resources as having a purpose distinct from being made solely for the use of humanity. It is contemporaneous with John Paul II's famous speech on World Peace Day on 1 January 1990, when he linked peace with God with peace and reconciliation with all creation. It was the first of his documents that focused on environmental issues. From then on, the environment would be integral to the vision of the Common Good. But, bearing in mind the contemporary lack of steam for the conciliar process of Justice, Peace and Integrity of Creation, *The Catholic Catechism* strongly advocates this in the context of the discussion of the seventh commandment.[55] Yet the statement is quite weak, referring to the fact that 'mineral, vegetable and animal resources of the universe cannot be divorced from respect for moral imperatives'. Because the statement is not in the context of social justice teaching it does not have the same force and impact.

Moving specifically to the ethics of liberation it is clear that here, as with previous approaches, we deal with an anthropocentric tradition. Leonard Boff, writing after the Rio Summit in 1992, is explicitly self-critical of himself, of liberation theology and of all developmental frameworks, in his book *Ecology and Liberation: A New Paradigm*.[56] He says that there is no global development framework capable of safeguarding all aspects of social ecology. The task for social ecology is to study social systems as interacting with ecosystems. He defines the task for ecopolitics, ecotechnology, for ethics, economics and ecology of the mind as the need to recover from the state of maimed human intimacy and to value and love nature. For this a revolution of the mind is needed. His new ethical project will be nurtured by a spiritual project that he calls *cosmic mysticism*. This means solidarity with all living things starting with the least favoured. (There are similarities here with the Pope's invoking of a mystical dimension to suffering.)

So the focus of ecological liberation ethics is on privileging the poor. But now, as Sallie McFague has also written, *nature is the new category of poverty*.[57] The suffering of the degraded environment, the polluted water systems along with the human communities affected, especially women, children and indigenous peoples (in India I would add caste-based poverty), has now to be the rightful goal of liberation struggles.

The last dimension I want to factor in is a feminist ethic of care. In Chapter 2, following Heidegger' parable, I reflected on care-for-life itself as a basic dimension of the spirituality I explore. Drawing on Carol Gilligan's early work in 1982,[58] I factored in Joan Tronto's more recent book *Moral Boundaries*,[59] which treats care as both disposition and activity. It is important also here as it includes in its scope care for humans and care for the environment. (And it is significant that Deane-Drummond integrates this into her virtue-centred approach.) Clearly there is scope here for pushing the parameters of ethics to include human and non-human worlds, and to begin to appreciate the reciprocal dimension of an ethic of care. We would not be able to care for nature unless nature had already cared for us with air, water, trees, growing plants.

And so we end where we began, with the recovery of connection, the deep appreciation of the giftedness of the earth without which all ethical attempts founder.

> 'All things begin in mysticism, end in politics only to begin again.' (Attributed to Péguy)

In coming to an end of this exploration, (at least in this chapter), the most one can say is that we need a multifaceted approach to reconciliation with the earth. Of the ideas I have discussed, Celia Deane-Drummond's appeal to tradition and re-visioning of Aquinas's virtue-centred ethics is extremely appealing – but will it stand up without a faith commitment matching Aquinas's theological basis? John Paul II's encyclicals draw also on Aquinas's virtue-ethics. For example, his advocacy of solidarity is very similar to Aquinas's stress on justice as a virtue that links the personal with the structural. The strength of a virtue-ethics approach is the fostering of the personal qualities of restraint/prudent deliberation/perseverance that act as checks on an overly egocentric perspective that masks a one-sided self-interested ethics. Virtue-ethics offers a bridge between personal and structural approaches. But without a more broadly based liberation-ethic and eco-feminist-ethic approach I cannot see how it can of itself be adequate to face the structural barriers to the eradication of poverty in the widest possible sense.

What is very evident is that without a common, shared understanding that human and non-human flourishing belong together, nature has no future. If the human person within his or her ecological setting in the widest sense, in Britain, the Sahara or India, is the starting point for ethical thinking and action, then there will be hope of achieving global structural justice. This is not a programme for a completely egalitarian redistribution of resources. At a very basic level the global situation of water, for example, demands a recognition of the fundamental right to a life of dignity of every human being and all earth's creatures, as well as a recognition that if there is a finite limit to water, the need for control and restraint, for appropriate water management, is an urgent mandate for all, not only for the poorest communities.

In terms of ecclesial documents, the approach that comes nearest is the document of the Catholic Bishops of Britain prior to the election in 1997, *The Common Good*. This was an attempt to offer an ethical language that communicated beyond the faith communities. Linked with that, in some way, an ethic of care – care of persons, care of interlinked ecological communities, care for the world's future – is fundamental. Maybe Gandhi's Talisman has again to be brought into play. Not, as he originally said, 'When you are about to make a decision, think of the poorest man you know and how your decision will affect him', but:

> Think of the poorest communities in their ecological con-
> text, and think how your decisions and institutional

structures affect the possibility of the living or perishing of both human and non-human communities.

Think how their flourishing affects the common good, even the flourishing of the planet itself for future generations.[60]

But, as I have been trying to show, how we think and perceive is exactly the issue. How deeply we are able to ground our consciousness in embodied realities, in 'the flesh of the world', will affect our integrity as ethical beings, our ability to make generous decisions, involving personal sacrifices. I cannot see another way for reconciling with the earth than through living out of a deep sense of connection, in Christian terms out of the vision of earth as God's beloved creation, a vision similar to the young Russian monk whose rapture sent him directly into the world to mend broken relations.

In Rwanda, *matter matters*, whether it be its people, rivers or land with its haunted memories. A spirituality with reconciliation at its core will reverence these deep connections and seek to link struggles for structural justice with a mystical cosmic vision. As Péguy hinted, the two should never be separated. The effective witness of the martyr Church, which Santmire tried to evoke, spoke of raging against injustice, but also of love of earth's most fragile people and places. And it is to the nature of this mystical love that works for justice that I now turn.

6 MOVING ON

How to Bring Back the Beauty of Life? How to Bring Back Hope?

Bread. A clean sky. Active peace. A woman's voice singing somewhere, melody drifting like smoke from the cook fires. The army disbanded, the harvest abundant. The wound healed, the child wanted, the prisoner freed, the body's integrity honoured, the lover returned . . . The labour equal, fair and valued. Delight in the challenge for consensus to solve problems. No hand raised in any gesture but greeting. Secure interiors – of heart, home, land – so firm as to make secure borders irrelevant at last. And everywhere, laughter, care, dancing, contentment. A humble, earthly paradise in the *now*.[1]

What's sacred is singular:
out of this dry fork, this
wreck of perspective
what's sacred tries itself
one more time.

Adrienne Rich[2]

I am sitting by the small river at the bottom of the garden where we live, in the stillness of early morning where the only noise is of water flowing over the stones and a few pigeons calling to each other. It is June and the promise of early summer surrounds me. Weeping willows dip into the flowing waters, concealing the hiding places of newborn ducklings. Ducks, brown trout, swans, pigeons and numerous birds form the river community: humans are not central. Hidden beneath the river edge, a patient moorhen sits on her nest and I hardly dare make a movement for fear of disturbing the process of bringing-to-birth. This is where I start each morning whenever possible, often in icy cold weather clutching a mug of coffee to keep warm. It feels edenic and never fails to give hope and inspiration for the day, although lowering river levels point to a harsher reality. Yet, if I focus on Rwanda, Iraq, the Sudan, Palestine or Afghanistan, the horror and brutality of the real world return to the radar screen in piercing focus. How to bring back the beauty of life to such places of devastation? This is the focus of this chapter. It will be an exploration beginning with examples of victims becoming agents of healing; then returning to Christian visions of reconciliation in a more radical way, by transforming our symbols of healing; and, finally, calling on the Holy Spirit as Spirit of Beauty, restoring hope in transformation and the fullness of life.

I express it in this way – 'How to bring back beauty?' – because it was also the question of Violette Nyirarukundo in Kigali, a minister speaking of the counselling ministry where people try to find healing from the memories of trauma. Rwanda, she told us, is now a country where reconciliation is happening on many levels. This is where hope of healing acquires tangibility, in a country where the prisons are still overflowing with people complicit in the genocide and where *gacaca* courts – mentioned earlier – have become part of day-to-day experience. There is a real attempt by the government to insist that '*there are now no Hutu or Tutsi divisions, we are all Rwandans*', as one survivor told us. Even if now this can serve to produce a one-sided restorative justice, as was hinted earlier, what has to be appreciated are the wondrous efforts of Rwandans themselves to move forward, to heal and be healed, in many diverse ways.[3]

Around the world, subsequent to the genocide, there are heart-warming stories of individuals whose families have been wiped out in the most appalling way, who are acting as bridges of healing. On a personal level the story of the young girl Immaculée Ilibagiza, whose deep faith in Christ saved her from being killed, is very poignant.[4] Her narrative reveals the horror of lifelong friends joining in the murder of neighbours. Another remarkable example of practical forgiveness, in England, is the inspiration of Mary Blewitt, fifty of whose family were murdered, who founded the Survivors' Fund, SURF.[5] In summer 2005, SURF mounted an exhibition in London telling four extraordinary stories of heroic survivors. These are only two examples from many heroic individuals, who, in rejecting the option of revenge, are seeking to move on, even with grief-filled hearts.

In Rwanda itself, Abbé Jean Marie is an outstanding example of this: he works with Caritas Gisenyi, trying to build bridges between the two communities.[6] We learnt that day from Violette Nyirarukundo and from our hosts in Kigali, that for victims to want to live again there must be some meaning, some reason to live and hope, and if the perpetrator held out a hand for this process, this might become possible. Caritas Gisenyi[7] (which began to respond to the devastated country by providing housing for survivors) is involved in a whole range of activities, including counselling for people suffering from the trauma of the genocide, small micro-credit projects, as well as facilitating a process where prisoners who committed acts of genocide could ask publicly for forgiveness from families who were willing to do this. Before I left, I spoke to representatives of Caritas in Kigali who told of the continuing process of reconciliation initiated by Caritas, working at grassroots level in every Catholic diocese and every parish in the country, with every faith group in the community. Knowing that this is a process fully backed by the Catholic hierarchy was heartening and is itself another sign of recon-ciling hope. The Abbé spoke of the desire to create a 'caritas spirit', characterising this as being a spirit of generosity and openness and felt it was a vital part of his work:

'Reconciliation does not happen suddenly. It happens little by little. But people are starting to realise that national renewal is not possible unless we do this.'

No one pretended that the process was easy. There is a horror of 'cheap reconciliation', reconciliation as 'quick fix', and a misuse of spirituality that takes refuge only in prayers, as if people were 'refugees in heaven'! Violette told us of the huge loss of dignity, innocence and humanity on the one hand, yet the difficulties of getting people to listen to the stories of pain on the other. *'Pain that is not transformed is pain transferred'*, she said, in a phrase that haunts me, emphasising that being told to 'forget about it' and get on with life left victims still imprisoned in the genocide experience.

This dilemma struck us continually. The pain of Rwanda is partly that the violence took such a monstrous character, when (as the story of Immaculée Ilibagiza showed starkly), neighbours killed neighbours, and husbands even killed wives and children. Nowhere did this stand out more clearly than in the Kigali Genocide Memorial, where more than 200,000 people are buried, *and remains are still being brought in. The memory of the genocide is a daily reality*. For me, the room where children are remembered was a stark proof of the depth of evil perpetrated. Huge photographs of small children are hung on large windows so that the daylight seems to bring a life-like quality to their faces. Beneath each picture hangs a text, telling us about each child, their name, favourite meal, favourite game, hymn or song, and then, chillingly, how they died. Axed with machetes, burnt alive, tortured, shot in the eyes and then beheaded were just some of the violent means used against these children, in some cases aged three and four years.

And where is the hope for the children who survived? Some 800,000 were orphaned and many have contracted AIDS. How can the beauty of life return for them? The challenge of facing life again with these memories is a real issue for children. And yet, as Beatha Uwazaninka says (she was fourteen at the time of the genocide), 'Remembering is important for everyone, even for the whole world, because the world knew, and did not stop the genocide.'[8] Her words strike a chord: everywhere in Rwanda are seen the defiant words 'Never Again!' But for these words to mean anything, for reconciliation to be a reality for orphans, for widows and for those with painful losses, more is needed than all the building blocks to spirituality I have explored up till now. To enable 'a mystical love that establishes justice' to bring back beauty to life, we need a new framework, a new symbol system enabling flourishing despite the devastation of society and culture.

A 'HUMBLE, EARTHLY PARADISE IN THE *NOW*'

What do we mean by fullness of life? What are our visions and dreams? How can we imagine the peace and justice of the Reign of God in our violent world? What does tradition tell us?

The Bible of Christianity, Judaism and Islam begins with a story in a garden – of Eden – from which humanity was expelled, a tragedy for which a woman, Eve, has frequently been blamed.[9] Unfortunately, this has had the effect that Christianity is troubled by a nostalgia for this lost Garden, for return to Eden, a pre-Fall state of affairs, and – as I explained in the last chapter – has constructed a belief system where human destiny is for the next world, for heaven, a place of bliss far removed from anything that is of the earth. Women became identified more with the earth, flesh (and sinful flesh at that), and with sexuality (negatively understood): the other side of the coin is that holiness and sanctity are viewed as being of the spirit (soul) not the body, and as being more masculine, not feminine.

But this view is not shared by Judaism, which has a more

positive exegesis of this part of the book of Genesis, one that does not include a Fall. (Although even within Judaism women have been considered inferior to and subject to men.) In Islam, the subjection of women that occurs in many Arab states is not ordained by the Qur'an. Nor are women blamed for the first sin:

> Both the man and the woman listened to the whisper of Satan, ate the fruit, repented and were sent out of the garden together.[10]

Yet, given the tradition of reading our Scriptures and sacred texts from within a patriarchal system, where, by and large, women have been the property of men until recent liberation and justice movements across the world, small wonder that in most of our religions the flourishing of women is not a major concern. So I began this chapter citing women's own dreams of flourishing, first with the 'Women's Creed', written for the WCC Assembly at Beijing in 1995.

In this text we see it all – true peace, food in plenty, celebration, bodily integrity – all within a situation of renewed and restored relation. Something definitely to be celebrated as a this-worldly reality, not endlessly deferred to eternal bliss. Nor should this be dismissed as the dream only of women who are confident of worldly prosperity, or as giving up on the whole dimension of eternity. For many poor communities this is a crucial issue: where no flourishing is experienced on earth, hope in heaven is all that sustains. In the embodied spirituality of reconciliation I am developing, I suggest that the transcendence and eternity of God, Sacred Being and Divine Presence will take care of eternity, with oceans of mercy and justice: for us, care and responsibility for this earth – the only one we have and cherish – and all earth dwellers, human and non-human, is (literally) the burning issue.

This religiously inspired vision springs from the binding, connecting, sustaining of all life through sacred power and

To Rwanda and Back

energy for its well-being and flourishing. Sacred spirit, sacred energy is the source and resource for this grounded, sustaining hope.

VISIONS OF FLOURISHING

I pause for a minute, reflecting on what is meant by flourishing, and why it is so significant.[11] Grace Jantzen, whose recent early death is sadly mourned – following Hannah Arendt, Luce Irigaray and Adriana Caverero – used the concept of flourishing to create a new symbolic order for the feminist philosophy of religion she was developing. Its importance here is its potential for a spirituality of reconciliation.[12] The English word 'flourish' is from the Latin, *florere*, French *flourir*, with hints of blossoming and beauty; a German synonym is *blühen*, or *gedeihen*, which is like the English word thrive, used in a technical sense to tell if a baby will live and grow in the quality of loving care provided. A Dutch equivalent is *bloeien* (to blossom), in *de bloeitjd zijn* (to be in blossom time), or simply *leven* (to be fully alive), with similar connotations of well-being and fullness of life. The word is deliberately chosen as a term with ecological roots, body/ earth/spirit belonging together in this life-determining process. Flourishing means all that is life-giving for people, earth and earth creatures together. It evokes Jewish *shalom* and Islamic *salam*. The Yoruba, a Nigerian people, use the word *alafia* (like Tanzanian *ubuntu*), meaning the 'fullness of life'. God is understood as source of *alafia*, grace, hospitality and compassion.[13] Aristotle's word was εὐδαιμονια, *eudaimonia*, which means well-being and happiness – but his usage does not cover all the meanings I want to evoke.

The concept of flourishing calls to mind sacred texts from many faiths and traditions: whereas Chapter 5 cited Isaiah with reference to the earth's suffering, the same prophet told of the flourishing of earth and people intertwined:

The wilderness and the dry land will be glad,
The desert shall rejoice and blossom;
Like the crocus it shall blossom abundantly,
and rejoice with joy and singing ...
Then the eyes of the blind shall be opened,
And the ears of the deaf be unstopped;
then shall the lame leap like a deer,
and the tongue of the speechless sing for joy,
For water shall break forth in the wilderness,
and streams in the desert. (Isaiah 35.1, 5–6)

This flourishing text has also been imaginatively adapted for the urban situation, bringing hope to the wilderness of the city:

Let the tenement and the derelict park land be glad,
Let the slums and ghettos rejoice and burst into comfort and
    beauty.
Let them flower with well-kept gardens,
let music and laughter be heard in the streets ...
Then there will be vision for those blinded by despair,
and the people who long for a friendly voice will hear love
    songs.
Those crippled with poverty will jump up and run into
    plenty ...
Free at last, God's people will possess the city
and shout out in delight at God's triumph
and their joy will last forever![14]

As Jews recall the promise of *shalom*, and the vision of plenty of the holy mountain (Isaiah 24), Muslims also recall a vision of flourishing, remembering the kindness of Muhammad to Muslim women:

God hath promised to believers,
Men and women, Gardens
under which rivers flow,

To swell therein,
and beautiful mansions
In Gardens of everlasting bliss.
But the greatest bliss
is the Good pleasure of God.[15]

But how do visions of flourishing fit with traumatised memories of genocide and war, with ongoing violence and injustice as in Palestine and Iraq? These are similar to the contexts faced by Adrienne Rich, a contemporary Jewish American poet, as she tried to cling on to some sense of vision, in the wreck of post-Holocaust, post-Hiroshima and post-Chernobyl survival in a poem called 'The Desert as Garden of Paradise':

What would it mean
to think you are part of a generation
that simply must pass on?
What would it mean to live
in the desert, try to live
a human life, something
to hand on to the children
to take up to the Land?
What would it mean to think
you were born in chains and only time,
nothing you can do
could redeem the slavery
you were born into?[16]

This sense of despair well evokes the impasse and traumatised deadlock experienced by survivors in Rwanda, Bosnia and post-conflict situations. It takes a multifaceted approach to break this deadlock. So, visions of flourishing are invoked not only for the sake of ecological well-being, but fully mindful of this time, this place with its wounded history, with all the specificity of the cultural and historical memories that constitute identity, costly here because it meant life or death.

These are memories enshrined in bone and blood, in the sight of skulls arrayed inside churches and museums, frayed garments, children's cups and toys, in the silent stories of a landscape, deforested hillsides, abandoned plantations and burnt-down houses. Texts are more than mere words. They are written in stone and wood, glimpsed as fragments of ruined houses, or in the drawings of children as they crouched in cellars hearing the bombs drop on their city. Here are the words of another woman poet (Christian with Jewish background), the late Denise Levertov, who combined a mystical awareness with a lifelong struggle for justice: they evoke Rwanda, Bosnia and the contemporary tragedies forcing people to leave their homes:

> In each house, imprinted,
> a journey,   Partings, tearing
>   apart: storm, loss, hands
>   upraised for rescue,
>   onrush of wave,
>   exile.
> Long-hidden, the time
> of arrival, plumb-line,
> first foundation.
>
> How does memory
> serve, serve the earth?
>   Columns
>   of turned wood place
>   among broken stones,
>   perches for companion
>   ravens. A way
>   of witness.[17]

Building on specific Christian inspiration for flourishing in the promise of Jesus – cited in Chapter 4 – that 'I came so that you may have life in the full' (John 10.10), and in the way that he gave redemption an embodied meaning, I focus now on its relevance for *bringing back the beauty of life*. People need to be fed, welcomed, treated with compassion, clothed and healed: this is the grounding for flourishing and well-being. Liberation spiritualities the world over call for the re-membering of this, insisting on honesty and truth-telling in the acknowledgement of the lack of honour and integrity given to women's bodies trafficked in the sex trade, to the bodies of the poor forced to sell vital organs so as to be able to eat, and to the traumatised spirits of genocide survivors.

OVERTURNING THE LOGIC OF SACRIFICE

But there is a further step. And now I return to the discussion in Chapter 2 where, in tackling the question of forgiveness and sacrifice in feminist theology, I suggested that sacrifice be understood as voluntary self-giving in suffering love. Then, in Chapter 5, I hinted that more was needed and I linked peace and reconciliation with fullness of life on earth. Within the understanding of reconciliation as the vision of the structural healing of the world, I want to take another step. I suggest embedding ourselves in this new symbolic core of flourishing and well-being (used instead of more traditional concepts like redemption and salvation), and explore how 'sacrifice' would be understood within this.[18]

What happens here is the invitation to perceive of Jesus' death and sacrifice differently, made possible on the basis of this new symbolic core, one which transforms the foundations of the systems of domination. In Chapter 2 I saw Jesus as setting his face voluntarily to Jerusalem to confront distorted power structures. He set out neither to be crucified nor to fulfil a predetermined script, but to end the necessity for crucifixions, motivated by self-giving love. Sadly, the systems of violence were not ended by his death, but continue to sanction domination, militarism and violence as a way to solve political problems: they have permitted rape as concomitant to war, allowed torture if it serves national interests, and encouraged the disappearance of truth from the public arena.

First, let us be clear about the way religion has appeared to sanction the logic of violence even in its sacred texts. The Bible is full of texts called 'redemptive violence' texts, which appear to sanction violence on the part of the Jews to achieve the Promised Land, as the late Michael Prior, who lived the last years of his life out in a passionate commitment to Palestine and its suffering people, eloquently pointed out.[19] How are peace-lovers supposed to read the text of Exodus 15, the Song of Moses, referring to the slaughter of the Egyptians, which Christians read every Easter vigil as preparation for the resurrection?

> I will sing to the Lord, for he has triumphed gloriously;
> Horse and rider he has thrown into the sea. (Exodus 15.1–2)[20]

This Song is not unique. In fact, the Bible is permeated with the myth of redemptive violence, the idea that violence is justified in the name of some greater gain for God's elect. This, one of the most influential ideas of history, that God blesses his chosen ones with victory, is still with us and is one of the reasons that we can remain blind and deaf to the contemporary plight of the Palestinians in Gaza and the West Bank, prisoners in their own land. It is only by the discerning reading of texts within a liberation hermeneutic of denunciation and reclamation – such as that of Elisabeth Schüssler Fiorenza – that a non-violent reconciling meaning will appear.

Second, still on the track of changing the symbolic matrix, feminist theology has constantly critiqued this love of redemptive violence, called by Mary Daly *necrophilia*, love of death. Paradoxically, this necrophilia is at the same time *necrophobia*, fear of death. One does not have to be much of a cultural analyst to notice how western society conceals and shuns death. People die in hospitals or homes for the elderly, rarely in their own homes surrounded by the extended family. The mourning period is almost non-existent compared with other cultures. Most children have never seen a dead body – except on TV. Much money and scientific research focuses on how to push back the approach of death. But, more serious is the symbolic focus on which this is built. A story is told of a headmasters' conference some years ago where each head-teacher was asked what was the aim of their school's education. The headmaster of a famous monastic school replied, 'To prepare the boys for death'. Wherever this story is told, it is done so to illustrate the moral superiority of this philosophy. What it really illustrates is religion's focus on the transcendent and the afterlife. For too long spirituality has been based on *contemptus mundi*, escape from the world, a privileging of the infinite over the finite, and not on *amor mundi*, love of the world with full acceptance of the demands of embodied life.

Grace Jantzen analysed this as *mortality*, *mortalité*, the privileging of death as the core of a symbolic order, which she proposed to replace by a focus on *natalité*, birth, birth-giving or creativity. She suggested that instead of calling ourselves *mortals*, we should use the term '*natals*'. This death-based symbolic order, which sanctions a system of interlocking oppressions (racism, sexism, militarism and so on), termed *a matrix of domination*, is actually based on the unacknowledged foundation of birth, of embodied and material dimensions and the body of the mother. Mythic and religious traditions have plenty of examples of the masculine reappropriation of birth, for example, the Greek legend of the birth of Athena from Zeus' head. Focus on death has not only encouraged military violence, the pressure to give one's life to save the country (whatever the cause), but has meant symbolising women as responsible for decay and death, at the same time as maintaining an indifference to women's own deaths.

In her more recent work Jantzen linked the silencing of birth and the displacement of beauty with this.[21] She asked what cultural difference it would make to focus on birth. It would mean a focus on *embodiment*, for example: instead of a focus on the soul's otherworldly destiny, attention focuses on the flourishing of the person in this life. Without denying life after death, the significance of bodily life here and now takes centre stage. Embodied life is gendered and particular, and lived out in webs of relationship. It also respects limits. Finitude, not infinity is at its heart. Lastly, Jantzen writes, with birth and creativity, hope is born anew, with new possibilities offered with each child.[22] She cites Arendt's phrase, 'Amo: volo ut sis', 'I love you: I want you to be.'[23] This means taking responsibility for the flourishing of the child situated in an entire web of relations:

> To act for love of the world is to act in such a way as to try to ensure that newcomers will not be worldless, that their uniqueness is valued, so that they need not lose themselves in 'the masses.'[24]

Acting responsibly in this way, in the face of whatever sorrow, deprivation or disaster should befall, is totally different from the traditional response of philosophers of religion, which has been to defend the honour and goodness of God in the face of 'evil'.

It should be emphasised that Jantzen is not exclusively focusing on mothers and mothering – even if what she writes expands the spirituality of mothering I developed in Chapter 3 – but has a wider connotation for birth-giving. In fact what she does has scriptural roots, where, for example, Isaiah speaks of the birthing of the new Israel. The people are writhing with birth pangs, unable to deliver, but God brings a new birth from their failure:

The dead shall live, their bodies shall rise.
O dwellers in the dust, awake and sing for joy! (Isaiah 26.19)

Third, within this symbolic core based on birth-giving, creativity, flourishing and hope, we can reclaim our sacred texts with *counter*-apocalyptic strands that emphasise the positive achievements of peace-lovers and conflict-resolution builders who listen and try to understand the truth of opposing factions, and place before them the possibility of sharing dreams of justice and dignity of living. Adrienne Rich well expresses the need to make the ancient symbols work differently, in a new context:

> Miriam, Aaron, Moses
> are somewhere else, marching
> You learn to live without prophets
> Without legends
> To live just where you are
> Your burning bush, your seven-branched candlestick
>
> What's sacred is singular . . .[25]

I argue now that the reclaiming of sacrifice has a positive meaning within this symbolic nexus of flourishing and well-being. Jesus' life and death does not save us from embodied life. (Jantzen points out that words like 'salvation' imply being rescued *from* the world.) Rather, inspired by compassionate love, and within an intimate sharing of God's suffering love for creation, contemporary Christology points to the hope of healed, restored embodied life for ravaged creation. This is sacrifice in its most life-enhancing meaning. Mercy Amba Oduyoye expressed it so well, in words cited in the last chapter: 'Not all sacrifice is victimization. Conscious self-sacrifice, which is related to resistance, embodies the hope of redemption, and may even bring joy to the one who is doing the letting-go.'[26]

Is it now possible to reclaim the cross symbol for feminist

spirituality? So often ignored or rejected as imposed by oppressive systems, 'taking up the cross' in costly discipleship means a willingness to struggle against evil, for the sake of fullness of life, for the 'bringing back of beauty'. It does not mean the passive acceptance of imposed suffering. Rather, it means resistance to any pain or violence unjustly inflicted, and an affirmation of abundant life for all. It means prioritising love and justice inseparably intertwined.

But if the aim is for the end of patriarchy and a post-patriarchal situation of flourishing, we have to start being honest with the way sacrificial concepts are still used to underpin violent use of power and to rethink the way traditional theology continues to use the concept to underpin asceticism and renunciation of the body as key values. In our eucharistic thinking, too, sacrifice still carries the overtones of the passive victim offered up, reinforcing categories of silence, the pain of the silenced, and their unjust suffering. Even if, officially, these cultic overtones are not the intention (think of Paul in Romans 12, and the offering of the body as our authentic sacrifice), yet the orchestration of Eucharist, with its altar and language of victimhood, reinforced the ideology, as well as pointed to the categories of people being offered up in the killing fields of the world.

THE SPIRIT OF BEAUTY

This new symbolic nexus of symbols of flourishing brings a new spirituality, or inclusive understanding of the Holy Spirit. Flourishing means the flourishing of all, within the larger earth story. The Holy Spirit, in the root meaning of life and breath, creates awareness of the woundedness of bodies and spirits that culturally sanctioned violence has inflicted all these years. The strength of flourishing language is to take us beyond the level of human rights language, to transform the unspoken, unsaid, many-layered levels of suffering. We have to make it clear that violence done to body, spirit and soul, human and non-human, is underpinned by the violent use of language, by metaphors of God emphasizing power and might, and by distorted models of salvation. Naming and uncovering these is the necessary first step towards their eradication, a step that frees the Spirit to cross the boundaries of human and non-human, of culture, race and ethnicity, to bring to birth something life-giving from this shipwreck of violence.[27]

But a dimension of the Spirit that is specially relevant in my search for 'bringing back the beauty of life', is the relationship between the Holy Spirit and beauty. Patrick Sherry believes that a failure to create beauty and a lack of appreciation of it are both signs of the absence of the Holy Spirit:[28] 'The Spirit of God communicates God's beauty to the world, both through Creation, in the case of natural beauty, and through inspiration, in the case of artistic beauty.'[29] In this exploration it is the Holy Spirit, in the role of creating *moral* beauty and in the awakening of the moral imagination, that is my focus. So, yes, the role of the Spirit in nature, as the Romantic poets experienced, is important: the Holy Spirit is the Green Face of God, revealed at this time of crisis to fire our deadened imaginations and uncaring hearts and inspire the kind of practice discussed in the last chapter.

The integral link between the human spirit and the Divine in the biblical tradition is vital here. The psalmist (Psalm 51) begs God not to remove his Spirit from the depths of the human heart:

> Create in me a clean heart, O God,
> and put a new and right spirit within me.
> Cast me not away from thy presence,
> and take not thy Holy Spirit from me. (Psalm 51.10–11)

From deep within us, 'Spirit' touches levels of truth and depth about humanity, creating dissatisfaction with societal values.

Spirit bores deeper than the superficial level at which we mostly exist, aiming for the truth of our being. But Spirit is not a synonym for the human person in the way that 'soul' (*nephesh*) or flesh/body (*basar*) function in the Scriptures, but is *an indwelling dimension that links us with what is most sacred.* For St John the indwelling Spirit is what links us with Christ and with God (1 John 3.24). And here it is the dimension of beauty that is the link. Calling on the Holy Spirit in the dimension of beauty may keep emotions and aesthetic sensibilities alive in a more dynamic way than theology ever could. It can also stimulate the imagination to rekindle hope and dreams of flourishing.

What can happen in the tragedy of genocide or disaster on the scale of the tsunami is that the spirit of an entire people is broken or crushed: this may mean despair and possibly the death of hope. Yet spirit is certainly not confined within one faith tradition. Rather, *spirit* appeals to the energy that can mobilise, move us out of deadlock and transform even what seems hopeless – always within a symbolic of flourishing – rather than removing us to the far-beyond. Spirit language seems to find its home at the edges between the personal and the non-personal. Wind, breath and fire are all images of movement with a symbolic appeal to a humanity deadlocked in bitterness, yet are linked too with the non-human.

For many ancient cultures there exists already a dynamic connection with the spirit world in nature and the spirits of the ancestors, where spirit world includes spirits of trees, spirits inhabiting rivers and wells, the spirit world of angels and wicked spirits. So the Christian Church, in banishing this connection as pagan, has risked the loss of the sense of the Spirit present to creation and to many-layered levels of beauty. In Christian tradition, 'Holy Spirit' belongs with the Trinity of Father and Son as the 'communing dimension' between the two, or, as John V. Taylor so felicitously put it, 'the go-between God'.[30] Feminist theology attempts to rise beyond the patriarchal imagery here in different ways, sometimes imaging Trinity in non-sexist ways as 'Creator', 'Redeemer' and 'Sustainer', or as being inclusive of the entire creation. Many contemporary theologians – not only feminist – see relatedness as the defining metaphor, both intra-trinitarian and as outpouring of liberating and compassionate love to the world.[31] But this needs to be understood within a wider understanding of the Spirit's role in enabling flourishing of the whole web of life.

In the Spirit as the depth principle of life – human and non-human – is the first link with the Divine creative Spirit. In the depth of the heart, as St Paul says, the Spirit prays with sighs too deep for words (Romans 8.26). Through this mutual indwelling at the depth of the human heart, the question is whether the Divine Spirit can rekindle the will to live and flourish of a broken people? In *Sacred Longings*, I asked how the Spirit could transform our misplaced, insatiable desires for consumer goods into longing for intimacy and longing for God.[32] Now the question is, how could the Spirit re-awaken humanity both within and after conflict situations, into desiring and yearning for what God holds sacred, the justice, peace and *beauty* of the Kingdom/Kin-dom, the flourishing of the whole earth and all its creatures? How could a renewed theology of the Spirit re-awaken the power of dreaming and imagining of a different reality, where the violence of patro-kyriarchy has given way to symbols of life and flourishing?

The first step is to re-imagine the centrality of the metaphor of relation and connectedness to include the dimension of otherness, of difference, even the otherness of the hostile other. Jantzen's critique of the symbolic system based on mortality centred on its need for uniformity and sameness. Inability to comprehend the sheer otherness of a conflicting group drives the urge for conquest and domination, in order to reinforce the logic of sameness. So metaphors of connection need expansion to find a way of relating to the 'hostile other'.

In Chapter 4 I told the story of peacemaking in Tajikistan, where honouring the mutual love of Sufi mysticism provided the catalyst for breaking the deadlock.[33] Jean Paul Lederach's work highlights the role of art, aesthetics and beauty in the work of peacemaking. A seasoned professional peace campaigner, he now finds himself writing poetry, drawing, trusting intuition and the sheer serendipity of the way the Spirit works.

The musician June Boyce-Tillman suggests a similar role for music.[34] With examples from many cultures she highlights music's role in therapy, conflict-resolution and healing: 'In a therapeutic group where a conflict had arisen, a man sang a lullaby. This was a very moving experience for all present, and involved a man holding the group safely through song.'[35] One of the most moving stories of the power of music to give strength in the most threatening of contexts comes from the story of the massacre at El Mozote in El Salvador (1981). A young girl was dying after having been raped several times, yet kept on singing even after being shot in the chest. Even though blood was flowing from her – on this, the hill called 'La Cruz' – she kept on singing until the soldiers could stand it no longer. So they hacked through her neck with a machete till at last the singing stopped.[36]

The power of music to stimulate the moral imagination and work towards reconciliation has also been shown dramatically by the Argentinian-Israeli conductor Daniel Barenboim, both through his founding of an orchestra of Palestinians and Israelis – an orchestra which has even played at Buchenwald – and most recently in his 2006 Reith Lectures, 'In the beginning was Sound'. The lectures were delivered in different sites, including Ramallah and Jerusalem. In his final lecture Barenboim opened up the area of the moral responsibility of listening. 'Compassionate listening' I understand as the work of the Spirit opening us up to each other. Rabbi Michael Lerner, in his book *Healing Israel/Palestine*, tells of the 'compassionate listening Project' that brings groups to the Middle East to hear both sides of the story.[37] But Barenboim's angle in his final lecture on 5 May 2006, 'The Power of Music', is slightly different. He introduces the idea of the 'moral responsibility of the ear':

> And here again we are confronted with what I like to see as the moral responsibility of the ear. After all, it is the ear that determines audibility and transparency in music. It is the ear that must guide us in *tempo rubato* to have the moral strength to give back what was inadvertently stolen. In other words, when taking time in parts of a phrase, we must find the right place to give it back. This is not unlike the moral responsibility to give back what has been stolen.[38]

In other words, he demonstrates the way that aesthetics (art, music, poetry and dance) can play a role in helping us to understand, heal and reconcile. This listening with attention and responsibility rather than letting the music role over us enables new understanding. Does it not evoke the cry of Jesus that people listen but do not hear, because they have dulled their hearing and hardened their hearts (Matthew 13.10–17, citing Isaiah 6.9–10)? It is the same with perception. The moral imagination enables a different seeing and perceiving, rather like the spiritual practice of 'seeing with the loving eye' discussed in the last chapter. The inspiration of Martin Buber is again with is, in inviting us to see the other as 'Thou' and not 'it', to develop the ability to perceive the divine spark in the other, which can never be completely obliterated. Thus the moral imagination is dependent on paying attention, the attentiveness alluded to by Simone Weil as a contemplative dimension that some would consider mystical. The philosopher and novelist Iris Murdoch certainly put great weight on this: 'I have used the word "attention" which I borrow from Simone Weil, to express the just and loving gaze directed upon an individual reality.'[39]

Listening, hearing into speech, reaching out across the silences spans the rhythms of nature and the seasons as well as political events and human interactions. Reflecting on what this attentiveness means, I understand it as a mode of total presence to what one is hearing or seeing. A presence which is empathic, sensitive, compassionate and responsive. Put within the context of the Spirit as great awakener of moral beauty, the *Spirit* becomes 'the power of life and space for living',[40] and inspires widened visions of reconciling truth.

THE SPIRIT OF BEAUTY AND THE HEALING OF WOUNDED MEMORIES

For many people in the tragic situations I discuss, all memories are wounded and these wounds originate deep in history in complex situations. How can the Spirit as inspirer of moral beauty act in this context, where frequently depression and pessimism is intergenerational and where forgetting, even amnesia, is sometimes necessary for the sake of survival?

In this context Lederach writes, surprisingly, that pessimism can sometimes be a gift. It is a reminder that engaging with the complex truth of a situation requires a long-term view. He distinguishes between a pessimism born of cynicism which actually avoides engagement and one which requires the horizon of hope, together with a certain indifference (not apathy) to violence.[41] The challenge for the moral imagination is to transcend what has been and what is now, while still living amidst cycles of violence, building on people's partici-pation, and to create spaces for authentic renewed relation-ships of trust, pregnant with the possibility of peacemaking, recognising that here we are in the realm of mystery and risk-taking.

For that to be enabled, a spiritual practice is needed, one that respects both the depth of woundedness and the need for daily strength just to survive. For this, women's spirituality has much to offer. I never cease to wonder at the women in drought situations in remote villages in Rajasthan, who somehow find the strength to rise before dawn and begin the endless toil to find water, wood for fuel, moving then to care for children, animals and work in the fields. Sometimes, they tell me, the very need to sustain the fabric of life itself keeps them going. And often it is the men-folk who succumb to deep-seated depression, relapsing into alcoholism and taking opium. (Rajasthan lies directly on the opium trade route from Afghanistan.) But, let it not be assumed that spirit is submerged in the weary daily round of women: on the contrary, the spirit keeps their dreams and hopes alive.

In some contexts it is a question of doing whatever is possible, however small. The story of Nobel Peace Prize-winner Professor Wangari Maathai makes that clear. Here she describes how she founded the Green Belt Movement:

> When I started the Green Belt Movement 27 years ago – the work for which I have been awarded the Nobel Peace Prize – I was teaching at the University of Nairobi. I was also a member of the National Council of Women of Kenya, and I would listen to women relating the realities of their lives: their need for water, wood (for fuel), and nutritious food. I came to understand that their problems were symptoms of a poorly managed environment leading to a lack of clean drinking water, an insufficient food supply and poor health. With these women, I hit on the idea of planting trees to provide food and fuel, slow soil erosion and desertification, offer shade and improve the aesthetic environment.
>
> Planting a tree is do-able. Anyone can dig a hole, put in a seedling and nurture it. When one plants a tree, one feels a connection to the Earth and has a stake in its survival.
>
> On World Environment Day in 1977, we planted seven

trees at a ceremony in Nairobi, and slowly the idea took off
... we established small tree nurseries close to homes which
women could manage. These nurseries evolved into the
Green Belt Movement, and in the process, a cadre of
women became 'foresters without diplomas'.[42]

The link with my theme of 'bringing back the beauty of life'
through the rekindled moral imagination is that planting trees
became one step in women's involvement with solving conflicts over land and building participative democracy. Similar
stories are told of planting healing gardens by survivors of the
Holocaust and torture situations. The Medical Foundation in
London and other parts of the UK works in this way with
psychotherapy and with nature.[43] No one pretends that the
scars and memories will disappear, nor that political and legal
action for justice and compensation are not essential parts of
the process, but all efforts are concentrated on finding ways for
the traumatised self to survive and discover reason to live.

Deep in faith traditions there are in fact resources for coping
with poverty, pain and the trauma of violence. The scriptural
writers spoke from a culture far more vulnerable to ecological
disasters than ours, at least until recently. Both our levels of
violence and ecological disasters have increased exponentially.
The stories of the eastern monks in the desert are full of
accounts of failure, despair and the desire to run away. One
monk, about to give up, was told to stay in his cell and endure:

> For three days the brother did just this, and then he was
> overcome with *akedia* (spiritual lassitude and apathy). But he
> found some little palm leaves and started trimming them.
> Next day he started plaiting them; when he felt hungry, he
> said, 'Here are some palm leaves; I'll prepare them and then
> have something to eat.' He finished them and said, 'Perhaps
> I'll read for a little bit before eating.' When he had done
> some reading he said, 'Now let's sing a few psalms and then
> I can eat with a clear conscience'.

And so, by God's help he went on little by little, until he had indeed become what he was meant to become.[44]

This may sound trivial compared with the immense project of Wangari Maathai, but is a well-trodden spiritual path, practised by saints and psychotherapists: *stay where you are, begin with the small tasks that are possible,* then other possibilities begin to open up. In overstressing the wonders of the Holy Spirit of a miraculous nature, we often overlook the humbler gifts of perseverance and staying power. These are the strengths seen in the many widows and orphans of Rwanda in the slow rebuilding of their lives. The beauty of the Spirit is in revealing God's longing for the healing of embodied life.

THE SUBALTERN CRY FOR JUSTICE

The book of Revelation (6.9–10) is the *locus classicus* for the cry for revenge of the slaughtered innocents, literally the *subalterns*, those under the altar:

> Under the altar the souls of those who had been slain for the word of God . . . cried put with a loud voice, 'O Sovereign Lord, holy and true, how long before thou wilt judge and avenge our blood on those who dwell upon the earth?'

Whereas some scholars want to dismiss this cry for revenge as 'sub-Christian', others understand it as a cry for justice and vindication.[45] Catherine Keller links this woundedness of the innocent sufferers with the Korean *han*, 'an emotion of the oppressed mixed of repressed rage, grief, and simmering resentment'.[46] *Han* is a complex concept in Korea, sometimes called the 'original wound'.[47] It is deeply felt both personally and collectively, and in this sense linked with the oppressions of classism, sexism and racism. It is also linked with *dan* or 'cutting off', the practice of self-denial by which one removes oneself from oppression and injustice. But the global systems of persecution are not overcome, so the woundedness of *han* festers on. Is there no narrative of hope to sustain those who await justice?

There is indeed another complex concept linked with my search for 'bringing back the beauty of life'. It is that of *jeong*. This cannot be identified simply with love, or with compassion. W. Anne Joh sees it as 'The power of eros that forges its presence in the interval between the self and other . . . *Jeong* is a supplement that comes in the interstitial site of relationality.'[48] The theologian Peter Hodgson links this eros with the Spirit of God and I would like to make the link with the Spirit as the creator of moral beauty. Thus, in W. Anne Joh's insistence that 'Jeong's call for vulnerability challenges us to identify with those we perceive to be the Other',[49] possibilities for connectedness and compassion are opened up, as well as possibilities for the unravelling of structural causes of *han*. Applied to the understanding of Jesus' death as desire for a new reality, 'a Christology of *jeong* seeks to go beyond by opening spaces of potent transformative possibilities in the interstitial spaces of hybrid realities'.[50]

Thus the subaltern innocents of the book of Revelation, and the thousands of genocidal victims, are offered a narrative of hope. They are re-membered with sorrow and love by the narratives of hope and transformation, by the Spirit's awakening of possibilities of moral beauty and the slow process of turning desire for vengeance into yearning for the birth of a new reality.

EPILOGUE

It was night. After a heavy day when it seemed impossible to take in yet another story of genocide and betrayal, our hosts in Kigali offered us some entertainment. But how could we now suddenly change from solidarity in re-membering killing into simply 'having a good time'? Rwanda taught me the way. Into the hall where we had been enjoying a wonderful meal came a troupe of dancers, both men and women, in beautiful traditional dress. Their joy, vitality and immense energy were overwhelming. They performed amazing dances for us, and then drew us in to participate – which we all attempted to do in a clumsy and inadequate way! Yet we were told that most of the members of this group had been killed in the genocide, and that they had had to start again, building up the team, literally to show that the peoples' spirit was not destroyed and that beauty could return to life. What I have been trying to express in words was danced into reality before my eyes.

7 STRUGGLING WITH RECONCILING HEARTS AND HOLDING FAST TO OUR DREAMS

> We face each other
> across a raw divide,
> the chasm of our anger
> filled with the bones
> of old hatreds.
>
> The wounded earth
> spews out our greed
> in acrid smoke.
> The gaping wound cries out in pain.
>
> The upward surge of birds in flight;
> wheeling and dancing
> in the sun,
> the sound of geese
> strung across an empty sky,
> the scent of blossom on the wind,
> gifts of a generous Creator,
> to lift, to call, to heal.

Kate McIlHagga[1]

I began this book in the context of reflecting on Rwanda, over ten years after the genocide. Throughout, I have been seeking a spirituality with reconciliation at its heart. But, as I approach the book's end, the world is still conflict-ridden, with continuing hostility between Palestine and Israel, Iraq descending ever deeper into civil war and a deteriorating situation in the Sudan that some say is genocidal in its pro-portions.[2] That is to mention only a few places in the world. It would be so easy to sink into hopelessness and despair. But what good would that do? How would that be keeping faith with the victims of genocide and war? I have been exploring a spirituality that tried to make a difference, bringing together prayer and praxis, one that created a sustaining hope, and light out of darkness and trauma, one that was not just about a personal journey, but trying to cross boundaries of race and community, asking where the resources are that enable the renewal of life after overwhelming suffering.

But I have also realised in the process of this writing that my own ideas of the spiritual journey have greatly changed over the last thirty years. It is not only a question of age. It is true that with progressing years certain options close; almost imperceptibly I find myself not so much looking forward into the great unknown, but looking backward, reflecting on choices, and beginning to dwell far more in the potential of the present, in what is given, its rich mixture of opportunity or limit, in the joys of relationship or the sorrow of loss, bereavement and estrangement. If I look to the future, it is one where I will probably not be alive for more than two decades (if I'm lucky!), so I imagine that because of this the level of my caring for future life on earth has intensified. This means not only my own children and grandchildren, but, following on the discussions in previous chapters, the quality of community life – in society and church – and the well-being and survival of the planet itself. In these days of global warming and climate change I ask myself continually if God's purposes for creation will ever be realised: I begin to understand spirituality in a far more God-centred way, in the sense that the sorrow of God for world suffering, the yearning of God for world-healing and flourishing have now become all-enveloping themes for me.

My conviction has ripened over the years that the values that I, in company with many other like-minded seekers, have discovered and developed in the spirituality of earlier writings – mutuality, connectedness, right relation, compassion, justice and wisdom – all these have solidly ripened in their urgency into prioritising the search for reconciliation as the most vital need for civilisation, at all possible levels. Second, it was feminist theology and spirituality that spurred and awakened in me the deepest spiritual awareness and challenge I have experienced in my life – even if some aspects had been previously intuited in earlier years. But feminist theology has developed, moved on – even if some consider it has run out of steam, and others would like it to do so – and is now part of a more complex approach to justice and liberation. How do these developments contribute to my current search? I will first sketch a general understanding of the current scene to show how this fits with the search for reconciliation, and then revisit an earlier attempt to reclaim the mystical path I explored twenty years ago, this time within a spirituality seeking reconciliation.[3]

First, feminism as a global movement has continued to stimulate gender consciousness in almost every area of society, even if the Roman Catholic Church continues to lag behind the wider society, not only in its continued refusal to ordain women, but also to allow juster participation in its decision-making structures.[4] But the initial movement of 'global sisterhood' has developed not only into awareness of the danger of white, western dominance – and hence the growth of contextually rooted women's theologies, such as womanist, Latina, mujerista, African[5] – but also of the complex interweaving of injustices, such as racism, colonialism, caste discrimination, militarism, heterosexism and discrimination against gay relationships. The particular context will define the contours of oppression: for example, in India – and other countries like Bangladesh and Nepal – it is the issue of caste that is the major key to desperate poverty, while within this situation, women will continue to bear its brunt, given the level of misogyny embedded within the caste-patriarchal system. Women theologians in many countries of the Two-Thirds World, often with the co-operation of male liberation theologians, continue to analyse the theological and economic structures and symbols that still underpin misogyny and 'the female face of poverty', while trying to reclaim more prophetic strands and enable justice. Meanwhile feminist theologians of the North and West have tried to work in solidarity, committed to the task of eradicating every trace of neo-colonialist thought and hegemonic tendencies. Reconciliation demands no less, and asks us never to stop digging ever deeper, to discover the prejudices blocking breakthrough.

My own position over the years has evolved considerably: aware that many continue, with great reluctance, to leave the Church, yet do so *often to save their faith in God*, I have struggled to maintain integrity by staying – through no great merit of my own, but more through the inspiration of some of my family and a large group of 'cradle Catholics' who refuse to give up hope that the prophetic, inclusive Church of their dreams will still come to birth. Despite the injustice and personal pain at the brick wall I and countless others face over issues like ordination, and still being forbidden to preach within my own church while being warmly welcomed in many other church communities, my decision to remain, while hoping and struggling for breakthrough, is actually inspired by movements *within the Church herself* since the Second Vatican Council. Though the despair I referred to in Chapter 1 frequently recurs, I take heart that it is official church teaching that encourages us to move into the healing of relationships with other Christians and beyond the Christian faith. As I write, the world's unanimous response to Pope Benedict's unfortunate comment about the Prophet Muhammad, in the context of a lecture at the University of Regensburg, Bavaria,[6] has prompted his invitation to Muslim representatives from all over the world to make amends.

Dialogue and reconciliation are still high on his agenda, even if some think the fallout from his remarks may take years to heal.

And, as regards my current theme, the call to repentance springs from the essential nature of Christian calling, even if it frequently fails to awaken the transformative action to bring peace out of conflict. I believe that the prophetic dimension is not completely stifled and that the richness of the Jewish and Christian prophetic and mystical traditions can still provide resources for this Dark Night and breakthrough to the dawn of reconciliation we seek.[7]

But there is a cost to both women and men who dream of a different church and remain obedient to the structures of the present one. This is the level of woundedness in the depths of the soul. At an official level, the hierarchy of the Church appear not to care that week after week, year after year, women listen to an exclusive liturgical language, singing hymns where they are not named, nor their experience recognised. Who has paid much attention to the consequences of centuries of powerlessness, inequality, misogyny, marginalisation and violence on the female psyche? Beverley Lanzetta has called this 'the oppression of women's soul' and names this spiritual oppression as the foundation of all her other oppressions.[8] From where will come healing and reconciliation? Lanzetta stresses the need for a contemplative wisdom to address these profound psychic wounds:

> Women's spiritual oppression, because it injures the site of a person's greatest holiness, sensitivity, and mutuality – their relationship with God – is frequently an unnamed, forbidden territory. The possession of women's ability to be relational, receptive and vulnerable – to reflect an outpouring of Divine Intimacy – is a form of spiritual violence maintained through complex relationships of blame and shame.[9]

To Rwanda and Back

How much more serious is this spiritual oppression when seen in the context of genocide: where solace and protection were expected, as we saw in the story of the Ntarama Chapel, betrayal and horrific violence were received. Correspondingly, how profound must be the understanding of the strategies of healing needed.

For these reasons I want to revisit the mystical path I began to trace twenty years ago, in my attempt to explore redemption within Christian feminism, in *Redeeming the Dream*,[10] but now with a different purpose. Twenty years ago I was exploring a spiritual path on the basis of nothingness and confusion, the lack of a healthy sense of female self that was offered by dominant philosophical and theological traditions. Then I sought a path to redemption in terms of self-affirmation, re-shaping the traditional stages in the mystical path. Admittedly this was only a partial solution: the following chapters went on to shape a theology where right relations of justice were put at the heart of a theology of redemption.

Now the goal is different: it is far less individualist, more community-oriented, embarked on with fellow peace-seekers with a passionate commitment to the earth herself; gender reconciliation is part of the journey, yet that itself is caught up with the realisation that reconciliation is a gift, dependent on the generosity of God, so that is where spirituality must begin: not with the individual's lonely struggle, but with God's gracious generosity, and giftedness. How does the mystical, contemplative journey now fare, if we consider the geography of the soul (the soul of both the individual and the communal soul), wounded through violence, and weave this healing together with the struggle for structural justice that is an integral part of reconciliation?

AWAKENING

The tools needed for the spiritual journey I have named earlier as, first, re-membering, second, the ability to develop the reflexive self, and third, the vision of the healed and redeemed city (symbolic of redeemed creation). I also stressed the role played by nature mysticism. In a spiritual journey of reconciliation, awakening to the needs and wounds of the earth is vital, as well as awakening to the limits of her resources, as we saw in Chapter 5. This process of awakening will never be completed. Earlier, I described it in terms of naturistic epiphanies, offered as a grace for the quest. Then I saw them in far rosier terms than now, given that the content of the epiphany is an awakened sense of human responsibility as to the crisis. Awakening to earth's limits makes inescapable claims on us. Our sense of vision is compromised at its very heart by the death of species, the sense of diminishment of earth's beauty by rivers running dry, the melting of the ice cap and devastation of the forests.

The healing of wounded memory has played an important part in this book. *Ibuka* is in fact the Kinyarwandan word for 'remember' and IBUKA is now an umbrella organisation working in Rwanda to keep the memory of the genocide alive – against those who deny that it happened – and to call for justice for the survivors. In a mystical, contemplative path, re-membering who we are, who we are called to be in God's eyes, is the focus. If reconciliation is God's dream for the earth, the ultimate symbol for redeemed and flourishing creation, for that to be enabled, this movement of awakening has to achieve one great task: whereas previously my stress was almost totally on connection and relation, what is now needed is awakening to the meaning of diversity and otherness. Diversity in creation is one thing. But respect for diverse ethnic groups is another and, as the last chapter began to discuss, a failure of respect for the other, seen as the hostile and threatening other, leaves the world's conflicts deadlocked. The ferocity of the killing in Rwanda was built on the deliberate destruction of the connection between three peoples, so that neighbours and friends became threatening others. In the Palestinian–Jewish–Lebanese conflict, fragile ceasefire may succeed fragile ceasefire. What is never faced is the deep-seated implacable hatred of *some* Israeli Jews for Arabs, and some say vice versa. How to change this hatred into respect for otherness and diversity, yet at the same time rebuild lost connections – in some cases connections that have never existed – is the challenge. Is the insight that the *eros* of *jeong*, the Korean concept of love undergirding sacrifice, discussed in the last chapter, of possible relevance here?

Reflecting on the ongoing struggles of survivors, the healing of child abuse, domestic violence, rape and war trauma, there is no doubt that spirituality has to come to terms with wounds that will not go away. There can never be a forgetting. Awakening may come to mean the process of remembering different levels of pain.[11] Creating communities for the safe telling of the stories, the acknowledging of their truth and the slow recovery of trust, is vital – as I have indicated. But how are we to move forward to heal the damaged psyche of persons and communities, the loss of the point of connection with the Divine source of wisdom? This is at the heart of the contemplative, mystical journey.

VIA PURGATIVA

In the traditional Christian mystical pathway, this second movement invited a focus on the stripping away of pride, arrogance, disobedience and any dimension blocking a Christ-centred personhood. But for many women, as I wrote earlier, the challenge was more to develop a healthy sense of self, on the basis of lack of self-esteem and sense of non-being, in the context of the dominant self of patriarchy. This spiritual journey is not embarked on in a straight linear progress in search of the pot of gold at the rainbow's end: these stages are not sequential, but more like interweaving strands in the depths of awakening interiority. The focus now in question is the search for the God of peace and reconciliation, the God who is already awakening, energising and nourishing humanity's shared longing for peace. So the *via purgativa* has a special role to play. What are the practices, personal and communal, that block the healing of the world and those that stimulate the process of its transformation?

Surely, the need for repentance and accountability as a movement of the heart must be an unquestioned priority for Churches and religious communities caught up in world conflicts? In Chapter 4 I asked how a church with reconciliation at its heart could build fragile bridges towards peace. The *via purgativa* builds on this as spiritual practice, imagining a self transformed through commitment to repentance, leading to communities transformed. The World Council of Church's Faith and Order Commission, as part of its decade against violence, asked the same question. In a powerful statement, the Commission argues:

> Are there reasons for the churches to undertake such a process of repentance? While generally opposing violence and affirming peace, churches are held responsible for their role − complicit, supportive and silent, in situations of violence. The legacies of Christian expansionism which were aggressively pursued alongside colonisation and the death and dehumanisation these have caused (e.g.: the Crusades and the Conquest), the historical nexus between churches and the political and economic powers that not only distorted the gospel but also caused, allowed and justified the violence of the powerful, and the hostile attitudes and actions towards people of other faiths, cultures and values, are but a few examples. Furthermore, the churches' silence and role in justifying various forms of structural violence − economic, political, cultural, psychological or

religious – is also cited. However, it must also be asserted that churches have also played and continue to play prophetic and transformative roles in many situations of violence. The historic peace churches and many others today are passionately committed to a witness of peace and nonviolence. The way churches all over the world have opposed the invasion of Iraq is one recent example.[12]

The WCC document calls for discernment in the ways in which some theological convictions and traditional attitudes that the Churches have cherished for too long have allowed or perpetrated or justified certain forms of violence. These issues include:

- the influence of some doctrines of creation, Fall and human being on Churches' attitudes towards racism, sexual discrimination, social hierarchies;
- the suppression of human freedom, and the conquest and subjugation of the powerless;
- the way atonement is understood and interpreted in contexts where violence and the suffering of the innocent are held inevitable for the ultimate good;
- Christian triumphalism that has left memories of violence, bloodshed besides hatred and suspicion and similar trends and attitudes today.[13]

The document specifically mentions the violence of certain biblical texts, which I have called 'redemptive violence texts', texts claiming violence as a divine attribute, and the way they have influenced Christian attitudes towards institutionalised violence, as well as strategies of evangelisation that encourage or allow silence and neutrality in situations of blatant assaults on life and denial of justice.[14] I add to this catalogue the need to repent of exploitative patterns of violence towards the earth.

The development of patterns of repentance that, far from

being notional, face-saving gestures, enable the integrity of the self-in-relation to overcome the hurdles and barriers of difference demands creativity, discipline, generosity and sacrifice. Recalling my renaming of sacrifice as suffering love in the context of the renewal of fullness of life for all, the *via purgativa* nurtures the praxis of this in terms of accountability and responsibility. The reconciling heart cannot develop accountability for the planet without disciplined practices like prayer and meditation, and developing the liturgical sacramental practices of Christian Churches to address the need to make peace. Obviously Christian Churches have urged their members to repent – but they have not sufficiently embraced the need for this to be a social phenomenon: indeed they sometimes seem to shun this possibility.[15] *Social repentance is the cornerstone for transformed life.*

This is why the *via purgativa* is truly mystical: it refuses to make a separation between a person's interiority and the fullness of her social relationships. There has never been a peacemaker who has not sought solitude to 'nurture the inner monasteries of the heart'.[16] 'To find the monastery within is to discover the place of rest out of which all other relations flourish and grow.'[17] This place of solitude may seem elusive, given that for both women and men solitude for reflection is often a receding possibility, a luxury experienced perhaps on holiday or on a rare visit to a retreat centre. The mushrooming of spirituality centres and quiet days and the popularity of pilgrimages witness to the longing for meditative solitude. For the sleep-deprived young mother, nurses on night shift, jet-lagged executives expected to work the clock round, it seems an impossibility. Somehow, if we long sufficiently, simple ways are found, sometimes painfully integrated within the daily round. Within this space there are three further practices for the reconciling heart that the *via purgativa* invites. For the reordering of our values from the pressure to consume, for example, solitude and silence are indispensable. If reconciliation is the goal, limiting consumption is not only a priority for the sake of the earth's resources, but to open our eyes to the suffering caused to others with whom we are in conflict by our over-consumption. No conflict is unrelated to loss of land, water scarcity, lack of food through unjust trade, lack of market, or inability to access food because of indebtedness and being forced into migration.

Second, solitude and silence are also necessary to re-centre ourselves as to what is the heart of life's meaning. Where are goodness, grace, love and wonder to be found? The very power and mystery of love is experienced in a deep need to cross boundaries, to refuse limits, to recall those paradoxical words 'Love your enemies'. So, the third practice of this mystical *via purgativa* in the context of reconciliation is to do exactly that, to embark upon forgiveness as daily practice. To many feminists this is a non-starter, for good reasons – discussed earlier – emerging from the trauma of abuse, violence and damaged subjectivity. It is also not a practice that Jews will admit in the context of post-Holocaust, because 'Only God can forgive'. And this is where forgiveness starts, with God's initiative.[18] It springs from the mysterious, God-given grace to forgive in order to move on and recover a sense of well-being. But it can never be forced on a victim. President Paul Kagame himself realised this when, in a recent speech, he said that it seems impossible to call on survivors to forgive what was done to them, yet he had no other choice, because of the need for the country to heal and move on. Immaculée Ilibagiza (mentioned earlier), after her appalling experiences, was brought face to face with her family's killer, Félicien, with the intention that she should denounce him: ' "He looted your parents's home and robbed your family's plantation, Immaculée ... After he killed Rose and Damascene, he came looking for you ... he wanted you dead so he could take over your property. Didn't you, pig?" '[19] Much to the fury of the burgomaster, Semana, who had brought the killer to

Immaculée, the survivor, all she would say was: ' "Forgiveness is all I have to offer." ' [20] Such a response is not explicable in the categories we normally live with. It emerges from deep mystical faith and the kind of vulnerable love with which the Korean *jeong* began to heal the affliction of *han*. There is a remarkable exhibition called 'The Forgiveness Project' touring the UK as I write, describing the willingness of survivors' of violence and trauma, like Immaculée, to forgive, in order for hatred not to have the last word, to enable some form of healing, and for the memory of their lost loved ones to become part of this process.[21] These include not only Mary Blewitt from Rwanda, but Anne Gallagher from Northern Ireland who founded Seeds of Hope, the parents of the 7-year-old murdered Victoria Climbié, Mariane Pearl, widow of Daniel Pearl, murdered by an Islamic militant fundamentalist group, who, in an effort not to be broken by hatred, has written a book, *A Mighty Heart: The Brave Life and Death of Daniel Pearl* – and many others.

To heal the community's wounded psyche, to discover somehow a shared way to the mutual grace of forgiveness is desperately needed. Liberation theologians like Jon Sobrino and Rodolfo Cardenal, cited earlier, have shown how poor communities, whom they call *the crucified peoples*, from their very abjection, have developed a capacity to forgive:

> The crucified peoples offer values that are not found anywhere else. The poor have a great humanising potential because they offer community instead of individualism, service instead of egoism, simplicity instead of opulence, creativity instead of cultural mimicry, openness to transcendence instead of positivism and crass positivism.[22]

Despite a certain idealising tendency, there is something precious here, something that, while respecting the sensibilities and depth of emotional suffering of those who can never forgive the horror of what has been done to them

To Rwanda and Back

personally, or collectively as an entire people through history, the mystical nature of the *via purgativa* is revealed here in this incredible practising of forgiveness in the service of a vision of healing that can only be Divine-inspired.

VIA ILLUMINATIVA

After the trials of the *via purgativa*, traditionally the joys of the vision of God are the consolation of the *via illuminativa*. This never happened automatically for women mystics. For the early mediaeval mystic, Hildegard of Bingen, it happened after she was forty years old, on what seemed like her deathbed, that she received a call 'Cry out and write!'[23] Similarly, Julian of Norwich, after a great sickness, received the visions which she would spend a lifetime explaining and deepening.[24] When I reflected on this stage in *Redeeming the Dream*, I saw it partly in terms of the mystical breakthrough of Martha Quest, protagonist of Doris Lessing's novels, *The Children of Violence*, in other words in a breakthrough of consciousness that led from a rather self-centred life to a commitment to others.[25]

The focus is different here: building on Grace Jantzen's arguments that William James's influence has caused us to think (misleadingly) of mysticism as the privatised experience of the individual, an approach that would have been alien to Hildegarde, Julian and the mystical, liturgical heart of the early Church, together with my own ideas that mysticism belongs with the community experience, I ask what are the God-graced moments and visions of illumination that continue to inspire and provide resources for reconciliation for community?[26] I find a congruence here between the mediaeval female mystical use of visions as a tool to confront the power structures of the Church, and the more contemporary witness of peace activists who derive strength from the mystical way of contemplation. I will reflect here on the witness of two women whose lives spanned the last century, both deeply committed to peace movements, Dorothy Day and Dorothee Soelle, both of whom could never separate the contemplative, mystical journey to God from the journey to peace and reconciliation.[27]

With American activist Dorothy Day (1897–1980), the striking point about this yearning for God that haunted her is that it was never separated from commitment to poor people with whom she was always identified: her commitment to 'the good life' and well-being drove her to live life in community, specifically with those rejected from 'respectable' society, the homeless, alcoholics, tramps and unemployed:

> I wanted the abundant life. I wanted it for others too. I did not want just the few, the missionary-minded people like the Salvation Army, to be kind to the poor, as the poor. I wanted everyone to be kind. I wanted every home to be open to the lame, the halt and the blind, the way it had been after the San Francisco earthquake. Only then did people really live, really love their brothers. In such love was the abundant life and I did not have the slightest idea how to find it.[28]

This search for the life abundant led her through socialism and communism into Catholicism and the founding of the Catholic Worker movement, with its astonishing achievement of numerous houses of hospitality and its thousands of daily battles against poverty, addictions of every sort, violence of all kinds and the attempt to live in genuine community with rejected people. *The Catholic Worker* – still in print – carried the stories of struggles every month: its pages and the pages of Day's writings are alive with names and stories of desperate people. For her, poor people have names, families, hopes and dreams that she shares. The struggle to find enough money to cook the daily soup for the community is told in gritty reality. Within the honesty and admission of failure, there is also a revolutionary sense of hope.

But what gives this a claim to be both mystical and political holiness? Unlike politically correct contemporary feminist theologians, Dorothy Day used the language of the times that was not gender sensitive. (This does not prevent her from being close to the sorrows of poor women, by which she herself was personally affected.) As we shall see with Dorothee Soelle, Day also loved literary texts, and was particularly influenced by Dostoevksy. After her conversion to Catholicism she became immersed in the mystical texts of Teresa of Avila and John of the Cross. But the deepest influence on her spiritual and philosophical education was the French philosopher Peter Maurin, who became her teacher and mentor for many years: through him she discovered Catholic social teaching (of which she had never heard), but also many of the French thinkers like Maritain and De Lubac. Peter Maurin was steeped in Aquinas and he wanted to make a totally new synthesis, a revolution comprising cult, culture and cultivation.[29] It was this synthesis of Aquinas, fashioning social transformation, that stimulated the political dimensions of Day and Maurin's thought and inspired houses of hospitality, Catholic Worker farms and what Peter Maurin termed 'agronomic universities'. People who reduce Day's achievements to schemes for the urban poor underestimate how her thought and that of Maurin's anticipated much of 'green thinking' today. 'Life abundant' meant the possibility of the very poorest people enjoying fresh air and eating nourishing food in surroundings that nurtured soul and spirit as well as body. This is something akin to 'bringing back the beauty of life' that is the focus and hope of Rwandan genocide survivors.

Hence Day came to appreciate the 'sacramentality of life' and all that made it possible. Influenced by Gandhi's ideas, sharing the humblest of household tasks was a principle, for example. But Maurin also aimed in the Catholic Worker farms for self-sufficiency with vegetables and keeping poultry. As well as baking their own bread there was an attempt to look for ethical sources of food.[30] Day's mysticism really lay in discovering God in these poor communities (although she does admit to some experiences when alone). She wrote:

> A mystic may be called a man in love with God. Not one who loves God, but who is *in love with God*. And this mystical love, which is an exalted emotion, leads one to love the things of Christ. His footsteps are sacred.[31]

Identification with the sufferings of Christ brings her to a mystical element in the love of a radical for his or her brother (and sister), so that this extended – as it did with Romero and the murdered Jesuits – to the scene of sufferings, and thus the places of their struggles and death became hallowed:

> You know this feeling, as does every other radical in the country. Through ignorance, perhaps, you do not acknowledge Christ's name. Yet I believe you are trying to love Christ in His poor, in His persecuted ones.[32]

It would be false to limit Day's attitude to practical charity on an individual basis. Though she did insist on beginning with a revolution of the heart, her achievement was to unite the personal with the political, the inner and outer expressions of mystical love. Until the end of her life the prophetic and mystical dimensions were held together by that indivisible love. Daniel Berrigan paid tribute to this after her death (while he was still on trial as one of eight Christians, for having destroyed two nuclear warheads):

> Without Dorothy, without that exemplary patience, courage, moral modesty, without this woman pounding on the locked door behind which the powerful mock the powerless ... the resistance we offered would have been simply unthinkable. She urged our consciences off the beaten track; she made the impossible ... probable, and then actual. She did this, first of all, by living as though the truth were true.[33]

This example of the mysticism of resistance links Dorothy Day with the mysticism of the late German political theologian, Dorothee Soelle. Many elements link these two peace activists: my principal focus will be the search for God within a mysticism seeking reconciliation, and in Soelle's case, the struggle to find a way to speak about God. I only met Dorothee Soelle once, at a conference in 1991 and was immediately struck by her saying that the only place to find God today was in the political struggle. She had discovered this painfully at a demonstration in Bonn in 1983 when the police turned water cannons against those protesting against the US nuclear weapons stationed in Germany. Somehow she had to find the courage to speak to the bedraggled protesters and she found herself screaming to God – 'Why have you forsaken us?' But then she found the answer coming: 'The God to whom this prayer was addressed was as grieved as we were, small like us, with no bank account or bombs in the background ... And yet God was with us that night.'[34]

Seeking a language to speak about this God mystically revealed in the political struggle was a lifelong quest for Dorothee Soelle, with its roots in her deep shame over the Nazi responsibility for the horror of the Holocaust. For, born in 1929 in Cologne, the bombings of the Second World War and the Holocaust formed the contours of her childhood and early adulthood. Her parents opposed the Nazi regime in private, but made it clear that their daughter had to keep her thoughts to herself or she would end up in a concentration camp. She found an outlet in a diary, and in her love of literature and poetry, where she found a Germany other than the fascist regime that surrounded her. Her initial studies were in literary criticism and, as she pursued higher study, she conflicted with the severely traditional and patriarchal system of German universities.

Soelle, like Jean Baptist Metz, was an *activist* theologian, a political theologian who could almost be considered a co-founder of political theology, but she soon changed to be fully identified with liberation theology and its different struggles. More than this, she was a genuine theologian of the struggle, never at home in the abstractions of systematic theology. Her theology was based on involvement with real people and experiences in the struggle. Keeping open a '*window of vulnerability*' to people and their suffering was always crucial to her. The German liberation theologian Luise Schottroff – Soelle's greatest friend – remembers how she initiated 'political evensongs' in Cologne from 1968 to 1972. Here forty people – from both Roman Catholic and Protestant traditions – came together in a new church community unconnected with parish structures. Through analysis, meditation and guidance towards praxis, they confronted the political scene – for example, the Soviet invasion of Czechoslovakia and the Vietnam war. Luise Schottroff thinks that this was the hour when liberation theology was born in a German – even a European – context.[35]

The move to the USA – in 1975, when offered a professorial post at Union Theological Seminary in New York – brought Soelle in touch with the women's movement, with which she had not yet been identified. Immediately she saw the relevance of patriarchy to the death-dealing systems of dominance: Rosemary Ruether believes that she integrated successfully a gender analysis into 'what remained a liberation theology steeped in Marxist critique'.[36] To the criticism that has been made that Soelle did not theorise at all about gender, or consider the significance of sex/gender in liberation theology, it can be retorted that she was far more interested in *what we do*, than in theorising on *who we are*. Yet she was passionately interested in the whole crucible of relationality:

> Personal inner deadness and lack of relationship as well as the religious and secular ideologies that sacralise submission to authorities both have their source in this dominating

power. Systems of oppression spring from and collectivise human arrogance, greed, fear and hate. These negative tendencies ... are organised and institutionalised as collective systems of death that hold humans themselves in bondage.[37]

So sin in collective form is seen as a demonic counter world to God's creation. A straight line can be drawn from Soelle's opposition to fascist domination in Germany, to opposing the US government's action in Vietnam and in Latin America, to her resistance to the economic domination of global capitalism. You could say that the most important dualism she unmasked was that between death-dealing dominating powers and life-giving love. *Choose life* was always the goal, abundant life for the most abandoned and brutalised peoples.

Another key to her life is the struggle to create an appropriate language for the project of liberation. Abstract and systematic argument does not feed the soul. Soelle gravitated to myth and poetry from many sources, but was also sensitive to where this was offered in the Bible. To say she loved the psalms is an understatement. She even spoke of 'eating the psalms':

> For me the psalms are one of the most important foods. I eat them, I drink them, I chew on them. Sometimes I spit them out and sometimes I repeat one to myself in the middle of the night. They are bread for me. Without them the spiritual anorexia that is so widespread among us sets in and often leads to a deadly impoverishment of the spirit and of the heart.[38]

Very early on in her search she visited Martin Buber in Jerusalem. On her telling him that she was a theologian, he disconcerted her by replying, 'Theo-logy – how do you do that? There is no logos of God.'[39] This prompted her lifelong exploration in poetry and myth, culminating in what would be recognised as a full-blown mystical theology. Her last book, *The Silent Cry: Mysticism and Resistance*,[40] is her most explicit expression of this yearning for God that fuels resistance to injustice and, eluding complete rational expression, is common to all faiths. In a way, she embodies the adage, cited earlier: *all things begin in mysticism and end in politics, only to begin again.*

In an early essay, 'Breaking the ice of the soul', Soelle complains on the inadequacy of most of theological language. I think she rediscovers the old meaning of poetry, as *remaking the world*. The Greek word ποιήσις (*poiesis*, poetry) translates as 'maker' – which is the old Scottish word for poet. But it also means recreating a different world, on the basis of memory:

> We always live in a house of language, built by previous generations. That is why the memory of a different life and the hope for less destructive ways of living can hardly be rooted out. Poetic, transforming, ice-melting speech is structured into language itself.[41]

Not only is this emphasis on language and memory germane to the theme of this book: in the struggle for liberation many have been inspired by the poems of Adrienne Rich, who in *The Dream of a Common Language* (1977) was challenging words like humanism, androgyny, as words she would never use again.[42] Soelle situates her search in the context of global capitalism where language has been corrupted, where a word like 'love' refers to a car, and the word 'purity' to laundry. Because the idols of money and power are marketing language in terms of ownership and commodification, there is no space for a language of being as opposed to that of having. With shame, despair and revulsion she comes to the biblical mythic-poetic language as a tool of resistance, to a rediscovery of prayer as poetry, and the challenge to sing different songs:

To sing of peace in the midst of war is, I believe, the secret
of the people in the New Testament, who, trembling under
an empire marked by a similar hostility towards human
beings, still sang their different songs.[43]

It has become familiar to see in poets and novelists using
naturistic epiphanies, a sense of mystical awakening. Soelle
offers us this mystical awakening in a context of the praying
community. 'If there is any verb for the language of mysticism,
it is praying', she wrote.[44] Only with this language is there a
hope of penetrating beyond domination and control. It is a
language drawing us into paradox, and silence. But it should
not be thought that she draws uncritically on biblical mytho-
poetry. Texts are revisited in a subversive way, in full
awareness of centuries of misinterpretation. For example, here
is how she writes poetically of resurrection:

O don't ask about resurrection
A tale of ages long ago
That will soon skip your mind
I listen to those
Who dry me out and diminish me
I accustom myself
To the creeping accommodation to being dead
In my well-heated abode
The big stone at my door.[45]

But later on in the poem, she cries:

O do ask me about resurrection;
O don't stop asking me.[46]

Joy, eros, justice, relationality and resistance are all embodied
in Soelle's poetry. As Carter Heyward wrote: 'She does not
accept mysticism as an "inward" journey taken by and on
behalf of the self. The mystical journey "leads into a healing
that is at the same time resistance".'[47]

Soelle's lifelong quest for justice and peace meant that she struggled for a new way to speak about God. I find a remarkable similarity with the words of the German poet, Rainer Maria Rilke, in his famous ninth Duino Elegy. The traveller, descending from the heights, leaving behind 'long-drawn encounters of love':

> He bears the sheer word won from the gentian; its message
>   of yellow, of blue.
> Were we put in this world here, truly, for speech? To say:
> House, Fountain, Bridge, Jug, Gate, Fruit tree; or Window?
>   . . .
>
>   Ours the age of the sayable. Ours its parish.
>   Speak and bear witness.[48]

In this bearing witness, the poet's mission is one of transformation. This is the heart of the *via illuminativa*: the sacramental imagination, in its mystical dimension, as awakening to the healing and transforming of the world. As with many poets, there comes a deepening awareness of Divine immanent presence, but in a way that opens up to what I name a *healing transcendent*. As Anne Primavesi pleaded, in *Sacred Gaia*, for room for God: for God 'to be transcendent to and at the same time present within a world no smaller than the whole in which we exist; a whole which can only be glimpsed with awe'.[49] The eco-mystical path she advocates is inspired by the experience of this cosmos as sacred. God present, but *not confused with the world*, is the clue here. Poets, mystics, Goddess disciples, peacemakers and prophetic resisters alike share the insight, and rejoice in the many-levelled dynamic sacred presence of the Divine in creation. Julian of Norwich recognised the entirety of God's creative goodness present in a small hazelnut – a classic example. But Soelle's mystic witness to the sacred begins with ordinary people recognising, in the faithful living out of their daily lives, that there is a hallowing, a sense of sacred presence in sharing a simple meal, enabling children to grow in safe spaces, after the desecration of war, with nourishing food, for the voices of victims to be heard, *no longer as victims*, and in sowing seeds and celebrating harvest after the environmental devastation of war.

The presence of God as healing transcendent in a culture of global violence is manifested as the kenotic or self-emptying presence of God, or the refusal of God to be a commodity within the system of global capitalism, as well as an invitation to our own process of self-emptying, as challenge to the way that a culture of violence has tried to occupy all available space. This language of voluntary self-emptying leads to recognising vulnerability, God's vulnerability and compassionate suffering shared with numerous vulnerable communities around the world. Soelle pleaded for keeping open this place of vulnerability:

> The window of vulnerability
> Must be closed –
> So the military say
> To justify the arms race.
>
> My skin is a window of vulnerability
> Without moisture, without touching
> I must die
>
> The window of vulnerability
> Is being walled up
> My land
> Cannot live
>
> We need light
> So we can think
> We need air
> So we can breathe
> We need a window
> Open toward heaven.[50]

Keeping a 'window open toward heaven', enables us as praying communities of resistance to allow the mystical experience of the *via illuminativa* to draw us into the cultural alternative that is the Divine healing transcendent. Our dreams of peace and reconciliation are nurtured and grounded by God's generosity. For it has always been a straight choice: choose life, or death. Acquiesce in the dominating culture of violence or keep alive the torch of the political and mystical spirituality of resistance. There is no Third Way.

THE DARK NIGHT OF THE SOUL

Writing about the traditional dark night stage of the mystical journey can act as a temptation to literary fiction. For when today's spiritual seeker reads John of the Cross's text, it is to know that after the anguish and desolation comes the joy and consolation of the *via unitiva*, Union with God. Even when I wrote earlier[51] that after the initial illumination that feminist awakening in the Church had brought me had disappeared into the despair of realising that nothing was changing, I still found a positive way forward in 'hanging on':

> It is to hang onto the insight that we are touched by God, who, as the process model suggests, is taking the initiative. We have lost that all-pervasive sense of Divine presence: but we are touching and being touched by the dark knowing of God, only made possible by the shattering of existing sexist and power-ridden images, and by our experiencing exis-tential loneliness so that new growth will occur.[52]

The temptation is to cling to this insight, that however des-pairing and angst-ridden is the present moment, that darkness and despair are the prelude to Divine light breaking through. And there is an artificiality in this presupposition.

As I write this morning, even though I believe what I have

written about 'holding onto dreams', existentially the dream seems very dead. Even though there are breakthroughs in, for example, Northern Ireland, the possibility of genuine peace elsewhere appears to have receded. The world is obsessed by what it considers an imminent terrorist threat. In our own project in drought-stressed Rajasthan, monsoon floods have just swept away the frail water-harvesting structures pains-takingly constructed by the villagers. The carcasses of 50,000 animals drowned in the floods are floating past, causing a terrible stench. Some people have drowned (figures are unclear) and thousands are homeless. The rain normally falling over five years has come in four days. I embarked on this book partly as a way of atonement for the neglect of Rwanda in her hour of need and partly as my own spiritual journey. Yet, the killing in the Sudan escalates almost to genocide proportions, and the world is as silent as we were in 1994. (There are a few heroic exceptions.) The voice of the Palestinians, whose agony goes back to the very beginning of the state of Israel, continues to be (mostly) ignored, as the most powerful politicians will not intervene effectively with the Israeli government.

On a personal level, when I wrote at the beginning of this chapter that I was at a different stage of the spiritual journey, I still believed in the spiritual journey as a dominant metaphor. But I am also convinced of the falsity of writing about the dark night with the presumption that after darkness, Divine light will come. The essence of the dark night is to be blocked, to experience impasse, to doubt the power of the journey motif, because one is going nowhere. I am not alone in raising questions about the journey metaphor. Michael Symmons Roberts, writing recently in *The Tablet*, describing the tourists stranded in Heathrow because of the (apparent) terrorist threat to blow up flights to the USA, wondered whether this was the end of flying, and indeed of journeying − in the sense of families taking summer holidays by air. Of course this is exactly what environmentalists long for − that flying would cease to be our chosen mode of travel. But something less obvious is going on. He cited the philosopher Galen Strawson who asked if we would then seek other metaphors to describe the spiritual life and what they would be.[53] The answer should not come glibly. Metaphors are tried and tested over hundreds of years.

Is there a way out of this impasse? Part of my sense of blockage, the sense that normal metaphors are not working, comes from the experience of serious illness, my own and that of family, friends and colleagues. Experiences of chronic pain and debilitating illness challenge accepted standards of wholeness and healing, and the inbuilt optimism of the journey motif. They even inspire a new reading of the Gospels. All my life I had been trying to live an activist version of Christianity, convinced that 'feeding the hungry', 'giving water to the least of the little ones', and so on, was the bedrock of faith. Being part of a group of believers who, while living out of deep faith, are experiencing one or multiple forms of disability has challenged me to a different expression of the 'journey to wholeness'. Feminist theology and spirituality has always privileged embodied faith, but I think there was still a presumption of an able body behind this, even if the artificial body of consumerism is rejected. Indeed all the notions of wholeness and well-being are still resting on the basis of this 'able body', or its nearest approximation. I now understand that there are as many varieties of 'wholeness' as there are with healing and that any notion of well-being must incorporate these. I have become more conscious, when reading the Gospels, of those whom Jesus did not heal, and still today are not healed. I ask, what meaning does the faith and ministry of those with debilitating conditions like multiple sclerosis and motor neurone diseases, those who are hearing- and sight-impaired, and those who live with chronic pain? Is it not an insult to them to make disability a metaphor for bad faith? When we overuse the condition of blindness, for example, as a metaphor for 'not seeing' the truth, the 'I was blind but now I see' of the famous hymn 'Amazing grace', not only do we implicitly ascribe an inferior mode of existence to sight-impaired people, but miss the contribution that is made to the life of faith and to church life by people of disability.

But if the sense of 'I'm going nowhere' is overwhelming, and undermines the journey motif of spirituality, what other metaphors could replace it? Must the Exodus metaphor that has held central place for so long, give way to stasis? Is it enough to continue to light candles in the dark, and accept impasse as the only state of affairs?

VIA UNITIVA

This, the glorious state of unity with God, is the final resting place of the *via mystica* for the Christian seeker, as enlightenment is for the Buddhist and nirvana for the Hindu. But if impasse, blockage and temptation to despair have undermined the journey motif, can there be any closure? Great emphasis is put on 'waiting', 'waiting on God' as an appropriate mode of being.[54] Adrienne Rich's 'Wait with sadness and with grave impatience' seems to sum up this stance.[55] How many great lives have reached their earthly closure in this mode, my own mother's for example?

What gives the spiritual life meaning, and becomes the source of new metaphors, not in replacing 'journeying' but in standing alongside it, is of course the centrality of reconciliation, because this is God's great hope for the world. Journeying will always be an important metaphor: after all, even if I may feel blocked, others do not; the journey is often one where we can be sustained by the action or solidarity of others. The energy of the quest, the passion for creation appear in different ways. I understand now that it matters not to be caught up into the ecstasy of the fullness of God's presence, wonderful though that might be. Our great inspirations for reconciliation, beginning with Jesus himself, did not die in that kind of ecstasy. Brother Roger of Taizé was murdered during the liturgy, Gandhi during his morning walk of prayer, Sister Dorothy Stang in her efforts to protect the Brazilian forest, and countless others in the struggle for peace and justice. Reconciliation is the great vision, the way God sustains, inspires and gives meaning to the myriad forms of witness over the ages. What matters is to be steadfast in this faith, and to draw strength from this integrity, this truthfulness that whatever path to reconciliation God has made concrete in our lives, be it from wheelchair, or pulpit – or both – that is our contribution to the *via unitiva*, or the process of reconciliation, that is the mighty hope for our planet.

Journeying, waiting, hoping, holding our ground so as to receive reconciliation as gift and vision, these are the modes of being that sustain the practices this book has advocated of remembering, of sacrifice as suffering love, caring and being compassionate, reconciling, forgiving, re-connecting with the earth, all within a symbolic core of flourishing, inspired by the Holy Spirit of beauty. But how does this count as mysticism, rather than concrete praxis for peacemaking? Throughout I have stressed the inseparability of justice from peace and reconciliation. I have also held together the prophetic, the contemplative and mystical. Lifestyle issues of simplicity and anti-consumerism are also integral to the process and to forming a culture of peace that promotes reconciliation.

But the most profound reason for calling this path to reconciliation mystical lies in what has been revealed about the trinitarian God. For Christians, God is hidden, *absconditus*, yet wonderfully revealed in the life and death of Christ, in the sacramental life of the Church that is not separated from Divine sacred presence in creation, but builds on this. It has become popular in recent years to build a theology of relationship and connection on the Divine relationships of the perichoretic movement of the Trinity; but in a theology of reconciliation drawing the world to unity, another interpretation offers more depth. Thomas Berry, in his book *The Dream of the Earth*, described the three principles on which the universe rests as increased subjectivity, communion and differentiation.[56] Whereas in the past we have tended to be inspired by the communion between Divine persons, now, in our search for peace, *differentiation* is the gift and grace offered by God. The diversity in creation gives glory to God, just as diversity between peoples is also part of the brilliance of creation, if liberated from a culture of violence, threat of terrorism and a deliberately fostered pathology of 'the threatening other'. But the grace of differentiation emanates from the trinitarian economy, offering itself as the very ground of communion, a communion that respects the boundaries of difference, and as the enhancement of an identity grounded in creation in the image of God.

EPILOGUE

The journey to Rwanda sparked this exploration of sacrifice as integral to reconciliation and challenged me as to where I was in the spiritual journey. So, where am I now? The *via mystica* seems to have provoked a radical questioning of the metaphor of the quest itself. The world around me seems as ever to be poised between recovering from old conflicts and embarking on new, thus making the spiritual life a perennial struggle to keep hope alive amidst despair. But in these contrast experiences, even if diminishment of life's quality is integral, there are still moments when faith and joy are deepened. I mourn the suffering of Rwanda – and will continue to do so – but rejoice in many heroic efforts to move on, and will always be grateful to have been put in touch with this country's ongoing struggle. And I know in my heart that this is what grace means: that you are given enough compassion – however inadequate you feel and are – to keep in solidarity and struggle with whatever people or situation that God has put you in touch with. And to trust that God will make room in your heart and energies for the next involvement, as well as keeping faith with existing loyalties, that's what it means to me to be part of the *kin-dom, the kinship of sisters and brothers and all forms of life in the planet.* That's a great joy, enough for one life, and to celebrate the coming messianic feast of life when all tears will be wiped away. Now, today, in communion with those who walked the earth before us, and those still to come.

But let the last words be from a courageous Rwandan, a Catholic bishop, Bishop Aloys Bigiruwami, whose voice was not heeded. Yet, can re-membering his urgent words in our own times of conflict be a stimulus to act now, before it is too late?

> Let us start by saving what was lost; let us stand up and look for friendliness of Rwandans among themselves; let us look ahead, the sky is getting dark, the storm is brewing, let us put under shelter what is not covered ... Let us strengthen the links of unity ... If we do not succeed at home, we will have nothing else to do but sink into the sea with the millstone round our necks.[57]

Yes – stark and tragic in their going unheeded. Yet faith, hope and love still beckon us onward, and tell us to 'hold fast to our dreams'.

NOTES

Introduction

1. Wells for India was founded in 1987 by my husband Dr Nicholas Grey and myself and focuses on water harvesting and related social projects in the semi-desert state of Rajasthan, North-West India. See www.wellsforindia.org

2. Alan Paton, *Ah But Your Land is Beautiful!* (London: Penguin 1983).

3. The source here is www.ambarwanda.co.uk (UK Rwandan embassy).

4. This story has become the subject of a moving film, *Hotel Rwanda*. Paul Rusesebagina has now written his own account, *An Ordinary Man: The True Story behind Hotel Rwanda* (London: Bloomsbury 2006). Some have criticised the claims he makes as overblown.

5. See M. Grey, *Redeeming the Dream* (London: SPCK 1989); *The Wisdom of Fools? Seeking Revelation for Today* (London: SPCK 1993).

6. See *Beyond the Dark Night: A Way Forward for the Church?* (London: Continuum 1997); *Prophecy and Mysticism: The Heart of the Post-modern Church* (Edinburgh: T & T Clark 1997).

7. See M. Grey, *The Unheard Scream: The Struggles of Dalit Women in India* (New Delhi: Centre for Dalit Theology 2004).

8. *The Outrageous Pursuit of Hope: Prophetic Dreams for the 21st Century* (London: Darton, Longman & Todd 2000).

9. See John W. De Gruchy, *Reconciliation: Restoring Justice* (London: SCM Press 2002).

10. Dan Cohn Sherbok and Mary Grey, *Pursuing the Dream: A Jewish–Christian Conversation* (London: Darton, Longman & Todd 2005).

I THE DYNAMICS OF THE RWANDAN GENOCIDE

1. Philippe Gaillard, 'Memory never forgets miracles' in Carol Rittner et al. (eds.), *Genocide in Rwanda: Complicity of the Churches?* (St Paul MN: Paragon House 2004), p. 111. At the time of the genocide Philippe Gaillard was the head of the delegation of the International Red Cross.

2. See Meg Guillebaud, *Rwanda: The Land God Forgot? Revival, Genocide and Hope* (London: Monarch Books 2002).

3. Hugh McCullum, *The Angels have Left Us: The Rwandan Tragedy and the Churches* (Geneva: WCC Publications, 2nd printing, 2004), ch. 1, pp. 2–3.

4. ibid., p. 2.

5. This is well documented by Mahmood Mamdani, *When Victims Become Killers: Colonialism, Racism and Genocide in Rwanda* (Princeton: Princeton University Press 2001).

6. Peter Uvin, *Aiding Violence: Development Enterprise in Rwanda* (Bloomfield CT: Kumarian Press 1998).

7. See – among other sources – Philippe Gourevitch, *We Wish to Inform You that Tomorrow We Will Be Killed with our Families: Stories from Rwanda* (New York: Picador 1999).

8. For documentation on the Decade, see www.wcc-coe.org

9. This will be developed in Chapter 3.

10. A. J. Ayer, *Language, Truth and Logic* (London: Gollancz 1936). This was considered the key text for logical positivism: Ayer himself was a formidable character who poured scorn on the possibility of religious beliefs making any sense to a rational human being.

11. Jean-Baptist Metz, *Faith in History and Society: Towards a Practical, Fundamental Theology* (New York: Crossroad 1980), pp. 66–7.

12. I used this idea as the basis of the my argument in M. Grey, *Redeeming the Dream* (London: SPCK 1989).

13. Elisabeth Schüssler Fiorenza, *In Memory of Her* (London: SCM Press 1980).

14. See Carol Christ, *She who Changes: Reimagining the Divine in the World* (New York: Palgrave Macmillan 2003).

15. Mercy Amba Oduyoye, *Introducing African Women's Theology* (Sheffield: Sheffield Academic Press 2001).

16. Toni Morrison, *Beloved* (London: Chatto & Windus 1987).

17. This next section is taken from the group report from Kigali: the full report – of which this is only a small part – was presented by the Faith and Order Commission at a Conference in 2005.

18. Maya Angelou, 'On the pulse of the morning', poem for the inauguration of the President of the USA (New York: Random House 1993; London: Virago 1993).

19. Cited in Fergus Finlay, *Mary Robinson: A President with a Purpose* (Dublin: The O'Brien Press 1990), p. 156.

20. Joseph Montville, 'Looking ahead: toward a new paradigm' in Douglas Johnston and Cynthia Sampson (eds.), *Religion: The Missing Dimension of Statecraft* (Oxford: Oxford University Press 1994), p. 332.

21. Thomas Merton, *Conjectures of a Guilty Bystander* (London, Burns & Oates 1995), p. 86.

22. Tharcisse Gatwa, *Rwanda: Eglises, Victimes ou Coupables?* (Yaounde: Editions CLE 2001), pp. 244–6.

23. Nicholas Frayling, *Pardon and Peace: A Reflection on the Making of Peace in N. Ireland* (London: SPCK 1995).
24. ibid.
25. Miroslav Volf, *Exclusion and Embrace* (Nashville: Abingdon Press 1996).
26. For some idea of the difficulties involved, see Peter Pelz and Donald Reeves, *A Tender Bridge: A Journey to Another Europe* (Sheffield: Cairns Publications 2001).
27. Adrienne Rich, 'For memory' in *A Wild Patience Has Taken Me Thus Far* (New York: W & W Norton 1980), p. 22.
28. See M. Grey, *The Wisdom of Fools?* (London: SPCK 1993), p. 116.
29. This is documented in *Rwanda: Not So Innocent: When Women Become Killers* (London: African Rights 1995).
30. See M. Grey, *Sacred Longings: Ecofeminist Theology and Globalisation* (London: SCM Press 2003).

2 THE GENOCIDE, THE CHURCHES AND THE BETRAYAL OF SACRED SPACE

1. Fergal Keane, *Season of Blood: A Rwandan Journey* (London: Penguin 1996), p. 78.
2. Mercy Amba Oduyoye, *Introducing African Women's Theology* (Sheffield: Sheffield Academic Press 2001), p. 106.
3. Dancilla's story can be found in James M. Smith (ed.), *A Time to Remember: Rwanda, Ten Years after the Genocide* (The Aegis Institute 2004). Details of the Ntarama massacre are also found in the Kigali Genocide Memorial.
4. MRND = National Republican Movement for Democracy and Development, the party of President Habyarimana, who made all Rwandans automatically members of it.
5. The story is related both in Fergal Keane's book *Season of Blood* and in the BBC Programme, *Rwanda Revisited*. See Cafod at www.cafod.org for links.
6. Christian Aid report, '*Rwanda: It's Time to Open Up*': Ten years after the Genocide in Rwanda, a report on government accountability, human rights and freedom of speech (London: March 2004), p. 10.
7. See the book resulting from this occasion of the same title: Mary-John Mananzan, Mercy Oduyoye, Elsa Tamez, Mary Grey (eds.) (Maryknoll: Orbis 1996).
8. An earlier version of this section appeared in *New Blackfriars*, vol. 85, no. 995, January 2004, pp. 56–73: M. Grey, 'To struggle with a reconciled heart: reconciliation and justice'.
9. Tacitus, *Agricola*, tr. H. Mattingly (London: Penguin Classics 1948), p. 80.
10. Marc Ellis, *Ending Auschwitz: The Future of Jewish and Christian Life* (Louisville KY: Westminster, John Knox 1994), p. 72.
11. Fyodor Dostoevsky, tr. Constance Garnett, *The Brothers Karamazov* (London: Heinemann 1912), Book V, p. 251.

12. See Mary Grey, *Redeeming the Dream* (London: SPCK 1989); Sally B. Purvis, *The Power of the Cross: Foundations for a Christian Feminist Ethic of Community* (Ashville: Abingdon Press 1993); Carol R. Bohn and Joanne Carlson Brown (eds.), *Christianity, Patriarchy and Abuse* (New York: Pilgrim Press 1989); Cynthia Crysdale, *Embracing Travail: Retrieving the Cross Today* (New York: Continuum 1999).

13. The phrase is Carter Heyward's, *Our Passion for Justice* (New York: Pilgrim Press 1984).

14. Personal conversation with Fr Paul Baird.

15. For information on this project, *Project Asha,* see the Newsletter of Wells for India, The Winchester Centre, 68 St George's Road, Winchester SO23, Hampshire. The project ran for 10 years.

16. For example: *Breaking the Silence on Violence against Women,* Religion and Violence against Women Working Group, Glasgow, March 1992; Forum Bulletin on Structural Violence, ed. Fiona Hulbert, Winter 1993/94; Rita Nakashima Brock and Susan Brooks Thistlethwaite, *Casting Stones: Prostitution and Liberation in Asia and the United States* (Minneapolis: Fortress Press 1996).

17. Kyriarchal = the law of domination. The phrase was invented by Elisabeth Schüssler Fiorenza.

18. The source is my personal conversation with the sociologist Dr Komal Ganotra, formerly of the College of Social Science, Udaipur, Rajasthan, who had conducted this research with her students,

19. Desmond Tutu, *No Future without Forgiveness* (London: Rider 1999).

20. Leslie Griffiths, *The Aristide Factor* (Oxford: Lion Publishing 1997), p. 73.

21. Charles Williams, *The Region of the Summer Stars* (London: Editions Poetry 1944), pp. 26–7. 'The Inklings' were the group of writers, namely Tolkien, Williams and C. S. Lewis, who met regularly to discuss ongoing work in an Oxford pub, 'The Eagle and Child'.

22. Rita Nakashima Brock, 'And a little child shall lead them' in Bohn and Brown (eds.), *Christianity, Patriarchy and Abuse,* pp. 42–61.

23. Grey, *Redeeming the Dream,* ch. 2.

24. Cited in Larry Rasmussen, *Earth Community, Earth Ethics* (Maryknoll NY: Orbis Books 1996), p. 209. He himself is citing Michael Perlmann, *The Power of Trees: The Reforesting of the Soul* (Dallas: Spring Publications 1994), p. 136.

25. David Jenkins, cited in Brian Frost, *The Politics of Peace* (London: Darton, Longman & Todd 1991), p. 3.

26. Haddon Wilmer, 'Forgiveness and politics', *Crucible,* July–September 1979, p. 105.

27. See Miroslav Volf, *Free of Charge: Giving and Forgiving in a Culture Stripped of Grace* (Michigan/Grand Rapids: Zondervan 2005).

28. www.theforgivenessproject.com – to be developed in Chapter 7.

29. Ralph Martin, commentary on 2 Corinthians 5 in *2 Corinthians,* Word Biblical Commentaries, vol. 40 (Texas, Waco: Word Books 1986), p. 146.

30. Links with environmental justice will be developed in Chapter 5.

31. Rodolfo Cardenal sj, 'The crucified people' in *Reclaiming Vision: Education, Liberation and Justice,* Papers of the Inaugural Summer School, ed. Mary Grey (Southampton: La Sainte Union 1994), pp. 12–18.

32. ibid.

33. E. Schumacher, *Small is Beautiful* (New York: Harperbusiness, 1989 [1973]).

34. See the CAFOD film, *Roses in December.*

35. Arundhati Roy, *The Cost of Living* (New York: The Modern Library 1999), pp.104–5.

36. Bikhu Parekh, 'Is Gandhi still relevant?' in Antony Copley and George Paxton (eds.), *Gandhi and the Contemporary World* (Chennai: Indo-British Historical Society 1997), pp. 372–82, quotation p. 376. I have written at greater length on Gandhi's alternative to consumerist lifestyle in M. Grey, *Sacred Longings: Ecofeminist Theology and Globalisation* (London: SCM Press 2003), ch. 9.

37. Anselm Min, *The Solidarity of Others in a Divided World: A Post-modern Theology after Postmodernism* (New York: T & T Clark International, Continuum imprint, 2004).

38. See M. K. Gandhi, *Selected Works of Mahatma Gandhi,* ed. Sriman Narayan (Ahmedabad: Navjivan Publishing House 1968), vol. 4. The following few lines are indebted to John Chathanatt sj,'Upon this foundation: Gandhian foundational bases for social transformation' in *Liberating the Vision,* Papers of the Summer School 1996, ed. Mary Grey (Southampton, La Sainte Union 1996), pp. 35–57.

39. ibid, pp. 50–53.

40. Desmond Tutu, *No Future without Forgiveness* (London: Rider 1999).

41. Beverley Harrison, 'The power of anger in the work of love' in *Making the Connections,* ed. Carol Robb (Boston: Beacon Press 1985), pp. 18–19.

42. Rodolfo Cardenal, 'The timeliness and the challenge of the theology of liberation' in *Reclaiming Vision,* ed. Grey, p. 21.

43. Marie Fortune, *Sexual Violence: The Unmentionable Sin* (New York: Pilgrim Press 1983), pp. 209–11.

44. Tertullian, *Treatise on Idolatry,* 19.

45. Hippolytus, *Apostolica Traditio,* cited in John Helgeland, Robert J. Daly and J. Patout Burns, *Christians and the Military: The Early Experience* (London: SCM Press 1985), p. 37. This section builds on earlier work. See M. Grey in John Bowker (ed.), *Conflict and Reconciliation: The Contribution of Religions* (The Key Publishing House Inc., 2008).

46. See Helgeland, Daly and Burns, *Christians and the Military,* pp. 40–41.

47. See Thomas A. Shannon (ed.), *War or Peace? The Search for New Answers,* Part 1 (Maryknoll NY: Orbis Books 1982).

48. See Ronald Musto, *The Catholic Peace Tradition* (Maryknoll NY: Orbis Books 1986), pp. 72–3.

49. John Paul Lederach, *Building Peace: Sustainable Reconciliation in a Diverse Society* (UN University 1995), p. 51ff. A paraphrase is given here.

50. Ronald Kraybill, 'The transition from Rhodesia to Zimbabwe' in Douglas Johnston and Cynthia Sampson (eds.), *Religion: The Missing*

Dimension of Statecraft (New York and Oxford: Oxford University Press 1994), pp. 208–57.

51. Cited in Johnston and Sampson, *Religion*, p. 332.
52. See Mario Marazitti, 'A miracle of two fish', *The Tablet*, 28 September 2002, p. 6.
53. ibid.
54. The source is an oral story from the theologian.
55. Antjie Krog, *A Country in My Skull* (London: Random House Vintage 1999), p. 423.
56. Naim Ateek, 'Suicide bombers: what is theologically and morally wrong with suicide bombers?' *Cornerstone* (Sabeel), Issue 25, Summer 2002, p. 16.
57. Moltmann calls this the 'Christus traditus' tradition. See *The Crucified God* (London: SCM Press 1974), p. 286, footnote 103.

3 THE WORLD WAS SILENT – AND ABANDONED

1. Roméo Dallaire, *Shake Hands with the Devil: The Failure of Humanity in Rwanda* (Canada: Random House 2003), pp. 4–5.
2. It is interesting to note, Margaret Brearley writes, that whereas reporting of the killing was ambiguous and haphazard in the religious press as a whole in Britain, *The Tablet* was unique in reporting the genocide fully and in depth. Margaret Brearley, 'The Rwandan genocide and the British religious press' in Carol Rittner, John Roth and Wendy Whitworth (eds.), *Genocide in Rwanda: Complicity of the Churches ?* (St Paul MN: Paragon House 2004), p. 172.
3. See Dallaire, *Shake Hands*.
4. ibid., pp. 515–16.
5. Hugh McCullum, *The Angels Have Left Us* (Geneva: WCC 2004), p. 49.
6. ibid., p. 50.
7. ibid., p. 51.
8. See Philip Gourevitch, *We Wish to Inform You that Tomorrow We Will be Killed with Our Families* (London: Picador 1999), pp. 188–200.
9. This part of the story is told poignantly by Fergal Keane, *Season of Blood: A Rwanda Journey* (London: Penguin 1996).
10. Cited in Neil Paynter (ed.), *This Is the Day: Readings and Meditations from the Iona Community* (Glasgow: Wild Goose Publications 2002), Month 1, Day 30.
11. ibid.
12. See Margaret Hebblethwaite, *Motherhood and God* (London: Geoffrey Chapman 1993). This book was one of the first to trace an almost forgotten dimension of Christian tradition.
13. This idea will be developed in Chapter 6.
14. See Luise Schottroff, *Lydia's Impatient Sisters: A Feminist Social History of Early Christianity*, tr. Barbara and Martin Rumscheidt (Westminster John Knox Press 1995).

15. Yvone Gebara and Maria Clara Bingemer, *Mary Mother of God and Mother of the Poor*, tr. Philip Berryman (Maryknoll NY: Orbis Books 1989).

16. Elizabeth Johnson, *Truly our Sister: A Theology of Mary in the Communion of Saints* (New York: Continuum 2004).

17. ibid., pp. 256.

18. Sally Purvis, 'Mothers, neighbours and strangers: another look at agape', *Journal of Feminist Studies in Religion*, vol. 7, no. 1, Spring 1991, pp. 19–34.

19. ibid., pp. 26–7.

20. See Carol Gilligan, *In a Different Voice? Psychological Theory and Women's Development* (Cambridge MA: Harvard University Press 1982).

21. ibid., p. 173.

22. Martin Heidegger, *Being and Time*, tr. John Macquarrie and Edward Robinson (Oxford: Blackwell 1962), p. 242.

23. This account owes much to the analysis of Joan C. Tronto, *Moral Boundaries: A Political Argument for an Ethic of Care* (New York: Routledge 1994).

24. Thomas Merton, *Conjectures of a Guilty Bystander* (London: Burns & Oates 1965), pp. 156–7.

25. This is now given contemporary expression in Christian Ecology Link's Rainbow Coalition for Climate Change.

26. Melissa Raphael, *The Female Face of God in Auschwitz* (London/New York: Routledge 2003).

27. Tronto, *Moral Boundaries*, pp. 134–5.

28. ibid., p. 137.

29. Simon Schama, 'Sorry Mr President: Katrina is not 9/11', *Guardian*, T2, 12 September 2005, p. 8.

30. ibid.

31. 'Shining India' was the name given by the former Prime Minister of India to describe the ambitious economic developments by which India would take a leading place in the world.

32. See M. Grey, *The Wisdom of Fools* (London: SPCK 1993), p. 115; Wendy Farley, *Tragic Vision and Divine Compassion: A Contemporary Theodicy* (Louisville KY: Westminster/John Knox Press 1990).

33. Farley, *Tragic Vision*, p. 93.

34. See Phyllis Trible, *God and the Rhetoric of Sexuality* (Philadelphia: Fortress Press 1978), pp. 41–59.

35. Jonathan Sacks, *To Heal a Fractured World* (London: Continuum 2005), p. 210.

36. See Schotroff, *Lydia's Impatient Sisters*.

37. For this section I am grateful to Mario Marazziti and Austin Ivereigh, 'A Church that is and works to be a Church for everyone, but particularly the poor' in Michael A. Hayes (ed.), *New Religious Movements in the Catholic Church* (London: Burns & Oates 2005), pp. 30–43.

38. ibid., p. 30.

39. ibid., p. 37.

---

1. Jean Paul Lederach, *The Moral Imagination: The Art and Soul of Building Peace* (Oxford: Oxford University Press 2005), pp. 146–7.
2. There are numerous sources for the behaviour of Fr Wenceslas Munyasyhaka. This is cited from Mahmood Mamdani, *When Victims Become Killers: Colonialism, Racism and Genocide in Rwanda* (Princeton: Princeton University Press 2001), p. 227. Mamdani is himself citing African Rights, *Rwanda: Death, Despair and Defiance* (London: African Rights, revised edition, 1995), pp. 381–5. Raymond Bonner, 'Clergy in Rwanda is accused of abetting atrocities', *New York Times*, 7 July 1995, Section A, p. 3.
3. Mamdani, *When Victims Become Killers*, p. 226.
4. ibid., p. 227.
5. For a fuller discussion of this controversial case, see African Rights, *Rwanda: Not so Innocent: When Women Become Killers* (London: African Rights 1995), pp. 156–8.
6. ibid., p. 157.
7. Martin (François) Neyt, 'Two convicted Rwandan nuns' in Carol Rittner, John Roth and Wendy Whitworth (eds.), *Genocide in Rwanda: Complicity of the Churches* (St Paul MN: Paragon House 2004), pp. 251–8.
8. From '*Rwanda, It's Time to Open Up*': Ten Years after the Genocide in Rwanda, a Christian Aid report on government accountability, human rights and freedom of speech (London: March 2004), p. 19.
9. ibid., p. 18.
10. ibid., p. 20.
11. See Francesco Fortunato 'Blackening a White Father's name', *The Tablet*, 24 September 2005, pp. 15–17.
12. Tharcisse Gatwa, *Rwanda: Eglises, Victimes ou Coupable? Les Eglises et L'Ideologie Ethnique au Rwanda* 1900–1994 (Yaoundé: Editions CLE 2001), p. 239. My translations are from the French edition, the English edition being published later (2005).
13. ibid., p. 235, my translation.
14. ibid., p. 250.
15. A. Dumas, *Théologies Politiques et Vie Spirituelle de l'Eglise* (Paris: Chollet 1977), p. 69.
16. Gatwa, *Rwanda*, p. 265.
17. Donald Shriver, *An Ethics for Enemies: Forgiveness in Politics* (New York/ London: Oxford University Press 1995), cited in Gatwa, *Rwanda*, p. 265.
18. Meg Guillebaud, *Rwanda – the Land God Forgot: Revival, Genocide and Hope* (London: Monarch Books 2002), p. 293.
19. Gatwa, *Rwanda*, pp. 269–71.
20. Jean-Paul Lederach, *The Moral Imagination: The Art and Soul of Building Peace* (New York: Oxford University Press 2005), pp. 146–7 (I have slightly rephrased this).
21. Gatwa, *Rwanda*, p. 243.
22. ibid., pp. 284–5.

23. I have written about *kenosis* in other contexts in M. Grey, *Sacred Longings: Ecofeminist Theology and Globalisation* (London: SCM Press 2003), ch. 5.
24. Johnson McMaster, cited in 'Realising mutuality and interdependence in a world of diverse identities', World Council of Churches Faith and Order Commission, 27–30 April 2005.
25. This is a Gandhian movement serving rural poor.
26. GRAVIS = Gramin Vikas Vigyan Samiti, or 'Village Self-help Organisation'.
27. His wife Shashi donated a kidney to another person, who donated one to Tyagiji. But he barely regained consciousness after the operation.
28. Lederach, *Moral Imagination*, pp. 17–19.
29. ibid., p. 19.
30. I Corinthians 1.18–25.
31. Rita Nakashima Brock, 'Communities of the cross: Christa and the communal nature of redemption, *Feminist Theology*, vol. 14, no. 1, September 2005, pp. 109–25.
32. ibid., pp. 112–13.
33. This is the title of David Nyonzima's book, *Unlocking Horns: Forgiveness and Reconciliation in Burundi* (Newberg OR: Barclay Press 2001).
34. ibid., p. 18.
35. ibid., pp. 10–12.
36. I have to be honest and say that it is not the same planks of wood that have survived – they have been repaired and replaced many times.
37. Karin Sporre, 'Women and agency: new arising images of motherhood in the context of the Christian tradition', unpublished text. Sporre is citing a colleague, Grønlien Zetterquist.
38. See the same text for a further spelling out of this idea.

5 LISTEN TO THE CRYING OF THE EARTH

1. Paul Santmire, *Nature Reborn: The Ecological and Cosmic Promise of Christian Theology* (Minneapolis: Fortress Augsburg Press 2000), pp. 119–20.
2. See M. Grey, *Sacred Longings: Ecofeminist Theology and Globalisation* (London: SCM Press 2003), ch. 1.
3. James Lovelock, *The Revenge of Gaia* (London: Penguin/Allen Lane 2006).
4. Mahmood Mamdani, *When Victims Become Killers: Colonialism, Racism and Genocide in Rwanda* (Princteon: Princeton University Press 2001), p. 197.
5. ibid.
6. Jared Diamond, in his recent book, regards agricultural and ecological factors as contributing to the genocide. See Diamond, *Collapse: How Societies Choose to Fail or Survive* (London: Penguin 2005).
7. As reported in *Tiempo: A Bulletin on Climate and Development*, issue 57, October 2005, p. 11. See www.tiempocyberclimate.org/newswatch/arnews
8. Papal texts on the environment have been collected by Sister Ancilla

Dent, *Ecology and Faith: Writings of John Paul II* (New Alresford: Arthur James 1997). This quotation is from a speech to the regional council of Lazio, Italy.

9. Mary Colwell, 'Green Witness', *The Tablet*, 16 September 2006, p. 15.

10. *Letter to the Churches* (Geneva: WCC, 1992), p. 10.

11. As his book indicates: *Ecology and Liberation: A New Paradigm*, tr. John Cumming (Maryknoll NY: Orbis Books 1995).

12. Donald Bruce and David Pickering, 'Ecology and ecumenism', *Ecotheology*, vol. 5, no. 6, pp. 9–21, p. 17.

13. This was influenced by *Kairos South Africa* and *Kairos Central America*.

14. *Kairos Europa* document (Salisbury: Sarum College Press 1998), p. 41.

15. Eamonn O'Brien, 'Editorial', *Vocation for Justice*, vol. 19, no. 3, Autumn 2005, p. 1.

16. See 'The gift of water', a statement from Catholic Earthcare Australia, endorsed by the Bishops of the Murray · Darling Basin. www.catholicearthcare.oz.net

17. Lovelock, *The Revenge of Gaia*, p. 137.

18. John 4.

19. Fyodor Dostoevksy, *The Brothers Karamazov* (New York: Dell Publishing Co. 1956), pp. 252–3.

20. Catherine Keller, 'Eschatology, ecology and a green ecumenacy', *Ecotheology* 2, January 1997, ed. Mary Grey, pp. 84–99.

21. See Sherry Ortner, 'Is female to male as nature is to culture?' in M. Z. Rosaldo and L. Lamphere (eds.), *Women, Culture and Society* (Stanford University Press 1974), pp. 67–89.

22. This word has been coined by Edward Echlin and expresses well the exclusive focus on humanity.

23. See Grey, *Sacred Longings*.

24. Sallie McFague, *Super, Natural Christians: How We Should Love Nature* (Minneapolis: Fortress Press 1997).

25. Cited by Sallie McFague, *The Body of God: An Ecological Theology* (London: SCM Press 1993), p. 26.

26. Alice Walker, *The Colour Purple* (London: The Women's Press 1983), cited by Catherine Keller, 'Feminism and the Ethic of Inseparability' in Barbara Hilkert Andolsen, Christine Gudorf and Mary Pellauer (eds.), *Women's Consciousness, Women's Conscience: A Reader in Feminist Ethics* (San Francisco: Harper & Row 1993), p. 251.

27. Martin Buber, *I and Thou* (Edinburgh: T & T Clark 1935), pp. 7–8.

28. Christian Ecology Link (CEL) promotes the LOAF principles: 'Locally grown, Organic, Animal-friendly and Fairly traded'.

29. Yvone Gebara, *Longing for Running Water* (Minneapolis: Fortress Press 1999), p. 2.

30. See Chapter 4.

31. Roger Gottlieb, *A Spirituality of Resistance* (New York: Rowman & Littlefield 2003), p. 180.

32. Deborah Bird Rose, *Reports from a Wild Country: Ethics for Decolonisation* (Sydney: University of New South Wales Press 2004).

33. Rosemary Radford Ruether, *Gaia and God* (New York: HarperSan-Francsico 1992).

34. I explored this trajectory in *Sacred Longings*, ch. 2.

35. Vandana Shiva, *Water Wars* (London: Pluto 2002).

36. Abelard was convinced that the monks were trying to poison him, and escaped in a small boat. He referred to the sea as a 'mer agitée'.

37. The source here is a lecture by Michael Northcott, who was working on a book on climate change – so far unpublished – at Oxford Brooks University, July 2005.

38. Denise Levertov, 'What time is made from' in *Sands of the Well* (New York: New Direction Books 1994), p. 120.

39. Andy Fisher, *Radical Ecopsychology: Psychology in the Service of Life* (New York: SUNY 2002), p. 141.

40. I have written about this in *Sacred Longings*, ch. 6.

41. Principles of Water Democracy –

    1 Water is nature's gift
    We owe it to nature to use this gift in accordance with our sustenance needs, to keep it clean and in adequate quantity.

    2 Water is essential to life
    All species and ecosystems have a right to their share of water on the planet.

    3 Life is interconnected through water
    Water connects all being and life forms through the water cycle. We have a duty to ensure that our actions do not cause harm to other species.

    4 Water must be free for sustenance needs
    Selling water for profit violates our inherent right to nature's gift and denies the poor of their human right.

    5 Water is limited and can be exhausted
    Water is exhaustible if used unsustainably. This means ...

    6 Water must be conserved
    Everyone has a duty to conserve water and to use water sustainably.

    7 Water is a commons
    Water cannot be owned as private property or sold as a commodity.

    8 No one holds a right to destroy
    No one has aright to overuse, abuse, waste, or pollute water systems. Tradable pollution permits violate the principle of sustainable and just use.

    9 Water cannot be substituted
    Water is different from everything else and cannot be treated as a commodity.
    (From Vandana Shiva, *Water Wars* (London: Pluto 2002), pp. 35–6.)

42. Aristotle, *Politics*, Book 1, ch. 5 (London: Penguin 1962), pp. 32–4.

43. See Charles Taylor, *Sources of the Self* (Cambridge: Cambridge University Press 1986).

44. See Anne Primavesi, *Gaia's Gift: Earth, Ourselves and God after Copernicus* (London: Routledge 2003).

45. Thomas Berry, *The Dream of the Earth* (San Francisco: Sierra Books 1986).

46. McFague, *The Body of God*; Hans Jonas, *The Imperative of Responsibility: In Search of an Ethics for the Technological Age* (Chicago: Chicago University Press 1984).

47. Michael Northcott, *The Environment and Christian Ethics* (Cambridge: Cambridge University Press 1996), p. 33.

48. ibid., p. 34.

49. See Laura Westra, *Living in Integrity: A Global Ethic to Restore a Fragmented Earth* (Lanham MD: Rowman & Littlefield 1998).

50. Celia Deane-Drummond, *The Ethics of Nature* (Oxford: Blackwell 2004), p. 40.

51. ibid., p. 43.

52. Lovelock, *The Revenge of Gaia*, pp. 149–50.

53. *Gaudium et Spes*, section 69, in Michael Walsh and Brian Davies (eds.), *Proclaiming Justice and Peace: Documents from John XXIII to John Paul II* (London: CAFOD/Collins 1984), p. 123.

54. John Paul II, *Centesimus Annus*, as cited by Clifford Longley, 'Structures of sin and the free market' in Paul Vallely (ed.), *The New Politics: Catholic Social Teaching for the 21st Century* (London: SCM Press 1998), p. 112.

55. *The Catholic Catechism*, sections 2415–2418.

56. Leonardo Boff, *Ecology and Liberation: A New Paradigm* (Maryknoll NY: Orbis Books 1995).

57. McFague, *The Body of God*.

58. Carol Gilligan, *In a Different Voice?* (Harvard University Press 1982).

59. Joan Tronto, *Moral Boundaries: A Political Argument for an Ethic of Care* (London: Routledge 1993).

60. My own reworking.

6 MOVING ON: HOW TO BRING BACK THE BEAUTY OF LIFE?

1. 'A woman's creed', cited in Beijing Preparatory documents, and quoted in Catherine Keller, *Apocalypse Now and Then: A Feminist Guide to the End of the World* (Boston: Beacon 1996), p. 268. Actually it was composed by Robin Morgan with a group of Third World women sponsored by a women's environment and development organisation.

2. Adrienne Rich, 'The desert as garden of paradise' in *Poems 1985–88* (New York: W & W Norton 1989), pp. 29–30.

3. This is related movingly by Wanda Nash, *A Fable for our Time* (Christians Aware – no date or place given: ISBN:1-873372-19-1).

4. Immaculée Ilibagiza, with Steve Irwin, *Left to Tell: One Woman's Story of Surviving the Rwandan Holocaust* (London: Hay House UK 2006).

5. See www.thesurvivors-fund.org

6. The source is personal conversation with Caritas in Kigali.

7. Caritas is funded by CAFOD.

8. Cited in *A Time to Remember: Rwanda, 10 years after the genocide*, Kigali Memorial Museum, www.kigalimemorial.org

9. Jewish exegesis interprets the story differently, more as a picture of how

human beings behave. We do sin, disobey and transgress limits, bring forth children in pain, and till the earth with great struggles.

10. Cited in Mukti Barton, *Scripture as Empowerment for Liberation and Justice: The Experience of Christian and Muslim Women in Bangladesh*, CCRSG Monograph Series 1 (Bristol: Department of Theology 1999), p .69.

11. I have written on the significance of flourishing earlier, in *The Outrageous Pursuit of Hope* (London: Darton, Longman & Todd 2000), but have never explored it in such a serious context as post-genocide Rwanda.

12. Grace Jantzen, *Becoming Divine: Towards a Feminist Philosophy of Religion* (Bloomington: Indian University Press 1999).

13. Mercy Amba Oduyoye, *Introducing African Women's Theology* (Sheffield: Sheffield Academic Press 2001), pp. 40, 113.

14. Heather Pencavel, 'An urban version of Isaiah 35' in Geoffrey Duncan (ed.), *Wisdom is Calling: An Anthology of Hope, an Agenda for Change* (Norwich: Canterbury Press 1999), pp. 20–21.

15. From Surah 9: At-Taubah: 71–72; The Holy Qur'an 461, cited in Rifat Hassan, 'Muslim women in post-patriarchal Islam' in Paula M. Cooey et al. (eds.), *After Patriarchy: Feminist Transformations of the World Religions* (Maryknoll NY: Orbis Books 1992), pp. 52–3.

16. Rich, *Poems 1985–88*, pp. 29–30.

17. Denise Levertov, 'Anamnesis at the fault-line' in *Sands at the Well* (New York: New Directions Books 1996), p.67.

18. This symbolic core of flourishing/well-being is being developed by many of us today. The late Grace Jantzen explored it theologically and the inspiration of Ina Praetorius, Michaela Moser and Maria Moser is important in applying the idea to a different economic understanding.

19. See Michael Prior, *Jesus the Liberator: A Nazareth Liberation Theology* (New York: Continuum 1995).

20. There have been different ways of 'softening' this text. Jewish midrash says that God forbade rejoicing, and wept. An Icelandic theologian recently told me that there is a legend in Iceland that God did not kill the Egyptians but turned them into seals!

21. Grace Jantzen, *Foundations of Violence* (London: Routledge 2004), p. 36.

22. ibid., pp. 35–7.

23. Jantzen, *Becoming Divine*, p. 153.

24. ibid.

25. Adrienne Rich, 'The desert'.

26. Oduyoye, *Introducing African Women's Theology*, p. 106.

27. Here I develop the ideas I expressed in *Sacred Longings: Ecofeminist Theology and Globalisation* (London: SCM Press 2003), ch. 6, specifically in the context of post-genocide Rwanda.

28. Patrick Sherry, *Spirit and Beauty* (London: Clarendon Press 1992), p. 165.

29. ibid., p. 2.

30. John V, Taylor, *The Go-between God* (London: Collins 1972).

31. Elizabeth Johnson, *She Who Is* (New York: Crossroad 1994), pp. 191–213.

32. Grey, *Sacred Longings*.

Notes

33. Jean Paul Lederach, *The Moral Imagination: The Art and Soul of Building Peace* (Oxford: Oxford University Press 2005), pp. 146–7.
34. June Boyce-Tillman, *Constructing Musical Healing: The Wounds that Sing* (London: Jessica Kingsley 2000).
35. ibid., p. 271.
36. M. Danner, *The Massacre at El Mozote* (New York: Vintage 1994), pp. 78–9.
37. Rabbi Michael Lerner, *Healing Israel/Palestine: A Path to Peace and Reconciliation* (Berkeley: North Atlantic Books 2003).
38. www.bbc.co.uk/reithlectures2006
39. Iris Murdoch, *The Sovereignty of the Good* (London: ARK Paperbacks 1970), p. 34
40. See Jürgen Moltmann, *The Spirit of Life: A Universal Affirmation*, tr. Margaret Kohl (London: SCM Press 1992).
41. Lederach, *The Moral Imagination*, p. 55.
42. Wangari Maathai in the *Guardian*, 1 November 2004.
43. Jenny Grut and Sonja Linden, *The Healing Fields: Working with Psychotherapy and Nature to Rebuild Shattered Lives* (New York: Woodstocker Books/Frances Linden 2003).
44. This is cited by Rowan Williams, *Silence and Honey Cakes: The Wisdom of the Desert* (Oxford: Lion Publishing 2003), pp. 86–7.
45. As does Elisabeth Schüssler Fiorenza, cited in Catherine Keller, *Apocalypse Now and Then: A Feminist Guide to the End of the World* (Boston: Beacon Press 1996), pp. 57–8.
46. Keller, *Apocalypse Now and Then*.
47. Jau Hoon Lee, cited in W. Anne Joh, 'The transgressive power of jeong' in Catherine Keller, Michael Nausner and Mayra Rivera (eds.), *Postcolonial Theologies: Divinity and Empire* (Missouri: Chalice Press 2004), pp. 149–63.
48. ibid., p. 153.
49. ibid., p. 153
50. ibid., p. 163.

7 STRUGGLING WITH RECONCILING HEARTS AND HOLDING FAST TO OUR DREAMS

1. Kate McIlHagga, 'Reconciliation as God's gift' in *The Green Heart of the Snowdrop* (Glasgow: Wild Goose Publications 2004), p. 67.
2. See Rebecca Tinsley: www.wagingpeace.org
3. See M. Grey, *Redeeming the Dream* (London: SPCK 1989).
4. See Editorial, 'The Vatican view of women', *The Tablet*, 26 August 2006, p. 2.
5. Womanist = the theology of African American women; Latina, of Latin American women; *mujerista*, of Hispanic American women; and African women refers to women from different African countries.

6. This was in the context of his visit to Germany, including his own village, in September 2006.

7. See M. Grey, *Beyond the Dark Night* (London: Continuum 1997); M. Grey, *Prophecy and Mysticism: The Heart of the Post-modern Church* (Edinburgh: T & T Clark 1997).

8. Beverley Lanzetta, *Radical Wisdom: A Feminist Mystical Theology* (Minneapolis: Augsburg Fortress Press 2005), p. 68.

9. ibid., p. 70.

10. Grey, *Redeeming the Dream*, pp. 61–83.

11. This is well discussed by Judith Lewis Herman, *Trauma and Recovery* (London: Pandora 1992).

12. Faith and Order Commission, *Nurturing Peace, Overcoming Violence: In the Way of Christ for the Sake of the World* (Geneva: WCC September 2003).

13. *Nurturing Peace.*

14. Additional points are: concepts that hold peace as inner tranquillity or as absence of conflict and thus trivialise violence, forgiveness and reconciliation; traditional forms of diakonia that limit Christian response to violence to merely binding the wounds of the victims and avoid resisting and transforming powers and forces that cause violence and suffering; the failure to internalise the values of justice, equality and fairness in the ways Churches pursue their ecclesial existence; and the meaning of denominational existence and loyalty to ecclesiastical traditions in situations of brokenness.

15. As in the current prohibition in the Roman Catholic Church against Rite Three of the sacrament of reconciliation thus preventing general absolution to the gathered community in the Rite of Reconciliation.

16. The phrase is Kate McIlhagga's, *The Green Heart of the Snowdrop.*

17. Lanzetta, *Radical Wisdom*, p. 169.

18. See Miroslav Wolf, *Free of Charge: Giving and Forgiving in a Culture Stripped of Grace* (Michigan/Grand Rapids: Zondervan 2005).

19. Immaculée Ibilibagiza, with Steve Irwin, *Left to Tell: One Woman's Story of Surviving the Rwandan Holocaust* (London: Hay House UK 2006), p. 204.

20. ibid.

21. See www.theforgivenessproject.com Text also available in book form with an introduction by Archbishop Tutu.

22. Rodolfo Cardenal SJ, 'The crucified people' in *Reclaiming Vision: Education, Liberation and Justice*, Papers of the Inaugural Summer School (Southampton: La Sainte Union 1994), ed. Mary Grey, pp. 12–18.

23. Edward Peter Nolan, *Cry Out and Write* (New York: Continuum 1984).

24. See Grace Jantzen, *Julian of Norwich* (London: SPCK 1987).

25. The key novel of Lessing's for mystical awakening is Doris Lessing, *The Four-Gated City* (London: Grafton 1972).

26. Grace Jantzen, *Power, Gender and Christian Mysticism* (Cambridge: Cambridge University Press 1995); Grey, *Prophecy and Mysticism.*

27. I have written about Day and Soelle in 'My yearning is for justice: moving beyond praxis in feminist theology' in Rosemary Radford

Ruether, Marion Grau (eds.), *Interpreting the Postmodern: Responses to Radical Orthodoxy* (New York: T & T Clark 2006), pp. 175–96.

28. Dorothy Day, *The Long Loneliness* (San Francisco: Harper & Row 1952), p. 39.
29. ibid., pp. 170–2.
30. It is interesting that Day's daughter Tamar chose an unusual education, learning crafts like spinning and weaving and how to budget for a poor family, at the same time ensuring that they were able to eat nourishing food.
31. Robert Ellsberg (ed.), *Dorothy Day: Selected Writings* (Maryknoll NY: Orbis Books 2001), p. 7.
32. ibid., p. 7.
33. Daniel Berrigan, in Day, *The Long Loneliness*, p. xxiii.
34. Dorothee Soelle, 'Liberating our God-talk: from authoritarian otherness to mystical inwardness' in Ursula King (ed.), *Liberating Women: New Theological Directions* (University of Bristol Press 1991), pp. 40–52.
35. Luise Schottroff, '"Come read with my eyes": Dorothee Soelle's biblical hermeneutics of liberation' in Sarah K. Pinnock (ed.), *The Theology of Dorothee Soelle* (London: Trinity Press International 2003), pp. 45–53.
36. Rosemary Radford Ruether, 'The feminist liberation theology of Dorothee Soelle' in ibid., pp. 205–17.
37. ibid., p. 213.
38. Dorothee Soelle and Luise Schottroff, *Den Himmel Erden. Eine ökofeministische Annährung an die Bibel* (Munich: Deutscher Taschenbuch Verlag 1996), p. 31.
39. Cited in Soelle, 'Breaking the ice of the soul' in Pinnock (ed.), *The Theology of Dorothee Soelle*, pp. 31–41.
40. Dorothee Soelle, *The Silent Cry: Mysticism and Resistance* (Minneapolis: Fortress Press 2001).
41. Soelle, 'Breaking the ice', p. 37.
42. Adrienne Rich, 'Natural resources' in *The Dream of a Common Language* (New York: W & W Norton 1978).
43. Soelle, 'Breaking the ice', pp. 40–41.
44. Soelle, *The Silent Cry*, pp. 292–3.
45. Dorothee Soelle, 'Über auferstehung' in *Fliegen Lernen* (Kleinmachnow: Wolfgang Fietkau Verlag 1979), p. 21.
46. ibid.
47. Carter Heyward, 'Crossing over' in Pinnock (ed.), *The Theology of Dorothee Soelle*, p. 235.
48. Rainer Maria Rilke, 'The Ninth Elegy' in *Duino Elegies*, tr. Stephen Cohn (Manchester: Carcanet Press 1989), p. 73.
49. Anne Primavesi, *Sacred Gaia* (London: Routledge 2000), p. 169.
50. Dorothee Soelle, 'The window of vulnerability' in *The Window of Vulnerability: A Political Spirituality* (Minneapolis: Fortress Press 1990), p. vii.
51. See Grey, *Redeeming the Dream*, pp. 78–80.
52. ibid., p. 80

53. Michael Symmons Roberts, 'Journey's end', *The Tablet*, 19 August 2006, pp. 4–5. He cites Galen Strawson, *Against Narrative*.
54. As with T. S. Eliot, 'East Coker' in *Poems* (London: Faber and Faber 1963), p. 202; Simone Weil, *Waiting on God* (London: Fontana 1949).
55. Adrienne Rich, 'The spirit of place' in *A Wild Patience has Taken Me This Far* (New York: Norton & Norton 1981), p. 44.
56. Thomas Berry, *The Dream of the Earth* (San Francisco: Sierra Club 1988), pp. 45–9.
57. Cited in Tom Ndahiro, 'The Church's blind eye to genocide" in Carol Rittner et al. (eds.), *Genocide in Rwanda: Complicity of the Churches* (St Paul MN: Paragon House 2004), p. 233.

BIBLIOGRAPHY

RWANDA/BURUNDI AND REFLECTION ON THE GENOCIDE

African Rights, *Rwanda: Not So Innocent. When Women Become Killers* (London: African Rights 1995).

Bonner, Raymond, 'Clergy in Rwanda is accused of abetting atrocities', *New York Times*, 7 July 1995, Section A, p. 3.

Brearley, Margaret, 'The Rwandan genocide and the British religious press' in Rittner et al. (eds.), *Genocide in Rwanda* (2004), pp. 169–80.

Christian Aid, *Rwanda: It's Time to Open Up: Ten Years after the Genocide in Rwanda*, a report on government accountability, human rights and freedom of speech (London: March 2004).

Dallaire, Roméo, *Shake Hands with the Devil: The Failure of Humanity in Rwanda* (Canada: Random House 2003).

Fortunato, Francesco, 'Blackening a White Father's name', *The Tablet*, 24 September 2005, p. 15.

Gaillard, Philippe, 'Memory never forgets miracles' in Rittner et al. (eds.), *Genocide in Rwanda* (2004).

Gatwa, Tharcisse, *Rwanda: Eglises, Victimes ou Coupables?* (Yaounde: Editions CLE, 2001).

Gatwa, Tharcisse, *The Churches and Ethnic Ideology in the Rwandan Crises 1900–1994* (Milton Keynes: Regnum Books International, 2005).

Gourevitch, Philippe, *We Wish to Inform You that Tomorrow we will be Killed with our Families: Stories from Rwanda* (New York: Picador 1999).

Guillebaud, Meg, *Rwanda: The Land God Forgot? Revival, Genocide and Hope* (London: Monarch Books 2002).

Ilibagiza, Immaculée, with Steve Irwin, *Left to Tell: One Woman's Story of Surviving the Rwandan Holocaust* (London: Hay House UK 2006).

Keane, Fergal, *Season of Blood: A Rwanda Journey* (London: Penguin 1996).

Kigali Memorial, *A Time To Remember: Rwanda, 10 years after the Genocide (Kigali Memorial Museum 2004).*

Mamdani, Mahmood, *When Victims Become Killers: Colonialism, Racism and Genocide in Rwanda* (Princeton: Princeton University Press 2001).

McCullum, Hugh, *The Angels Have Left Us: The Rwandan Tragedy and the Churches* (Geneva: WCC Publications, 2nd printing, 2004).

Nash, Wanda, *A Fable for our Time* (Christians Aware: no date or place given; ISBN:1-873372-19-1).

Ndahiro, Tom, 'The Church's blind eye to genocide' in Rittner et al. (eds.), *Genocide in Rwanda* (2004), pp. 229–49.

Neyt, Martin (François), 'Two convicted Rwandan nuns' in Rittner et al. (eds.), *Genocide in Rwanda* (2004), pp. 251–8.

Nyonzima, David, *Unlocking Horns: Forgiveness and Reconciliation in Burundi* (Newberg, OR: Barclay Press 2001).

Rittner, Carol, Roth, John and Whitworth, Wendy (eds.), *Genocide in Rwanda: Complicity of the Churches?* (Paragon House 2004).

Temple-Raston, Diana, *Justice in the Grass: Three Rwandan Journalists, their Trial for War Crimes, and a Nation's Quest for Redemption* (New York: Free Press 2005).

Salem, Richard A. (ed.), *Witness to Genocide: The Children of Rwanda – Drawings by Child Survivors* (New York: Friendship Press 2000).

Smith, James A. (ed.), *A Time to Remember: Rwanda, Ten Years after the Genocide* (The Aegis Institute 2004).

Uvin, Peter, *Aiding Violence: Development Enterprise in Rwanda* (Bloomfield CT: Kumarian Press 1998).

THEOLOGY, PHILOSOPHY AND SPIRITUALITY

Andolsen, Barbara Hilkert, Gudorf, Christine and Pellauer, Mary (eds.), *Women's Consciousness, Women's Conscience: A Reader in Feminist Ethics* (San Francisco: Harper & Row 1993).

Ateek, Naim, 'Suicide Bombers: what is theologically and morally wrong with suicide bombers?' *Cornerstone* (Sabeel), issue 25, Summer 2002, p. 16.

Ayer, A. J., *Language, Truth and Logic* (London: Gollancz 1936).

Barton, Mukti, *Scripture as Empowerment for Liberation and Justice: The Experience of Christian and Muslim Women in Bangladesh*, CCRSG Monograph Series 1 (Bristol: Department of Theology 1999).

Berry, Thomas, *The Dream of the Earth* (San Francisco: Sierra Books 1986).

Boff, Leonardo, *Ecology and Liberation: A New Paradigm*, tr. John Cumming (Maryknoll NY: Orbis Books 1995).

Bohn, Carol R. and Brown, Joanne Carlson (eds.), *Christianity, Patriarchy and Abuse* (New York: Pilgrim Press 1989).

Boyce-Tillman, June, *Constructing Musical Healing: The Wounds that Sing* (London: Jessica Kingsley 2000).

Brock, Rita Nakashima and Brooks Thistlethwaite, Susan, *Casting Stones: Prostitution and Liberation in Asia and the United States* (Minneapolis: Fortress Press 1996).

'Communities of the cross: Christa and the communal nature of redemption', *Feminist Theology*, 14/1, September 2005, pp. 127–49.

Bruce, Donald and Pickering, David, 'Ecology and ecumenism', *Ecotheology* 5/6, ed. Mary Grey, pp. 9–21.

Buber, Martin, *I and Thou* (Edinburgh: T & T Clark 1935).

Cardenal sj, Rodolfo, 'The crucified people' in Grey (ed.), *Reclaiming Vision* (1994), pp. 12–18.

Catechism of the Catholic Church, The (London: Geoffrey Chapman 1994).

Chathanatt sj, John, 'Upon this foundation: Gandhian foundational bases for social transformation' in Grey (ed.), *Liberating the Vision* (1996), pp. 35–57.

Christ, Carol, *She who Changes: Reimagining the Divine in the World* (New York: Palgrave Macmillan 2003).

Cooey, Paula M., Eakin, William R., McDaniel, Jay B., (eds.), *After Patriarchy: Feminist Transformations of the World Religions* (Maryknoll NY: Orbis Books 1992).

Copley, Antony and Paxton, George (eds.), *Gandhi and the Contemporary World* (Chennai: Indo-British Historical Society 1997).

Cose, Ellis, *Bone to Pick: Of Forgiveness, Reconciliation, Reparation and Revenge* (New York: Washington Square Press 2004).

Crysdale, Cynthia, *Embracing Travail: Retrieving the Cross Today* (New York: Continuum 1999).

Danner, M., *The Massacre at El Mozote* (New York: Vintage 1994).

Day, Dorothy, *The Long Loneliness* (San Francisco: Harper & Row 1952).

Deane-Drummond, Celia, *The Ethics of Nature* (Oxford: Blackwell 2004).

De Gruchy, John W., *Reconciliation: Restoring Justice* (London: SCM Press 2002).

Dent, Sister Ancilla, *Ecology and Faith: Writings of John Paul II* (New Alresford: Arthur James 1997).

Diamond, Irene and Orenstein, Gloria Feman (eds.), *Reweaving the World: The Emergence of Ecofeminism* (San Francisco: Sierra Books 1990).

Dumas, A., *Théologies Politiques et Vie Spirituelle de l'Eglise* (Paris: Chollet 1977).

Duncan, Geoffrey (ed.), *Wisdom is Calling: An Anthology of Hope, an Agenda for Change* (Norwich: Canterbury Press 1999).

Ellis, Marc, *Ending Auschwitz: The Future of Jewish and Christian Life* (Louisville KY: Westminster/John Knox Press 1994).

Ellsberg, Robert (ed.), *Dorothy Day: Selected Writings* (Maryknoll NY: Orbis Books 2001).

Faith and Order Commission, World Council of Churches, *Nurturing Peace, Overcoming Violence: In the Way of Christ for the Sake of the World* (Geneva: WCC September 2003).

Farley, Wendy, *Tragic Vision and Divine Compassion: A Contemporary Theodicy* (Louisville KY: Westminster/John Knox Press 1990).

Fiorenza, Elisabeth Schüssler, *In Memory of Her* (London: SCM Press 1980).

Fisher, Andy, *Radical Ecopsychology: Psychology in the Service of Life* (New York: SUNY 2002).

Fortune, Marie, *Sexual Violence: The Unmentionable Sin* (New York: Pilgrim Press 1983).

Frayling, Nicholas, *Pardon and Peace: A Reflection on the Making of Peace in N. Ireland* (London: SPCK 1995).

Frost, Brian, *The Politics of Peace* (London: Darton, Longman & Todd 1991).

Gandhi, M. K., *Selected Works of Mahatma Gandhi*, ed. Sriman Narayan (Ahmedabad: Navjivan Publishing House 1968).

Gebara, Yvone, *Longing for Running Water* (Minneapolis: Fortress Press 1999).

Gebara, Yvone and Bingemer, Maria Clara, *Mary Mother of God and Mother of the Poor*, tr. Philip Berryman (Maryknoll NY: Orbis Books 1989).

Gilligan, Carol, *In a Different Voice? Psychological Theory and Women's Development* (Cambridge MA: Harvard University Press 1982).

Gottlieb, Roger, *A Spirituality of Resistance* (New York: Rowman & Littlefield 2003).

Grey, Mary, *Redeeming the Dream: Christianity, Feminism and Redemption* (London: SPCK 1989; Gujurat: Sahitya Prakash 2000).

Grey, Mary, *The Wisdom of Fools* (London: SPCK 1993).

Grey, Mary, *Beyond the Dark Night* (London: Continuum 1997).

Grey, Mary, *Prophecy and Mysticism: The Heart of the Post-modern Church* (Edinburgh: T & T Clark 1997).

Grey, Mary, *Sacred Longings: Ecofeminist Theology and Globalisation* (London: SCM Press 2003).

Grey, Mary, 'To struggle with a reconciled heart: reconciliation and justice', *New Blackfriars*, vol. 85, no. 995, January 2004, pp. 56–73.

Grey, Mary, 'My yearning is for justice: moving beyond praxis in feminist theology' in Rosemary Radford Ruether and Marion Grau (eds.), *Interpreting the Postmodern: Responses to Radical Orthodoxy* (New York: T & T Clark 2006), pp.175–96.

Grey, Mary (ed.), *Reclaiming Vision: Education,Liberation and Justice,* Papers of the Inaugural Summer School (Southampton: La Sainte Union 1994).

Grey, Mary (ed.), *Liberating the Vision*, Papers of the Summer School 1996, (Southampton: La Sainte Union 1996).

Harrison, Beverley, 'The power of anger in the work of love' in Carol Robb (ed.), *Making the Connections* (Boston: Beacon Press 1986), pp. 3–21.

Hassan, Riffat, 'Muslim women in post-patriarchal Islam in Cooey et al. (eds.), *After Patriarchy* (1992), pp. 52–3.

Hayes, Michael A. (ed.), *New Religious Movements in the Catholic Church* (London: Burns & Oates 2005).

Hebblethwaite, Margaret, *Motherhood and God* (London: Geoffrey Chapman 1993).

Heidegger, Martin, *Being and Time*, tr. John Macquarrie and Edward Robinson (Oxford: Blackwell 1962).

Helgeland, John, Daly, Robert J. and Burns, Patout J., *Christians and the Military: The Early Experience* (London: SCM Press 1985).

Heyward, Carter, *Our Passion for Justice* (New York: Pilgrim Press 1984).

Heyward, Carter, 'Crossing over' in Pinnock (ed.), *The Theology of Dorothee Soelle* (2003).

Hippolytus, *Apostolica Traditio,* cited in Helgeland et al. (eds.), *Christians and the Military*.

Hulbert, Fiona (ed.), *Breaking the Silence on Violence against Women,* Religion and Violence against Women Working Group, Glasgow, March 1992.

Bibliography

Isasi-Diaz, Ada-Maria, 'Reconciliation: an intrinsic element of justice' in Tombs and Liechty (eds.), *Explorations in Reconciliation* (2006).

Jantzen, Grace, *Julian of Norwich* (London: SPCK 1987).

Jantzen, Grace, *Becoming Divine: Towards a Feminist Philosophy of Religion* (Bloomington: Indian University Press 1999).

Jantzen, Grace, *Foundations of Violence* (London: Routledge 2004).

Johnson, Elizabeth, *Truly our Sister: A Theology of Mary in the Communion of Saints* (New York: Continuum 2004).

Johnston, Douglas and Sampson, Cynthia (eds.), *Religion, The Missing Dimension of Statecraft* (Oxford: Oxford University Press 1994).

Jonas, Hans, *The Imperative of Responsibility: In Search of an Ethics for the Technological Age* (Chicago: Chicago University Press 1984).

Kairos Europa document (Salisbury: Sarum College Press 1998).

Keller, Catherine, *Apocalypse Now and Then: A Feminist Guide to the End of the World* (Boston: Beacon 1996).

Keller, Catherine, 'Eschatology, ecology and a green ecumenacy', *Ecology* 2, ed. Mary Grey, January 1997, pp. 84–99.

Keller, Catherine, 'Feminism and the ethic of inseparability' in Andolsen et al. (eds.), *Women's Consciousness, Women's Conscience* (1993).

Keller, Catherine, Nausner, Michael and Rivera, Mayra (eds.), *Postcolonial Theologies: Divinity and Empire* (Missouri: Chalice Press 2004).

King, Ursula (ed.), *Liberating Women: New Theological Directions* (University of Bristol Press 1991), pp. 40–52.

Kraybill, Ronald, 'The transition from Rhodesia to Zimbabwe' in Johnston and Sampson (eds.) *Religion* (1994), pp. 208–57.

Lanzetta, Beverley, *Radical Wisdom: A Feminist Mystical Theology* (Minneapolis: Augsburg Fortress Press 2005).

Lederach, Jean-Paul, *The Moral Imagination: The Art and Soul of Building Peace* (New York: Oxford University Press 2005).

Lederach, Jean-Paul, *Building Peace: Sustainable Reconciliation in a Diverse Society* (UN University 1995).

Lee, Jau Hoon, cited in W. Anne Joh, 'The transgressive power of jeong' in Keller et. al. (eds.), *Postcolonial Theologies* (2004), pp.149–63.

Lerner, Rabbi Michael, *Healing Israel/Palestine: A Path to Peace and Reconciliation* (Berkeley: North Atlantic Books 2003).

Longley, Clifford, 'Structures of sin and the free market' in Vallely (ed.), *The New Politics* (1998).

Lovelock, James, *The Revenge of Gaia* (London: Penguin/Allen Lane 2006).

Mananzan, Mary-John, Oduyoye, Mercy, Tamez, Elsa, Grey, Mary (eds.), *Women Struggling against Violence: A Spirituality for Life* (Maryknoll NY: Orbis Books 1996).

Marazziti, Mario and Ivereigh, Austin, 'A Church that is and works to be a Church for everyone, but particularly the poor' in Hayes (ed.), *New Religious* (2005), pp. 30–43.

Martin, Ralph, *2 Corinthians*, Word Biblical Commentaries, vol. 40 (Texas, Waco: Word Books 1986).

Bibliography

McFague, Sallie, *The Body of God: An Ecological Theology* (London: SCM Press 1993).

McFague, Sallie, *Super, Natural Christians: How We should Love Nature*, (Minneapolis: Fortress Press 1997).

McMaster, Johnson, 'Realising mutuality and interdependence in a world of diverse identities', World Council of Churches Faith and Order Commission, 27–30 April 2005.

Merton, Thomas, *Conjectures of a Guilty Bystander* (London: Burns & Oates 1995).

Metz, Jean-Baptist, *Faith in History and Society: Towards a Practical, Fundamental Theology* (New York: Crossroad 1980).

Min, Anselm, *The Solidarity of Others in a Divided World: A Post-modern Theology after Postmodernism.* (New York: T & T Clark International, Continuum imprint, 2004).

Moltmann, Jürgen, *The Crucified God* (London: SCM Press 1974).

Moltmann, Jürgen, *The Spirit of Life: A Universal Affirmation*, tr. Margaret Kohl (London: SCM Press 1992).

Montville, Joseph, 'Looking ahead: toward a new paradigm' in Johnston and Sampson (eds.) *Religion* (1994).

Murdoch, Iris, *The Sovereignty of the Good* (London: ARK Paperbacks 1970).

Musto, Ronald, *The Catholic Peace Tradition* (Maryknoll NY: Orbis Books 1986).

Nolan, Edward Peter, *Cry Out and Write* (New York: Continuum 1984).

Northcott, Michael, *The Environment and Christian Ethics* (Cambridge: Cambridge University Press 1996).

O'Brien, Eamonn, 'Editorial', *Vocation for Justice*, vol. 19, no. 3, Autumn 2005, p. 1.

Oduyoye, Mercy Amba, *Introducing African Women's Theology* (Sheffield: Sheffield Academic Press 2001).

Ortner, Sherry, 'Is female to male as nature is to culture?' in Rosaldo and Lamphere (eds.), *Women, Culture and Society* (1974), pp. 67–89.

Parekh, Bhikhu, 'Is Gandhi still relevant?' in Copley and Paxton (eds.), *Gandhi* (1997), pp. 372–82.

Paynter, Neil (ed.), *This is the Day: Readings and Meditations from the Iona Community* (Glasgow: Wild Goose Publications 2002).

Pelz, Peter and Reeves, Donald, *A Tender Bridge: A Journey to Another Europe* (Sheffield: Cairns Publications 2001).

Pencavel, Heather, 'An urban version of Isaiah 35' in Duncan (ed.), *Wisdom is Calling* (1999), pp. 20–21.

Pinnock, Sarah K. (ed.), *The Theology of Dorothee Soelle* (London: Trinity Press International 2003).

Primavesi, Anne, *Sacred Gaia* (London: Routledge 2000).

Primavesi, Anne, *Gaia's Gift: Earth, Ourselves and God after Copernicus* (London: Routledge 2003).

Prior, Michael, *Jesus the Liberator: A Nazareth Liberation Theology* (New York: Continuum 1995).

Purvis, Sally B., 'Mothers, neighbours and strangers: another look at agape', *Journal of Feminist Studies in Religion*, vol. 7, no.1, Spring 1991, pp. 19–34.

Purvis, Sally B., *The Power of the Cross: Foundations for a Christian Feminist Ethic of Community* (Ashville: Abingdon Press 1993).

Raphael, Melissa, *The Female Face of God in Auschwitz* (London/New York: Routledge 2003).

Rasmussen, Larry, *Earth Community, Earth Ethics* (Maryknoll NY: Orbis Books 1996).

Rosaldo, M. and Lamphere, L. (eds.), *Women, Culture and Society* (Stanford University Press 1974).

Rose, Deborah Bird, *Reports from a Wild Country: Ethics for Decolonisation* (Sydney: University of New South Wales Press 2004).

Ruether, Rosemary Radford, *Gaia and God: An Ecofeminist Theology of Earth Healing* (New York: HarperCollins 1992).

Sacks, Jonathan, *To Heal a Fractured World* (London: Continuum 2005).

Santmire, Paul, *Nature Reborn: The Ecological and Cosmic Promise of Christian Theology* (Minneapolis: Fortress Augsburg 2000).

Schottroff, Luise, *Lydia's Impatient Sisters: A Feminist Social History of Early Christianity*, tr. Barbara and Martin Rumscheidt (Westminster John Knox Press 1995).

Schottroff, Luise, '"Come read with my eyes": Dorothee Soelle's biblical hermeneutics of liberation' in Pinnock (ed.), *The Theology of Dorothee Soelle* (2003), pp. 45–53.

Shannon, Thomas A., (ed.), *War or Peace? The Search for New Answers*, Part 1, (Maryknoll NY: Orbis Books 1982).

Sherbok, Dan Cohn and Grey, Mary, *Pursuing the Dream: A Jewish Christian Conversation* (London: Darton, Longman & Todd 2005).

Sherry, Patrick, *Spirit and Beauty* (London: Clarendon Press 1992).

Shiva, Vandana, *Water Wars* (London: Pluto 2002).

Shriver, Donald, *An Ethics for Enemies: Forgiveness in Politics* (New York/London: Oxford University Press 1995).

Soelle, Dorothee, 'Liberating our God-talk: from authoritarian otherness to mystical inwardness' in King (ed.,), *Liberating Women* (1991), pp. 40–52.

Soelle, Dorothee, *The Silent Cry: Mysticism and Resistance* (Minneapolis: Fortress Press 2001).

Soelle, Dorothee, *Fliegen Lernen* (Kleinmachnow: Wolfgang Fietkau Verlag 1979).

Soelle, Dorothee, 'Breaking the ice of the soul: theology and literature in search of a new language, in Pinnock (ed.), *The Theology of Dorothee Soelle* (2003), pp. 31–41.

Soelle, Dorothee, *The Window of Vulnerability: A Political Spirituality* (Minneapolis: Fortress Press 1990).

Soelle, Dorothee and Schottroff, Luise, *Den Himmel Erden. Eine ökofeministische Annährung an die Bibel* (Munich: Deutscher Taschenbuch Verlag 1996), p. 31.

Sporre, Karin, 'Women and agency: new arising images of motherhood in the context of the Christian tradition', unpublished text.

Bibliography

Taylor, Charles, *Sources of the Self* (Cambridge: Cambridge University Press 1986).

Taylor, John V., *The Go-between God* (London: Collins 1972).

Tombs, David and Liechty, Joseph, *Explorations in Reconciliation: New Directions in Theology* (Aldershot: Ashgate 2006).

Trible, Phyllis, *God and the Rhetoric of Sexuality* (Philadelphia: Fortress Press 1978).

Tronto, Joan C., *Moral Boundaries: A Political Argument for an Ethic of Care* (New York: Routledge 1994).

Tutu, Desmond, *No Future without Forgiveness* (London: Rider 1999).

Vallely, Paul (ed.), *The New Politics: Catholic Social Teaching for the 21ˢᵗ Century* (London: SCM Press 1998).

Volf, Miroslav, *Exclusion and Embrace* (Nashville: Abingdon Press 1996).

Volf, Miroslav, *Free of Charge: Giving and Forgiving in a Culture Stripped of Grace* (Michigan/Grand Rapids: Zondervan 2005).

Walsh, Michael and Davies, Brian (eds.), *Proclaiming Justice and Peace: Documents from John XXIII to John Paul II* (London: CAFOD/Collins 1984).

Weil, Simone, *Waiting on God*, tr. Emma Crauford (London: Fontana 1949).

Westra, Laura, *Living in Integrity: A Global Ethic to Restore a Fragmented Earth* (Lanham MD: Rowman and Littlefield 1998).

Williams, Rowan, *Silence and Honey Cakes: The Wisdom of the Desert* (Oxford: Lion Publishing 2003).

Wilmer, Haddon, 'Forgiveness and Politics', *Crucible*, July–September 1979, p. 105.

World Council of Churches, *Letter to the Churches* (Geneva: WCC 1992).

GENERAL

Angelou, Maya, 'On the pulse of the morning', poem for the inauguration of the President of the USA (New York: Random House 1993; London: Virago 1993).

Diamond, Jared, *Collapse: How Societies Choose to Fail or Survive* (London: Penguin 2005).

Dostoevsky, Fyodor, *The Brothers Karamazov* (London: Heinemann 1912).

Eliot, T. S., 'East Coker' in *Poems* (London: Faber & Faber 1963).

Finlay, Fergus, *Mary Robinson: A President with a Purpose* (Dublin: The O'Brien Press 1990).

Griffiths, Leslie, *The Aristide Factor* (Oxford: Lion Publishing 1997).

Grut, Jenny and Linden, Sonja, *The Healing Fields: Working with Psychotherapy and Nature to Rebuild Shattered Lives* (New York: Woodstocker Books/ Frances Linden 2003).

Herman, Judith Lewis, *Trauma and Recovery* (London: Pandora 1992).

Krog, Antije, *A Country in My Skull* (London: Random House/Vintage 1999).

Lessing, Doris, *The Four-Gated City* (London: Grafton 1972).

Bibliography   223

Levertov, Denise, 'Anamnesis at the fault-line' in *Sands of the Well* (New York: New Directions Books 1996), p. 67.

Levertov, Denise, 'What time is made from' in *Sands of the Well*, p. 120.

McIlHagga, Kate, *The Green Heart of the Snowdrop* (Glasgow: Wild Goose Publications 2004).

Marazitti, Mario, 'A miracle of two fish', *The Tablet*, 28 September 2002, p. 6.

Morrison, Toni, *Beloved* (London: Chatto & Windus 1987).

Rich, Adrienne, 'Natural resources' in *The Dream of a Common Language* (New York: W & W. Norton 1978).

Rich, Adrienne, 'For memory' in *A Wild Patience Has Taken Me Thus Far* (New York: W & W Norton 1980).

Rich, Adrienne, *Poems 1985–88* (New York: W & W Norton 1989).

Rich, Adrienne, 'The spirit of place' in *A Wild Patience* (1981), p. 44.

Rilke, Rainer Maria, *Duino Elegies*, tr. Stephen Cohn (Manchester: Carcanet Press 1989).

Roberts, Michael Symmonds, 'Journey's end', *The Tablet*, 19 August 2006, pp. 4–5.

Schama, Simon, 'Sorry Mr President: Katrina is not 9/11', *Guardian*, T2, 12 September 2005, p. 8.

Schumacher, E. F., *Small is Beautiful: A Study of Economics as if People Mattered* (New York: Harperbusiness 1989 [1973]).

Roy, Arundhati, *The Cost of Living* (New York: The Modern Library 1999).

Tacitus, *Agricola*, tr. H. Mattingly (London: Penguin Classics 1948).

Walker, Alice, *The Colour Purple* (London: The Women's Press 1983).

Williams, Charles, *The Region of the Summer Stars* (London: Editions Poetry 1944).

WEBSITES

www.ambarwanda.co.uk
www.bbc.co.uk/reithlectures2006
www.cafod.org
www.catholicearthcare.oz.net
www.Christian-aid.org
www.christian-ecology.org
www.theforgivenessproject.com
www.kigalimemorialcentre.org
www.tiempocyberclimate.org/newswatch/arnews
www.thesurvivors-fund.org
www.wagingpeace.org
www.wcc-coe.org
www.wellsforindia.org

INDEX

Abbé Pierre 9
Amnesia, structural 10–11
Angelou, Maya 10, 200n
Arendt, Hannah 147, 154
Arusha Accord and Trials 3, 58, 84
Ateek, Naim 52, 204n
Attfield, Robin 133
Ayer, Alfred J. 7, 200n

Barenboim, Daniel 160–1, 212n
Benedict XVI, Pope ix, 171, 212n
Berrigan, Daniel 184, 214n
Berry, Thomas 124, 132, 197, 209n,
    215n
Bigiruwami, Bishop Aloys 198, 215n
Bingemer, Maria Clara 65, 204n
Bingen, Hildegarde of 181
Blewitt, Mary 143, 210n
Boff, Leonardo 114, 137, 208n, 210n
Boyce-Tillman, June 160, 212n
Brock, Rita Nakashima 33, 103,
    202n, 207n
Bruce, Donald 114–15, 208n
Buber, Martin 161, 187, 212n
Burundi xii, xviii, 4, 104–6

Cardenal sj, Rodolfo 39, 180, 203n,
    213n
Caritas Gisenyi 143–4, 210n
Catholic Bishops of Britain, *The
    Common Good* 140
Catholic Catechism, The 137, 210n
Catholic devotions 8
Catholic Earthcare Australia 117,
    208n

Catholic Institute of International
    Relations (now *Progressio*) 49
Caverero, Adriana 147
Christ, Carol 10, 200n
Christian Aid (Rwandan Report)
    24–5, 201n
Colwell, Mary 114, 208n
Compassion 61–2; and motherhood
    63–6; and the suffering mother 66–9

Dallaire, General Roméo xii, xviii,
    56–8, 204n
Day, Dorothy 182–5, 213n, 214n
Deane-Drummond, Celia 133–5,
    138, 210n
De Gruchy, John 51
Donovan, Jean 40
Dostoevsky, Fyodor 28, 117–18,
    183, 201n, 208n

EATWOT (Women's Commission)
    25–6, 201n
El Mozote, massacre of 160, 212n
Ellis, Marc 27, 46, 201n
Exodus paradigm 18–19

Farley, Wendy 76, 205n
Feminist theology, and reconciliation
    29–33, 54; and Christologies of
    justice 35–8; and sacrifice 38–44,
    151–3; and violence against
    women 45–6; and the suffering
    mother 67–9; and justice and care
    70–1; and recent developments
    170–1

Fiorenza, Elisabeth Schüssler 10, 200n
Fisher, Andy 128, 209n
Fortune, Marie 30, 45, 49, 202n, 203n
Frayling Nicholas 15–16, 201n

Gacaca courts 84–7, 92
Galloway, Kathy 61, 204n
Gandhi, the Mahatma 40–3, 54, 98–9, 129, 183, 196, 203n; and his Talisman 139–40
Gatwa, Tharcisse 15, 200n; and N. Ireland 15; and models of Church 81, 88–96, 123, 206n
Gebara, Yvone 65, 123, 204n, 208n
Gildas, St and Celtic monks 126–7, 129, 130
Gilligan, Carol 70, 138, 205n, 210n
Grey, Ben 74
Grey, Nicholas 63
Griffin, Susan 121–2, 208n
Griffiths, Leslie 13, 202n
Guillebaud, Meg 91, 93, 206n

Habyarimana, President 3
Harrison, Beverley 44, 203n
Hassan, Margaret 40
Hayes, Diana 66
Heidegger, Martin 71–2, 138, 205n
Heyward, Carter 189, 214n
Holy Spirit xviii, 20, 96–7, 130, 142; and beauty 157– 62; and healing of wounded memories 162–5
Hurley, Archbishop Denis 9
Hurricane Katrina 75–6

Ilibagiza, Immaculée 143, 144, 179–80, 210n, 213n
India 'Shining' 76, 205n
Isaiah 8, 34, 35, 109–10, 126, 130, 147–8, 154–5
Islam, and flourishing 148–9, 211n

James, William 181
Jantzen, Grace 147, 181, 211n, 213n; and mortalité, natalité 153–4, 159, 211n

Jenkins, David 37, 202n
Joh, W. Ann 65–6, 212n
John Paul II, Pope ix, 27, 113–14, 136–7, 138, 210n
John XXIII, Pope 50
Johnson, Elizabeth 65, 66, 205n
Jonas, Hans 132, 210n
Julian of Norwich 181

Kagame, President Paul xiv, 6, 57–8
Kairos Europa 115, 208n
Karamaga, André 96–7
Karamazov, Ivan 27–8
Karamazov, Alyosha 117–18, 121
Keane, Fergal 21, 23, 201n
Keller, Catherine 119, 165, 208n, 210n, 212n
kenosis 93, 107
Kibeho massacre 60
Kohlberg, Lawrence 70, 205n
Kraybill, Ronald 49, 203n
Krog, Antije 51–2, 204n
Kuan Yin (Goddess) 36
kyriarchy 30

Lazar, Prince of Serbia 19
Lederach, Jean Paul 49, 81, 93, 102–3, 160, 162, 203n, 206n, 212n
Leopold, Aldo 132
Lerner, Rabbi Michael 160–1, 212n
Lessing, Doris 181, 213n
Letter to the Churches 114, 208n
Levertov, Denise 128, 150, 209n, 211n
Lovelock, James 111, 126, 131, 134–5, 207n

Maathai, Wangari 163–4, 212n
Mamdani, Mahmood 82, 206n
McCullum, Hugh 59, 204n
McFague, Sallie 121, 132, 209n, 210n
McIlhagga, Kate 168, 212n
McMaster, Johnson 96–7, 98, 107, 207n
Make Poverty History xvii
Martin, Ralph 38, 202n

Mary, Virgin and Mother 62, 64–5, 71,
Maryknoll missionaries 40
Maurin, Peter, and synthesis of Aquinas 183
Medical Foundation, The 164, 212n
Memory, and spirituality 7–10; metanoic 18
Merleau–Ponty, Maurice 127–8, 129
Merton, Thomas 14, 48, 72–73, 200n, 205n
Metz, Jean-Baptist 9, 185, 200n
Min, Anselm 41, 203n
Montville, Joseph 49, 203n
Morrison, Toni 10, 35–6, 67, 200n
Murdoch, Iris 72, 161, 212n
Museveni, President 6

Ndahiro, Tom 24
Northcott, Michael 127, 130, 132–3, 209n, 210n
Ntarama xviii; massacre at Chapel 22–4, 53–4, 55
Nyirarukundo, Violette 142–4
Nyonzima, David 104–6, 207n

Obote, President 6
O'Brien, Eamon 116, 208n
Oduyoye, Mercy Amba 10, 21, 155, 200n, 201n, 211n

Paton, Alan xi, 199n
Peace, early traditions of 46–8, 203n; and just war 48; contemporary movements 48–9, 203n
Péguy, Charles 138, 140
Pickering, David 114–15, 208n
Primavesi, Anne 131, 190, 209n, 214n
Prior, Michael 152, 211n
Purvis, Sally 69, 205n

Raphael, Melissa 73–4, 205n
Rasmussen, Larry 35, 202n
Recovery of Historical Memory Project xvi, 17
Reeves, Donald 16, 201n

Rich, Adrienne 17, 141, 149, 155, 188, 195, 201n, 210n, 211n, 214n, 215n
Rilke, Rainer Maria 190, 214n
Robinson, Mary 13, 200n
Roman Catholic encyclicals, *Rerum Novarum* 131, 136; *Gaudium et Spes* 136; *Sollicitudo Rei Socialis* 136; *Centesimus Annus* 136
Rose, Deborah Bird 125, 208n
Roy, Arundhati 40–1, 203n
Ruether, Rosemary Radford 126, 186, 209n, 214n
Rusesebagina, Paul xiii, 199n
Rwandan genocide ix–xv, 1, 2–7, 11, 14–15, 22–5, 56–8, 67–8; and the churches 56–7, 84–8, 206n; and the refugee camps 59–61; and ecology 112; and healing 142–5; and Kigali Memorial 144–5

Sacks, Jonathan, Chief Rabbi 77, 205n
Sant'Egidio 49, 43, 204n; and Andrea Riccardi 50; and reconciliation 79–80, 81, 205n
Santmire, Paul 109, 127, 140, 207n
satyagraha 41–2
Schama, Simon 75–6, 205n
Schotroff, Luise 186, 214n
Sherbok, Rabbi Dan Cohn xvi–xvii
Sherry, Patrick 157, 211n
Shiva, Vandana 126, 130, 132, 209n
Sobrino sj, Jon 39, 180
Soelle, Dorothee 182, 185–92, 214n
Spirituality, and compassion 61–2, 75–80; and caring 71–5; of peace and non-violence 96–7; and ministry of reconciliation 100–2; and fullness of life 103–4, 147–51; and reconciliation with the earth 111ff.; and the theme of journeying 169–72, 193–5; and the mystical journey revisited 173ff.
Sporre, Karin 107, 207n
Stang, Dorothy 40, 196
Swimme, Brian 12

Tacitus 27, 201n
Taizé and reconciliation 44–5, 48, 53, 196
Taylor, John V. 158, 211n
The Forgiveness Project 38, 180, 202n, 213n
Theunis, Guy 87–8, 206n
Thistlethwaite, Susan 30, 202n
Thomas Aquinas and virtue ethics 133–5, 138–9
tikkun olam 36
Tronto, Joan 72–4, 138, 205n, 210n
Truth and Reconciliation Commission xvi, 16, 31, 42, 51, 92, 110
Tutu, Archbishop Desmond 14, 91, 203n
Tyagi, Laxmi 98–100, 207n

UNAMIR 57

Volf, Miroslav 16, 52, 201n

Walker, Alice 122, 208n
Weil, Simone 72, 161
Weizäcker, Richer, President 91
Wells for India x, 22, 30, 31, 68, 98, 130, 193, 202n
Westra, Laura 133, 210n
Williams, Charles 32, 202n
Wilmer, Haddon 37, 202n
Woodcock, Brian 61, 204n
World Council of Churches, Faith and Order Commission xi, 6, 116, 176–7, 213n; *Justice, Peace and Integrity of Creation* 116; and Women's' Creed 141, 146, 210n
Wresinski, Joseph 9
Wychalls, Abigail 38

Index